Galileo
Observed

For
Louisa and Bruce

Galileo
Observed

Science and the
Politics of Belief

WILLIAM R. SHEA & MARIANO ARTIGAS

Science History Publications/USA
Sagamore Beach
2006

First published in the United States of America
by Science History Publications/USA
a division of Watson Publishing International
Post Office Box 1240, Sagamore Beach, MA 02562-1240, USA
www.shpusa.com

© 2006 Watson Publishing International

Library of Congress Cataloging-in-Publication Data

Shea, William R.
   Galileo observed: science and the poitics of belief / William R. Shea & Mariano Artigas.
      p. cm.
   Includes bibliographical references and index.
   ISBN 0-88135-356-6 (alk. paper)
      1. Galilei, Galileo, 1564–1642.   2. Astronomers—Biography.   3. Religion and science—
Italy—Rome—History—16th century.   4. Religion and science—Italy—Rome—
History—17th century.   5. Trials (Heresy)—Italy—Rome—History—17th century.
I. Artigas, Mariano.   II. Title.

QB36.G2S459 2006
520.92—dc22
[B]

                                                                                    2006604521

Designed and typeset by Publishers' Design and Production Services, Inc.

Designed, typeset, and printed in the USA.

Contents

List of Illustrations

Palazzo Barberini. F. Bonanni, *Numismata Summorum Pontificum Templi Vaticani Fabricam Indicantia*, 2nd ed. (Rome: Ex Typographia Dominici Antonii Herculis in via Parionis, 1700). Courtesy of the Library of the University of Navarra. Page 123.

Portrait of Galileo by Ottavio Leoni, painted in 1624 when Galileo was fifty years old. From an engraving by the painter. Page 136.

Villa Borghese, built by Flaminio Ponzio and Giovanni Vasanzio, 1608–1613 (photo Paolo Soriani, Archivio Roma Sacra). Page 137.

Sister Maria Celeste, Galileo's daughter, portrait not signed or dated, but around 1630. Page 147.

Galileo's Villa *Il Gioiello* on the outskirts of Florence. Page 155.

Villa Medici in Rome, attributed to Bartolomeo Ammannati, end of the 16th century (photo Vasari). Page 169.

Portrait of Galileo by Giusto Sustermans, painted in 1640 when Galileo was seventy-six years old. From an old engraving of a copy.   page 172.

Galileo's tomb in Santa Croce. Page 187.

Preface

Radically different accounts of Galileo's trial have been offered by historians, philosophers, novelists, playwrights and journalists, who usually stress one aspect of the story at the expense of other equally important ones. In this book we try to set the record straight in the belief that truth is more satisfying, and more challenging, than propaganda or media hype.

In Chapter One, *Science and Religion: a Story of Warfare*, we discuss the nineteenth-century commonplace that science and religion are at war with each other. This view was advocated by John Draper, the author of the *History of the Conflict Between Science and Religion* (1874), and Andrew Dickson White, the first president of Cornell University, who wrote a detailed, two-volume work with the inflammatory title, *The History of Warfare Between Science and Theology in Christendom* (1896). Draper was convinced that the Roman Catholic Church had ferociously suppressed "by the sword and the stake" every attempt at progress, and White saw the Galileo Affair as an episode in "a war waged longer, with battles fiercer, with sieges more persistent, with strategy more shrewd than any of the comparatively transient warfare of Caesar or Napoleon." The warfare model became entrenched and exerted considerable influence throughout the twentieth century, particularly in America where even today divergent views about science and religion tend to be more radical than in other Western countries.

Chapter Two, *Did it Have to Happen?*, considers the bold hypothesis of Arthur Koestler, one of the most influential scientific journalists of the twentieth century. In his widely read book, *The Sleepwalkers*, he argues that Galileo's trial should not be seen as the outcome of a deeply-seated ideological opposition between science and religion, but as the result of personality clashes between an arrogant scientist and an equally proud pope. Chapter Three, *Brecht and the Revolutionary Who Moved the Earth*, is concerned with a playwright who felt quite differently, and whose play, *The Life of Galileo*, is still part of the repertoire of many theaters. Generally considered a faithful account of what happened, Brecht's play is largely a work of propaganda. Chapter Four, *Foul Play?*, asks whether Galileo was put in chains and subjected to torture, and whether a controversial document that was brought forward at Galileo's trial is a forgery, as some historians have claimed.

Chapter Five, *The Courtier Who Promised More than He Could Deliver*, examines the argument, made by Pierre Duhem and others that Galileo overstated his case and that the Church was right to censure him. We also consider the work of social historians of science, particularly Mario Biagioli, who stress the role of patrons in the unfolding of Galileo's career. We ponder the significance of Galileo's position as a courtier in Florence, and we question whether this played an essential role in the way he presented his views about the motion of the Earth. Chapter Six, *Galileo Another Bruno*, compares Galileo and the famous friar who held a variety of unconventional views about Christianity and was burned at the stake in Rome in 1600. We show what these men had in common and how they differed on religious and scientific issues.

In Chapter Seven, *Galileo Son of the Church*, we turn to Dava Sobel's *Galileo's Daughter. A Historical Memoir of Science, Faith and Love*, a recent biography of Galileo. Based on the letters that Galileo's daughter wrote to him, it offers new insights into the view they shared about science and religion. Chapter Eight is devoted to Pietro Redondi's *Galileo Heretic*, a work that claims that Galileo was not condemned for affirming that the Earth moves but for the worse crime of denying, as a consequence of his atomistic views, the Catholic formulation of the doctrine of the Eucharist. This radical view is re-examined in the light of a document related to the trial that was recently discovered by Mariano Artigas. Chapter Nine, *The Man to Whom the Church Apologized*, deals with the recognition by the Catholic Church that Galileo's views on science and religion are not only sound but commendable. Some authors feel that the Vatican did not go far enough. We outline their criticisms and weigh some of their proposals.

Demystifying is not an easy task and we are deeply grateful to friends and scholars who have helped us in a variety of ways. Rafael Martínez combed the Roman libraries to ensure that we had not overlooked important material; George Coyne and Ernan McMullin dispelled a few mysteries; Francesco Beretta and Thomas Cerbu cast light into dark corners;

Louisa Shea made a number of alterations to our draft in the interest of clarity and (we trust) the good name of the authors; our editor, Neale Watson, reminded us that plain language is the road to plain truth; and Anna Menna, our devoted secretary, taught us that a well-formated text is a pleasure to the eye and a safeguard against mystification.

We are happy to acknowledge the continuing support of the Templeton Foundation, and we owe particular thanks to Cardinal Paul Poupard, Monsignor Melchor Sánchez de Toca y Alameda and the dedicated staff of the Pontifical Council for Culture for making available recent material on the Galileo Affair. We are grateful to Evelyn Shea for raising important questions and never allowing us to escape with facile answers. To the numerous scholars, students and friends who have helped us, all that can be said here, and is not less true for being routine, is that the virtues of the book are due to them. The errors of fact, taste and logic are poor things, but our own.

William R. Shea

Mariano Artigas

CHAPTER ONE

Science and Religion:
A Story of Warfare?

Is Galileo's trial and condemnation the prime example of the conflict between science and religion? Was science, which is based on reason and experiment, bound to clash with religion, which relies on authority and dogma? How is it that honest inquirers still ask, Why did the Church try to silence Galileo? These questions are often raised because the Galileo Affair was a dramatic incident in the history of the relations between science and religion. It was also an isolated case. Galileo was a loyal member of the Catholic Church and it never occurred to him to attack the institution to which he belonged. He was eager to be heard within the Church, and he saw the rise of the new science as an opportunity for believers to gain a better insight into the workings of God in nature. He was worried that the Church might look foolish if it failed to understand the significance of the new astronomy and rashly condemned Copernicanism. Events proved him right, and the Church took a long time to recover from the blow.

Rome resisted the idea that it is the Earth and not the Sun that is in motion. Yet this historical opposition was not inevitable. If theologians had learned to respect their proper field of competence (as they later did), a fruitful dialogue might have been initiated in Galileo's own day. The pioneers of the Scientific Revolution were people for whom religion mattered. Copernicus was not an ordained priest, but he was a member of the clergy and a canon of his diocese in Poland. He was convinced that the motion of the Earth was not incompatible with the Christian Faith, and he dedicated his famous work, *On the Revolutions of the Heavenly Spheres*, to Pope Paul III. The German astronomer, Johannes Kepler, who discovered the three laws that describe how planets move around the sun, wanted to become a pastor in the Lutheran Church, and he saw himself as an interpreter of God's works in nature. The man who thought of universal gravitation, Isaac Newton, spent more time commenting on Scripture than working on problems of physics and mathematics.

The tension between what science was beginning to discover and what the Bible appeared to teach can be studied from a variety of viewpoints. A popular one is the warfare model that we owe to two nineteenth-century historians: John William Draper (1811–1882), and Andrew Dickson White (1832–1918). Draper published a *History of the Conflict Between Religion and Science*, and White a two-volume *A History of the Warfare of Science with Theology in Christendom*. For these writers, the opposition to Copernicanism was overwhelming evidence of the incompatibility of Christian theology with science. Reliance on authoritative texts and ecclesiastical control, they declared, produced a mind-set that precluded genuine knowledge of nature. War was not only inevitable; it was a duty for anyone who loved truth. We shall look closer at this position, but it will be helpful if we first consider the background against which Draper and White carried out their task. Theirs was the age of positivism, whose foremost exponent was the French philosopher Auguste Comte (1798–1857).

Three Stages of Human Development

According to Comte, the human mind developed through a succession of three stages that he called theological, metaphysical, and positivist. The first stage, the theological, was understood by Comte as the early phase of mental development in which the ultimate causes of events are found in the wills of superhuman beings or in the will of one such being. It is the age of the gods or of God, and it usually progresses from fetishism through polytheism to monotheism, which fuses several deities into the concept of one God.

The second stage, which Comte termed metaphysical, is the transformation of personal deities or of God into the abstract entities of an all-inclusive Nature such as force, attraction and repulsion. The third stage is the positive stage, namely that of the scientific outlook or mentality. Here there is no attempt to find unobservable causes of things. The mind

concerns itself with phenomena or observed facts, which are grouped together under general descriptive laws, such as the law of gravitation. The
search for ultimate causes is abandoned, for even if they existed they
could not be known. What can be known is only what can be observed. A
mature mind does not waste time in profitless theological and metaphysical speculation.

Each stage is associated by Comte with a distinct form of social orga-
nization. The theological stage is characterized by the imposition of authority from above, the metaphysical by the dominion of imagined law,
and the positive by the rise of a practical and scientific meritocracy whose
vocation is to organize and regulate industrial society in a peaceful and rational manner. In this scheme of things, religion falls by the wayside, not
because the existence of God has been refuted, but because there is no
positive reason for assuming that there is such a being. It is an unverifi-
able hypothesis that can only hinder scientific progress.

There is no doubt that Comte's theory captures some interesting features of intellectual history, but it cannot accommodate a number of important facts, such as the deep religious commitment of the founders of
modern science. Comte's description is far from neutral: it is a recon-
struction of the history of intellectual development on the assumption that
knowledge that is not "positive" is condemned to wither away.

Two Contending Powers

The son of a Wesleyan clergyman, John William Draper was born near Liv-
erpool in 1811. He studied chemistry at the University of London, but the
death of his father prevented his taking a degree. In 1832 he emigrated to
the United States with his mother and his sister and settled in a Wesleyan
colony in Christiansville, Virginia. He graduated in medicine at the University of Pennsylvania, and was appointed professor of chemistry in the
medical department of the University of New York in 1839. This was
the year that Daguerre announced his discovery of the action of sunlight
on silver, and Draper promptly made it his special study. He was the first
to apply the new technique of photography to an individual (his sister
Catherine) and to photograph the Moon's surface. He also investigated the
action of light on the growth of plants, and he was actively engaged with
Samuel F.B. Morse in the development of the telegraph. In 1839 he became
professor of chemistry at the University of New York. Later on he was

professor of physiology, and published a book on human physiology. In 1877 he was elected to the National Academy of Sciences.

Draper was fascinated with clashes of ideas, and devoted his energies to the study of intellectual battlegrounds. In 1860, one year after the publication of Darwin's *The Origin of Species*, Draper played a role in the famous debate between Thomas Henry Huxley, Darwin's bulldog, and Samuel Wilberforce, the Anglican bishop of Oxford. Two years later, he published his *History of the Intellectual Development of Europe*, the forerunner of his best-selling *History of the Conflict between Religion and Science* (1874) that passed through twenty editions and was translated into nine languages.

Draper's heavy artillery was reserved for the Catholic Church, which he considered the arch-enemy of science, ferociously suppressing by the sword and stake every attempt at progress. Stephen Jay Gould comments:

> Draper, following a lamentable tradition in the history of American prejudice, wrote his book as a Protestant "old American," fearful of Catholic influence, as particularly expressed in the foreign and proletarian origins of most American Catholics. His book, little more than an anti-papist diatribe, argued that the liberal spirit of Protestantism could make peace with the beneficial, and in any case ineluctable, advance of science, whereas dogmatic Catholicism could reach no such accommodation and had to be superseded or crushed.[1]

Every thoughtful person, according to Draper, must take part in the struggle between evil, which is manifested in religion, and goodness, which is revealed in science. "The history of Science," he writes,

> is not a mere record of isolated discoveries; it is a narrative of the conflict of two contending powers, the expansive force of the human intellect on one side, and the compression arising from traditionary faith and human interests on the other. No one has hitherto treated the subject from this point of view. Yet from this point it presents itself to us as a living issue—in fact, as the most important of all living issues.[2]

Convinced that he should face this challenge, Draper shows his credentials for doing so:

> Though deeply impressed with such thoughts, I should not have presumed to write this book, or to intrude on the public the ideas it

presents, had I not made the facts with which it deals a subject of long and earnest meditation. And I have gathered a strong incentive to undertake this duty from the circumstance that a *History of the Intellectual Development of Europe*, published by me several years ago, which has passed through many editions in America, and has been reprinted in numerous European languages, English, French, German, Russian, Polish, Serbian, etc., is everywhere received with favor.[3]

Draper declares that it was mainly the teaching of science that prepared him to present an objective account of the views and acts of the two contending parties. "What I have sought to do," he declares,

is, to present a clear and impartial statement of the views and acts of the two contending parties. In one sense I have tried to identify myself with each, so as to comprehend thoroughly their motives; but in another and higher sense I have endeavored to stand aloof, and relate with impartiality their actions. I therefore trust that those, who may be disposed to criticize this book, will bear in mind that its object is not to advocate the views and pretensions of either party, but to explain clearly, and without shrinking, those of both.[4]

The Shape of the Earth

Draper discusses Galileo's share in changing our views about nature in Chapter Six of his *History of the Conflict between Religion and Science*, titled "Conflict respecting the nature of the world" that opens with a description of the beliefs of primitive people who took it for granted that the Earth was flat and that they were the pinnacle of creation. They assumed that the heavenly bodies—the Sun, the Moon, the stars—revolve around the Earth and that beyond the celestial dome lies a region of eternal light and happiness (heaven), the abode of God and the angelic hosts. Beneath the Earth is a region of darkness and misery (hell), the habitation of those who are evil. It is on the basis of this primitive cosmology that the world's great religious systems were founded, and this is why they resist any change that might threaten the localization of heaven and hell. Although the ancient Greeks had realized that the Earth is round and had even speculated about its possible motion, Christians ignored them because of their belief that the Scriptures contain the sum of all knowledge.

Draper's indictment of the Middle Ages is ferocious. It is also completely out of step with recent scholarly assessment of that period, as we can see from the following passage by the American historian of science Thomas Kuhn:

> By modern standards the practice of science during the Middle Ages was incredibly inefficient. But how else could science have been reborn in the West? The centuries of scholasticism are the centuries in which the tradition of ancient science and philosophy was simultaneously reconstituted, assimilated, and tested for adequacy. As weak spots were discovered, they immediately became foci for the first effective research in the modern world. The great new scientific theories of the sixteenth and seventeenth centuries all originate from rents torn by scholastic criticism in the fabric of Aristotelian thought. Most of those theories also embody key concepts created by scholastic science. And more important even than these is the attitude that modern scientists inherited from their medieval predecessors: an unbounded faith in the power of human reason to solve the problems of nature. As the late Professor Whitehead remarked, "Faith in the possibility of science, generated antecedently to the development of modern scientific theory, is an unconscious derivative from medieval theology."[5]

Some periods of the Middle Ages are now considered models of international co-operation that brought together the contributions of the Greeks, the Arabs and the Latins. The point is well made by Edward Grant, a distinguished medieval historian:

> The collective achievement of these three civilizations, despite their significant linguistic, religious, and cultural differences, stands as one of the greatest examples of multiculturalism in recorded history. It is an example of multiculturalism in its best sense. It was possible only because scholars in one civilization recognized the need to learn from scholars of another civilization.[6]

The quotation is found in the last section of the book, devoted to comment on the scientific synthesis of the Greek, Arab and Latin elements, under the title: "Greco-Arabic-Latin science: A triumph of three civilizations." Draper would have none of this. For him the reasons to pursue science originated in commercial rivalries, and the question of the shape of the Earth was settled by Columbus, Vasco de Gama, and

GALILAEUS·GALILAEI PATRICIUS FLÓR.
AET, SUAE
ANNUM AGENS QUADRAGESIMUM

ILLUSTRATION 1   Portrait of Galileo by Santi di Tito, painted around 1603.

Ferdinand Magellan. This statement is completely wrong. The great explorers only set sail because they knew that the Earth is round, a fact that had been recognized since antiquity in the light of three simple observations: (a) the top of the mast of a ship approaching the shore becomes visible before the hull, (b) more of a ship and of the sea is seen from a mountain by the seaside than from the beach, and (c) the shadow that the Earth casts on the Moon during a lunar eclipse always has a circular shape.

Did Copernicus Establish the Heliocentric System?

The unquestioned herald of the Scientific Revolution for Draper is Copernicus, whose book *On the Revolutions of the Heavenly Spheres* appeared in 1543. Draper was convinced that he had understood this great work, but he brought his own convictions to bear on the issue when he declared that it incontestably established the heliocentric system, and that those who opposed it were fools or knaves: "Astronomers justly affirm," he wrote, "that the book of Copernicus, *De Revolutionibus*, changed the face of their science. It incontestably established the heliocentric theory."[7] The truth of the matter is that in Copernicus's day the overwhelming majority of astronomers considered his system to be no more than a clever idea. As a calculating device to determine where the planets would show up on a given night, it worked rather well. As a physical description of how the planets actually moved, it posed as many problems as it solved. The reason is that the orbits of the planets around the sun are elliptical, not circular, as Copernicus maintained. Hence, he could not work out precisely the orbits they follow.

The great astronomical novelty of the seventeenth century was the invention of the telescope that enabled Galileo to see what had never been seen by anyone before. Galileo discovered that the Moon is covered with mountains and craters, that Jupiter has four satellites, that the number of stars is simply enormous, and that Venus has phases like those of the Moon. "These and many other beautiful telescopic discoveries," comments Draper,

> tended to the establishment of the truth of the Copernican theory and gave unbounded alarm to the Church. By the low and ignorant ecclesiastics they were denounced as deceptions or frauds. . . . Galileo

was accused of imposture, heresy, blasphemy, atheism. With a view of defending himself, he addressed a letter to the Abbe Castelli. . . . He was summoned before the Holy Inquisition. . . . He was directed to desist from teaching and advocating the Copernican theory, and pledge himself that he would neither publish nor defend it for the future. Knowing well that Truth has no need of martyrs, he assented to the required recantation, and gave the promise demanded.[8]

Draper is led astray by what he believes *must* have happened. He states that Galileo made many other telescopic discoveries, when the only one to be added is the observation of sunspots, which was also made by the Jesuit Christopher Scheiner. Galileo's discoveries did not give "unbounded alarm to the Church," nor were they "denounced as deceptions or frauds." Neither was he "accused of imposture, heresy, blasphemy, atheism" for seeing what no human eye had beheld. On the contrary, when Galileo went to Rome in the spring of 1611, he was given a triumphal welcome, and the Jesuits of the Roman College gave a public lecture in praise of his achievement. The large audience included high church dignitaries as well as scientists. "If we were still in the ancient Roman Republic," Cardinal Francesco Maria del Monte wrote to the Grand Duke of Tuscany, "I am certain that a statue would have been erected in his honor on the Capitol."[9]

The letter to Castelli to which Draper refers in the quotation above was written in the following circumstances. A young Benedictine priest named Castelli, who had studied with Galileo in Padua, was appointed professor at the University of Pisa in November 1613. Shortly thereafter he was invited to dine with the Grand Duke Cosimo II and his mother, the dowager Grand Duchess Christina of Lorraine, a genuinely devout woman and a matriarchal figure of great influence at court. The Grand Duke asked about the University and the conversation turned to Galileo's celestial discoveries. Everyone praised them except the Grand Duchess who, prompted by a professor of philosophy, began to raise objections from Scripture against the motion of the Earth. Castelli replied as best he could, and promptly reported the conversation to Galileo, who felt it was important that the case for Copernicanism be made by himself rather than by an assistant professor. He immediately sent Castelli a long letter in which he clearly stated his views on the relations between science and religion. A Dominican friar named Niccolò Lorini got hold of a copy and sent it to the Holy Office without Galileo's permission or knowledge.

It is important to understand that although Galileo enjoyed a high position and a large salary as the Grand Duke's personal astronomer, no one saw him as the Father of Modern Science, quite simply because modern science was not yet born. His telescopic discoveries had ushered in a wealth of new facts, but an empirically based science needs not only fresh observational data but also a set of new laws and a theory to interpret them. Galileo had been working on two laws that were eventually to play a crucial role in the new science. The first is the law of free fall, which states that the distance that a body covers when it is dropped is proportional to the square of the time of descent. The second is that the shape of the flight of any projectile is a parabola, be it an arrow, a cannonball or a missile. Galileo had not published these laws as yet, and only a few knew about them. In any case, no one was to grasp their deep significance until Newton showed, at the end of the seventeenth century, that they followed from his more general laws of motion.

Galileo thought that the tides, by rising and falling as they do, provide evidence that the Earth both turns upon itself and goes around the Sun. The idea, however ingenious, is wrong, and it convinced few people. Some theologians began pondering the impact of the new astronomy on the interpretation of Scripture, but they would have been unwise to accept as established proof what virtually all astronomers considered a wild conjecture. In 1615, a priest by the name of Paolo Antonio Foscarini sent Cardinal Robert Bellarmine a pamphlet in which he argued that the Copernican hypothesis was not at variance with the Bible. The Cardinal replied in friendly terms that, to the best of his knowledge, there was no proof that the Earth really moved, but he did not rule out the possibility altogether:

> If there were a true demonstration that the Sun is at the centre of the world and the Earth in the third sphere, and that the Sun does not revolve around the Earth but the Earth around the Sun, then we would have to use great care in explaining those passages of Scripture that seem contrary. . . . But I cannot assume that there is such a demonstration unless someone shows me one.[10]

Although we can calculate the position of the planets by assuming that the Earth moves, this, by itself, is not enough to assert that it actually does. Cardinal Bellarmine was unmoved by the analogy, already invoked by Copernicus, with the beach that appears to recede when we leave the harbor aboard a ship. No one, Bellarmine jested, ever argued that what really moves is the shore and not the ship. As far as he was concerned, the Copernican, the Ptolemaic or other astronomical systems were not a detailed description of reality, but more like a map to help us get around. To mistake the map for the territory is a serious error, and the Cardinal thought there would always be a gap between our models of science and the reality they represent. Galileo's position was very different. He believed that Nature spoke plainly about who she was and that she could be clearly understood by those who understood her language. "This grand book, the universe," he wrote, "stands continually open to our gaze but it cannot be understood unless one first learns the language in which it is composed. It is written in the language of mathematics, and its characters are triangles, circles and other geometrical figures, without which it is humanly impossible to understand a single word of it."[11] In his masterpiece, the *Dialogue on the Two Chief World Systems*, Galileo took the further step of claiming that mathematical insight is so powerful that it provides us with knowledge that is as certain as the one that God has.

Galileo's Trial

For over seventy years after the publication of Copernicus's *On the Revolutions of the Heavenly Spheres*, the Church did not worry about whether the motion of the Earth went against what the Bible taught, but in 1616 the work was included in the Index of forbidden books. As much as we may regret the measure, there is more of indignation than truth in Draper's description of how Copernicus's work was handled: "Its fate was such as he had anticipated. The Inquisition condemned it as heretical. In their decree, prohibiting it, the Congregation of the Index denounced his system as 'that false Pythagorean doctrine utterly contrary to the Holy Scriptures.' "[12]

As we have by now come to suspect, matters were more complicated than Draper assumes. In 1616, the Inquisition took matters in hand and appointed a review panel of eleven experts, who met on 24 February 1616 to assess two statements. The first, "That the Sun is the centre of the world, and therefore does not move," was unanimously judged "foolish and absurd in philosophy and heretical since it explicitly contradicts in many places the sense of Holy Scripture, according to the literal meaning of the words and according to the common interpretation and understanding of the Holy Fathers and the doctors of theology." The second statement, "The Earth is not the centre of the world, nor motionless, but moves as a whole and also with diurnal motion," received "the same qualification in philosophy," and in regard to theological truth was described "as at least erroneous in faith."[13]

The assessment of the experts was communicated to Pope Paul V, who immediately instructed Cardinal Bellarmine to make it clear to Galileo that he was to abstain from teaching or even discussing Copernicanism. On 5 March 1616, a decree of the Congregation of the Index (not the Inquisition) appeared, which read: "The Congregation has decided that the books by Nicolaus Copernicus (*On the Revolutions of the Heavenly Spheres*) and Diego de Zuñiga (*Commentary on Job*) be suspended until corrected."[14] There was no mention of heresy. Although no Catholic publisher rushed to publish a corrected edition of the book, a reprint of the original appeared in Protestant Amsterdam in 1617, the year after the book had been placed on the Index.

Galileo was personally informed by Cardinal Bellarmine that Copernicanism had been banned and he was told, courteously but firmly, not to go about teaching that the Earth moves. He was not asked to stop doing what all astronomers did, namely using the heliocentric system as a tool to make calculations. All that was formally asked of Galileo was that he treat the Copernican system as a convenient geometrical device until such a day as he found real arguments for presenting it as physically true. As of the time when Bellarmine died in 1621, that day had not yet come. Neither had it in 1624 when Cardinal Maffeo Barberini, a Florentine and a friend of Galileo, was elected Pope and took the name of Urban VIII. Galileo was excited at the prospects this opened, and he went to Rome where he was warmly received by the new Pope, who granted him six interviews in six weeks, a rare favor. Urban VIII shared Cardinal Bellarmine's conviction that our access to scientific knowledge is limited to conditions that are forever short of completeness. He expressed this in theological terms by saying that it is an error to "impose necessity" on the Creator, who could have designed the universe in a variety of ways about which we know little or nothing. The Pope's overriding concern was that scientists should recognize that our view of nature is constructed from what we observe, and that we cannot claim at any time to have the whole picture. He assumed that Galileo agreed with him, whereas Galileo thought that the Pope would allow a defense of Copernicanism if it were presented in the guise of a mere hypothesis. What could have been a comedy of errors turned out, unfortunately, to be the first act of a tragedy.

A man of no small ego, Galileo had been elated by the Pope's warm reception, and upon his return to Florence he drafted his brilliant *Dialogue on the Two Chief World Systems*, in which he set out his best arguments. It appeared in 1632, but this time, unlike in 1616, Galileo was summoned to Rome by the Inquisition. After much procrastination, he arrived in Rome in the spring of 1633. Draper describes the outcome as follows:

> What a spectacle! This venerable man, the most illustrious of his age, forced by the threat of death to deny facts which his judges as well as himself knew to be true! He was then committed to prison, treated with remorseless severity during the remaining ten years of his life, and was denied burial in consecrated ground. Must not that be false which requires for its support so much imposture, so much barbarity?[15]

Galileo was condemned for disobeying the order enjoined to him in 1616 not to teach Copernicanism. The rest is what Draper's jaundiced view of Rome told him must have happened. In fact, Galileo never spent a single day in a prison cell. Before the trial, he was the guest of the Florentine Ambassador in the Palazzo Firenze in the heart of Rome. During the trial he was given a private suite in the main building of the Holy Office, and after the trial he was once more the official guest of the Tuscan government, but this time in the Villa Medici. He was allowed to leave Rome for Siena where Archbishop Ascanio Piccolomini made him welcome in the episcopal palace. At the end of 1633, Galileo was granted his request to return to his own house in Arcetri on the outskirts of Florence. He was placed under house arrest, in the sense that he could only leave his home with the permission of the ecclesiastical authorities. Urban VIII was repeatedly asked to lift this sanction, but the Pope remained adamant even after Galileo became blind, and he was still confined to his residence when he died in 1642. Galileo was buried in consecrated ground (in spite of Draper's assertion to the contrary) in the church of Santa Croce in Florence, but in a side chapel, not in the family vault in the nave. Urban VIII, with a regrettable lack of generosity, had objected to his being buried with his forefathers. Yet neither papal intransigence nor the condemnation of the *Dialogue on the Two Chief World Systems* put an end to the spread of Copernicanism. Indeed, the ban was much less effective than Draper surmised.

13

From Conflict to Warfare

Draper's book had appeared in 1874. Twenty-two years later, it was followed by a much more ambitious work, a two-volume *History of the Warfare of Science with Theology in Christendom* by Andrew Dickson White. Born in 1832, White had studied at Yale, and after serving as an attaché at the U.S. legation in Saint Petersburg, he became professor of history and English literature at the University of Michigan in Ann Arbor. He campaigned for a state university based on liberal principles, and unhampered by religious dogma. In 1865, at the age of thirty-three, he was given the possibility of fulfilling his dream when he was appointed the first president of Cornell University. He later served on numerous government commissions, and was U.S. minister to Germany (1879–1881) and Russia (1892–1894), and Ambassador to Germany (1898–1902). In 1899 he acted as president of the U.S. delegation at the Hague Peace Conference.

White went to Cornell with the passionate conviction that university education should be completely separated from religion. This caused something of an uproar and White defended his views in lectures, essays and articles in which he tried to show the disastrous effects of opening the door of Academe to religion. In this way he accumulated polemical material for his book *A History of the Warfare of Science with Theology in Christendom*. White's battle horse was the history of modern science, with which he rode roughshod over facts in order to drive his point home. Whereas Draper's contempt was reserved for Roman Catholicism, White extended his withering scorn to all Christian denominations. Owen Gingerich comments that White "was eager to discredit what he believed was religion's antipathy toward the march of science, so he got his graduate students to dig up as many cases as they could find. The so-called Galileo Affair played a central role in his account."[16]

Chapter 3 of White's book is devoted to astronomy, and includes a section on Galileo. White claimed to offer a fresh interpretation of Galileo's trial in the light of documents that had recently been published:

> I shall present this warfare at some length because, so far as I can find, no careful summary of it has been given in our language, since the whole history was placed in a new light by the revelations of the trial documents in the Vatican Library, honestly published for the first time by L'Épinois in 1867, and since that by Gebler, Berti, Favaro, and others.[17]

ILLUSTRATION 2   Portrait of Galileo by Domenico Tintoretto, painted around 1605.

In spite of his repeated good intentions and his appearance of rigor, White takes great liberties with history. He affirms, for instance, that Galileo's discoveries "had clearly taken the Copernican theory out of the list of hypotheses, and placed it before the world as a truth."[18] We have already seen that this assertion, which Draper also made, is wishful thinking. Galileo dealt a mortal blow to the astronomical system of Ptolemy, but he utterly failed to demonstrate the truth of Copernicanism. At the time, the system uppermost in the mind of astronomers was Tycho Brahe's compromise, in which the planets revolve around the Sun, which itself goes around the stationary Earth.

White assumes that the widespread rejection of the belief that the Earth moves entailed an equally strong denial of what could be seen through the telescope. We quote the following passage at length to give the reader the flavor of White's prose:

> The first important attack on Galileo began in 1610, when he announced that his telescope had revealed the moons of the planet Jupiter. The enemy saw that this took the Copernican theory out of the realm of hypothesis, and they gave battle immediately. They denounced both his method and its results as absurd and impious. As to his method, professors bred in the "safe science" favored by the Church argued that the divinely appointed way of arriving at the truth in astronomy was by theological reasoning on texts of Scripture; and, to his results, they insisted, first, that Aristotle knew nothing of these new revelations; and, next, that the Bible showed by all applicable types that there could be only seven planets; that this was proved by the seven golden candlesticks of the Apocalypse, by the seven-branched candlestick of the tabernacle, and by the seven churches of Asia; that from Galileo's doctrine consequences must logically result destructive to Christian truth. Bishops and priests therefore warned their flocks, and multitudes of the faithful besought the Inquisition to deal speedily and sharply with the heretic.[19]

This story fits White's idea of how history must have unfolded. But Galileo's discoveries met with very little resistance. They were rapidly acknowledged by scientists everywhere and, where they were doubted, this was only for a brief period of time by people who did not have decent telescopes or did not know how to focus them. In spite of what White claims, the satellites of Jupiter were never denounced, and the Church never invoked the symbolism of the number seven as an argument against Copernicanism. The "enemy" that gave battle consisted of two Dominican friars, Niccolò Lorini and Tommaso Caccini, who took it upon themselves to inform the Holy Office in 1615 (five years after Galileo's telescopic discoveries) that Galileo's views about the motion of the earth were at variance with Scripture.

White's outrageous disregard for facts can be explained by his overriding political agenda. He was dedicated to the creation of a center of higher knowledge that was entirely free of religious influence. In an age when the American establishment was still largely Protestant, this raised comprehensible opposition, and White came to see himself as another Galileo battling the arrayed forces of obscurantism. The Yankee divines, who objected to his plans behaved, on his view, like the Italian priests who had persecuted Galileo. Positivism, the reigning ideology of Academe, comforted White in this belief, and he trusted that he would overcome. He also hoped that this would be during his lifetime, and not after his death like Galileo. White writes with such self-assurance that his hectoring passes muster for careful scrutiny to the present day. In a recent biography of Galileo, James Reston quotes White as an authoritative source and attributes words and statements to different characters of the story relying on White, who never provided any source for his assertions.[20]

The New Heavens

The facts become unrecognizable in White's account. Speaking of the satellites of Jupiter he writes:

> In vain did Galileo try to prove the existence of satellites by showing them to the doubters through his telescope: they either declared it impious to look, or, if they did look, denounced the satellites as illusions from the devil. Good Father Clavius declared that "to see satellites of Jupiter, men had to make an instrument which would create them." In vain did Galileo try to save the great truths he had discovered by his letters to the Benedictine Castelli and the Grand-Duchess Christine, in which he argued that literal biblical interpretation should not be applied to science; it was answered that such an argument only made his heresy more detestable; that he was "worse than Luther or Calvin."[21]

White was fond of rumors. The quotation in the text above, "to see satellites of Jupiter, men had to make an instrument which would create them," comes from a letter that the painter Ludovico Cardi, known as Cigoli from his native town, wrote to Galileo from Rome on 1 October 1610. Cigoli was not quoting what Clavius had said before him but what he had heard from someone who had been told that Clavius had made such a remark to a friend. The facts are as follows. Galileo's *Sidereus Nuncius* was published in Venice in March 1610. The edition of 550 copies sold out almost immediately, and it may have taken some time for a copy to become available in Rome where Clavius taught astronomy. But by the autumn of 1610 the Jesuits had confirmed Galileo's discoveries, and Clavius wrote to Galileo on 17 December to say that he had observed the satellites several times. He even enclosed diagrams of their positions showing that they actually orbited Jupiter.[22]

Galileo passed on this good news to Mark Welser, a wealthy friend and patron in Augsburg, who promptly asked Clavius for confirmation. On 11 January 1611, Clavius replied that although he had been skeptical at first, all doubt had been dispelled when a friend sent him a good instrument.[23] Clavius's initial difficulties were clearly due to a telescope of inferior quality or poor mounting. In a letter of 17 September 1610, Galileo had given him some pointers on the effective use of a telescope for astronomical observation. He stressed that a firm mounting is necessary for a hand-held telescope. Even steadied on a windowsill, it is difficult to focus and the mere motion of one's heartbeat or breathing can render objects unrecognizable. Galileo closed by expressing the hope of going to Rome and personally demonstrating the truth of his discoveries,[24] but it was to be six months before he could fulfill that wish.

It is important to bear in mind that Galileo never understood how the telescope works or, more precisely, that he was never able to explain the geometrical properties of lenses. He knew that there are two main types: convex lenses that are thicker in the middle than at the edge and cause light to converge, and concave lenses that are thinner in the middle than at the edge and cause light to diverge. He did not realize that the position of the image formed by a convex lens can be calculated from the simple relations between the focal length of the lens, and the distances of the object and image from the lens. When Galileo claimed that he built his first telescope "on the basis of the science of refraction,"[25] he was not saying more than that he realized that a combination of a convex (converging) lens and a concave (diverging) lens produced an enlarged, erect image. Just how this worked escaped him. His good fortune was that he found a lens grinder who could produce lenses of superior quality.

We are now in a better position to appreciate Clavius's remark that to see the Jovian satellites one would have to build an instrument to create them. If he really said this, by the time it was related to Galileo by Cigoli, Clavius and the Jesuits had already reproduced Galileo's observations with a telescope of their own devising. Even if we accept Clavius's alleged remark at face value, his skepticism is understandable given the inferior quality of the instrument he had first used. As soon as he got a good telescope, he was more than delighted to confirm and praise Galileo's discoveries. It should also be mentioned that Clavius was already seventy-two years old when he first peered into a telescope, and his eyesight may not have been as keen as that of his younger colleagues. Nonetheless, in the summer of 1611, shortly before the onset of the illness that was to carry him away on 6 February 1612, Clavius provided an account of Galileo's discoveries in a revised edition of his popular textbook of astronomy. He recommended consulting

> the reliable little book by Galileo Galilei, printed at Venice in 1610 and called *Sidereus Nuncius*, which describes various observations of the stars first made by him. One of the most important things seen with this instrument is that Venus receives its light from the Sun as does the Moon, so that it has a more or less crescent shape according to its distance from the Sun. I have observed this in Rome in company of others several times. . . . Finally, Jupiter has four roving stars, which vary in a remarkable way their place both among themselves and with respect to Jupiter, as Galileo Galilei carefully and accurately describes. Since things are thus, astronomers ought to consider how the celestial orbs may be arranged in order to save these phenomena.[26]

The last sentence makes it clear that Clavius was willing to entertain the possibility of a radical change in astronomy.

Worse than Luther or Calvin

Let us now return to the passage from White's book that we cited above and examine his claim that what Galileo wrote in his letters to Castelli and the Grand Duchess was answered by denouncing his "heresy" and declaring that he was "worse than Luther or Calvin." White's disregard for chronology leads him astray once again. Galileo's letters to Castelli and the Grand Duchess were written between 1613 and 1615, but the reference to Luther and Calvin is much later, and is hearsay evidence. It is found in a letter that Galileo wrote to a Protestant friend in January 1633 as he was about to go to Rome to face his trial: "I know from a reliable source that the Jesuit Fathers have managed to create, in the highest quarters, the impression that my book is execrable and more injurious to the Church than the writings of Luther and Calvin."[27] Galileo had given some Jesuits a hard ride for disagreeing with him, and he assumed that they would deal with him in the same currency.

White's difficulty in seeing things in a non-polemical context is illustrated in the way he interprets an artist's depiction of Galileo's discovery that the surface of the Moon is not smooth but rough. "To make matters worse," White writes, "a painter, placing the Moon in a religious picture in its usual position beneath the feet of the Blessed Virgin, outlined on its surface mountains and valleys; this was denounced as a sacrilege logically resulting from the astronomer's heresy."[28] White is referring to Cigoli, who had been commissioned by Pope Paul V to decorate the Pauline Chapel in the Basilica of Santa Maria Maggiore in Rome. In the lantern of the dome, Cigoli painted his greatest and most beautiful work, a representation of the Virgin Mary with her feet on the moon. The striking feature is the surface of the Moon, which is covered with craters as Galileo had observed them. This work was never considered a sacrilege, and it continues to be admired to the present day by faithful and visitors alike. White thought it would have created a storm, and his fancy did the rest.

To set the historical record straight, let us briefly examine three other claims made by White. The first concerns the discovery of sunspots by Galileo and Christopher Scheiner, a German Jesuit. According to White, neither Scheiner nor any professor in a Catholic University was allowed to divulge their existence. This is sheer nonsense. Galileo's *Letters on Sunspots* were published in Rome with the *imprimatur* (official license to print) of the ecclesiastical authorities in 1613, and Christopher Scheiner's *Rosa Ursina*, with 70 copper engravings of sunspots, appeared in 1630 with the same kind of religious approval.

Second, White maintains that the Pope's infallibility was involved in the Inquisition's denial that the Earth moves, but papal infallibility is irrelevant in this case. The Roman Church distinguishes between doctrinal and administrative decisions, and the condemnation of Copernicanism was generally considered an administrative act, even though it might be seen as having doctrinal implications. There is not a single ecclesiastical document that makes the claim that papal infallibility was involved in Galileo's condemnation.

Third, White offers, in the light of allegedly new evidence, a dramatic account of Galileo's treatment when he was taken to the headquarters of the Inquisition:

There, as was too long concealed, but as is now fully revealed, he was menaced with torture again and again by express order of Pope Urban, and, as is also thoroughly established from the trial documents themselves, forced to abjure under threats, and subjected to imprisonment by command of the Pope; the Inquisition deferring in this whole matter to the papal authority. All the long series of attempts made in the supposed interest of the Church to mystify these transactions have at last failed. The world knows now that Galileo was subjected certainly to indignities, to imprisonment, and to threats equivalent to torture.[29]

If White had read the documents, he would have known that the trial was not conducted the way he claims. The facts are as follows. On 12 April 1633, Galileo was summoned to the Holy Office and interrogated by the Commissary General, the Dominican Francesco Maculano, in the presence of his assistant, Carolo Sinceri.[30] After the hearing, Galileo was detained in the Holy Office but he was not placed in one of the cells usually reserved for criminals. He was given a three-room suite with free access to the inner courtyard.[31] During the next few days, the Commissary General met informally with him and arranged a deal whereby Galileo agreed to admit some wrongdoing in order to be treated with leniency.[32] On 30 April, Galileo signed a statement in which he recognized that he had erred, but without any malicious intent, in writing his *Dialogue*.[33] He was then allowed to leave the headquarters of the Inquisition and go to the Palazzo Firenze, the residence of the Florentine ambassador, but he was enjoined not to discuss the matter with anyone. Summoned back on 10 May, he made a third deposition in which he tried to justify himself.[34] The outcome of the hearings was presented on 16 June at a meeting of the Inquisition (at which Galileo was not present) presided over by Urban VIII. The minutes record that:

> His Holiness decided that Galileo be examined on his intentions, even to the extent of threatening him with torture. Having undergone this interrogation, he is to abjure them before the whole Congregation of the Holy Office, as vehemently suspect of heresy. He is then to be condemned to imprisonment at the pleasure of the Sacred Congregation, and ordered, under penalty of relapse, never again to discuss, by word or in writing, the motion of the Earth or the stability of the Sun.[35]

The Pope also decreed that the *Dialogue* be prohibited and that, as a deterrent, the sentence be sent to apostolic nuncios and inquisitors in order that it might be read out at meetings of professors of science. Galileo's error was qualified as "vehemently suspect of heresy," an expression that calls for a brief explanation. The Inquisition dealt with other offences such as witchcraft, but it was mainly interested in doctrinal deviancy of two kinds: formal heresy and suspicion of heresy. The term *suspicion* does not have here the modern legal meaning of allegation as opposed to proof. The distinction between formal heresy and suspicion of heresy was the seriousness of the matter. For instance, to deny the divinity of Christ was a formal heresy, to read books forbidden by the Inquisition was to incur suspicion of heresy. Furthermore, suspicion of heresy was further subdivided (again according to the gravity of the offence) into *vehement* suspicion of heresy and *slight* suspicion of heresy. The term *vehement* used by the Inquisition indicates that the motion of the Earth was perceived as a serious threat to the traditional interpretation of the Bible.

On 21 June, Galileo returned to the headquarters of the Inquisition to be interrogated on his intentions by the Commissary General, in the presence of his assistant as before. Galileo declared that he did not hold the opinion of Copernicus after he had been enjoined to abandon it. He was then "told to tell the truth, otherwise one would have to have recourse to torture."[36] Galileo confirmed what he had said, signed his deposition, and was allowed to leave. Torture was not used, although the Inquisition manual published in 1621 has a whole chapter "On the Manner of Interrogating Culprits by Torture" that shows that it was not always an empty threat. It begins by saying:

> The culprit having denied the crimes with which he has been charged, and the latter not having been fully proved, in order to learn the truth it is necessary to proceed against him by means of a rigorous examination; in fact, the function of torture is to make up for the shortcoming of witnesses, when they cannot adduce a conclusive proof against the culprit.[37]

The melancholy truth is that the Pontifical States, which were a temporal as well as a spiritual power, dealt with dissent like other countries in Europe. The rules of procedure in seventeenth-century Rome were not far removed from those that were found in Paris or London. Confession, obtained under torture, was considered valid. In most cases, the ecclesiastical authorities did not forget their Christian duty of leniency, but as public officials they had the right to use torture.

On the day following his last meeting with Maculano and Sinceri, Galileo was brought to the convent of Santa Maria sopra Minerva where he faced, for the first and only time, the Cardinal Inquisitors, who numbered seven out of ten on that morning. He was made to kneel before the assembled prelates and read out a solemn recantation of "the false opinion that the Sun is the centre of the universe and does not move, and that the Earth is not the centre of the same and moves." He also promised, "never again to say or assert, orally or in writing, anything that might cause a similar suspicion."[38] His punishment consisted in the ban of his *Dialogue*, formal arrest at the pleasure of the Holy Office, and a religious penance that required that he recite the seven penitential palms once a week for three years. The sentence of imprisonment was immediately commuted to house arrest, and he was shortly thereafter relieved of the recital of the seven penitential psalms by his daughter, Sister Maria Celeste, who offered to say them for him. So things were bad, but not as iniquitous as White made them out.

The Conflict Thesis

"For nearly a century," writes Colin A. Russell,

> the notion of mutual hostility (the Draper-White thesis) has been routinely employed in popular-science writing, by the media, and in a few older histories of science. Only in the last thirty years of the twentieth century did historians of science mount a sustained attack on the thesis, and only gradually has a wider public begun to recognize its deficiencies.[39]

A case in point is the late Stephen Jay Gould, a paleontologist and the author of popular books on science, who was also the advocate of peaceful relationships between science and religion. Here is how he judges the Draper-White thesis:

> I cannot emphasize too strongly that the old model of all-out warfare between science and religion—the "standard" view of my secular education, and founded upon two wildly successful books of the mid–to late nineteenth century simply does not fit this issue, and represents an absurdly false and caricatured dichotomy that can only disrespect both supposed sides of this nonexistent conflict. "Religion," as

a coherent entity, never opposed "science" in any general or comprehensive way.[40]

Gould sums up, "This model of warfare between science and religion . . . fails on both possible rationales: as a defendable antithesis in logic, and as an accurate description in history."[41] Without claiming special expertise about the Galileo Affair, Gould has captured the complexity of the case. He also offers another example of the alleged antagonism between science and religion:

> As so many scholars have documented, the standard episodes in the supposed warfare of science and religion are either greatly distorted or entirely fictional. For example, the historian J. B. Russell (*Inventing the Earth*, Praeger, 1991) devotes an entire book to showing how Draper, White, and other architects of the "warfare" model simply invented the old tale of Columbus's brave conflict, as a scientifically savvy navigator, against religious authorities who insisted that he would sail off the edge of a flat earth. In fact, Christian consensus had never lost or challenged Greek and Roman knowledge of the earth's spherical shape. Columbus did hold a celebrated dispute with clerics at Salamanca and other places, but no one questioned the earth's roundness. . . . Moreover, his questioners were right, and Columbus entirely wrong. The debaters argued about the earth's diameter, not its shape.[42]

White and Draper were strident about abuses of power, which they saw as coming mainly from religious institutions. They were justified in denouncing the curtailment of freedom of speech and research, but they distorted facts in order to win at all cost. A reappraisal of the felicitous and less felicitous encounters between science and religion must begin with the willingness to be guided by history, not ideology.

NOTES

1. Stephen Jay Gould, *The Hedgehog, the Fox, and the Magister's Pox. Mending the Gap between Science and the Humanities* (New York: Harmony Books, 2003), p. 86.
2. John William Draper, *History of the Conflict between Religion and Science* (New York: D. Appleton and Co., 1890), pp. vi–vii.
3. *Ibid.*, p. viii.

4. *Ibid.*, pp. ix–x.
5. Thomas S. Kuhn, *The Copernican Revolution: Planetary Astronomy in the Development of Western Thought* (Cambridge, Mass.: Harvard University Press, 1957), p. 122.
6. Edward Grant, *The Foundations of Modern Science in the Middle Ages. Their Religious, Institutional, and Intellectual Contexts* (Cambridge: Cambridge University Press, 1996), p. 206.
7. Draper, *History of the Conflict between Religion and Science*, p. 168.
8. *Ibid.*, pp. 170–171.
9. Francesco Maria del Monte to Cosimo II, 31 May 1611, *Le Opere di Galileo*, ed. Antonio Favaro, 1890–1909, reprint (Florence: Barbèra, 1968), vol. XI, p. 119.
10. Robert Bellarmine to Paolo Antonio Foscarini, 12 April 1615, *ibid.*, vol. XII, p. 172.
11. Galileo Galilei, *The Assayer*, *ibid.*, vol. VI, p. 232.
12. Draper, *History of the Conflict between Religion and Science*, p. 168.
13. *Opere di Galileo*, vol. XIX, pp. 320–321.
14. *Ibid.*, vol. XIX, p. 323.
15. Draper, *History of the Conflict between Religion and Science*, pp. 171–172.
16. Owen Gingerich, *The Book Nobody Read. Chasing the Revolutions of Nicolaus Copernicus* (New York: Walker & Company, 2004), p. 137.
17. Andrew Dickson White, *A History of the Warfare of Science with Theology in Christendom* (Buffalo, N.Y.: Prometheus Books, 1993), vol. 1, p. 131.
18. *Ibid.*, vol. 1, p. 130.
19. *Ibid.*, vol. 1, p. 131.
20. Compare: James Reston, *Galileo: A Life* (London: Cassell, 1994), pp. 111, 120 and 292; White, *A History of the Warfare of Science with Theology in Christendom*, vol. 1, pp. 132–134.
21. White, *A History of the Warfare of Science with Theology in Christendom*, vol. 1, p. 132.
22. Christopher Clavius to Galileo Galilei, 17 December 1610: *Opere di Galileo*, vol. X, pp. 484–485.
23. Mark Welser to Christopher Clavius, 11 February 1611, *ibid.*, vol. XI, p. 45; Mark Welser to Galileo Galilei, 18 February 1611, *ibid.*, vol. XI, p. 52.
24. Galileo Galilei to Christopher Clavius, 17 September 1610, *ibid.*, vol. X, pp. 431–432.
25. Galileo Galilei, *Sidereus Nuncius*, *ibid.*, vol. III-1, p. 60.
26. Christopher Clavius, *Commentarius in Sphaeram Joannis de Sacro Bosco*, in his *Opera Mathematica*, vol. 3, Mainz, 1612, p. 75.
27. Galileo Galilei to Elia Diodati, 15 January 1633, *Opere di Galileo*, vol. XV, p. 25.
28. White, *A History of the Warfare of Science with Theology in Christendom*, vol. 1, p. 115.
29. *Ibid.*, vol. 1, p. 123.
30. *Opere di Galileo*, vol. XIX, pp. 336–342.

31. Galileo Galilei to Geri Bocchineri, 16 April 1633, *ibid.*, vol. XV, p. 88; Francesco Niccolini to Andrea Cioli, 16 April 1633, *ibid.*, p. 94.
32. Letter of Vincenzo Maculano to Cardinal Francesco Barberini, 28 April 1633, *ibid.*, vol. XV, pp. 106–107.
33. *Ibid.*, vol. XIX, pp. 342–344.
34. *Ibid.*, vol. XIX, pp. 345–347.
35. *Ibid.*, vol. XIX, p. 283.
36. *Ibid.*, vol. XIX, p. 362.
37. Eliseo Masini, *Sacro arsenale overo Prattica dell'officio della Santa Inquisizione* (Genoa: Giovanni Pavoni, 1621), quoted in Maurice A. Finocchiaro, *The Galileo Affair* (Berkeley: University of California Press, 1989), p. 363.
38. *Opere di Galileo*, vol. XIX, pp. 406–407.
39. Colin A. Russell, "The Conflict of Science and Religion," in *Science and Religion. A Historical Introduction*, Gary B. Ferngren, ed. (Baltimore: The Johns Hopkins University Press, 2002), p. 4.
40. Stephen Jay Gould, *The Hedgehog, the Fox, and the Magister's Pox. Mending the Gap between Science and the Humanities*, p. 29.
41. *Ibid.*, p. 87.
42. *Ibid.*, p. 88.

CHAPTER TWO

Did it Have to Happen?

In *The Sleepwalkers*, which appeared in 1959, Arthur Koestler (1905–1983) argues that the Galileo Affair does not illustrate a deep-seated opposition between science and religion.[1] He stresses the importance of local circumstances and idiosyncratic elements, and the story he tells is one of personality clashes, not all-out warfare between two worldviews. "It is my conviction," he writes,

> that the conflict between the Church and Galileo (or Copernicus) was not inevitable; that it was not in the nature of a fatal collision between opposite philosophies of existence, which was bound to occur sooner or later, but rather a clash of individual temperaments aggravated by unlucky coincidences. In other words, I believe the idea that Galileo's trial was a kind of Greek tragedy, a showdown between "blind faith" and "enlightened reason", to be naively erroneous. It is this conviction—or bias—that informs the following narrative.[2]

It is refreshing to find someone who openly acknowledges that his research is informed by a strong conviction that amounts to a methodological bias. Too many of those who write about Galileo would have us believe that they are paragons of objectivity when their mind is already made up. Koestler is convinced, of course, that the evidence is on his side, but he does not conceal that his working hypothesis is that the clash between science and religion was not written in the stars.

Why Incompatibility?

One of the curious aspects of the Galileo Affair is the difficulty scholars experience in answering what would appear to be an easy question: When was the incompatibility of Copernicanism with Scripture recognized? The answer is important if we are to understand the risks (if any) that Galileo was taking when he embraced the theory that the Earth moves. So let us inquire about the biblical texts that clearly state that the Earth is at rest and the Sun in motion. The answer is that there are none. We find scriptural passages such as: "Generations come and generations go, but the Earth remains forever. The Sun rises and the sun sets, and hurries back to where it rises" (*Ecclesiastes* 1, 4–5), but expressions like "the Sun rises" or "the Sun sets" are still common today, and no one would think of banning them although we know that they are literally false. The only passage in the whole Bible that could be said to make an unambiguous statement to the contrary is one from *Joshuah*, "The Sun stood in the middle of the sky and delayed its setting for almost a full day" (*Joshua* 10,13). If Joshua made the Sun stand still, it must have been moving!

We have long come to recognize that if the Sun appears to rise in the east and set in the west this is not because the Sun moves in the sky but because the Earth turns on its axis from west to east. Everyday language should not be confused with scientific utterances. Astronomy is not discussed in Scripture for, as a contemporary of Galileo put it, "The Bible teaches how to go to Heaven, not how the heavens go."[3] Already in the first centuries theologians interpreted passages in the Bible that refer to natural events as popular rather than scientific ways of speaking. St. Augustine, the most famous of the early Church Fathers, maintained that the six days of creation in the first chapter of *Genesis* are not natural days but a figure of speech intended to convey the truth of creation in simple and accessible language. Augustine went even further and warned against invoking Scripture too quickly to refute positions in natural philosophy, lest the ignorance of Christians put off those who have solid knowledge.[4]

So what went wrong? Why the sudden rigidity? Part of the answer lies in the climate of the age. Copernicus's book *On the Revolutions of the Heavenly Spheres* appeared in 1543, a few years after Martin Luther had initiated the Protestant Reformation that challenged the authority of the Papacy. The Catholic response was initially weak and confused but it gained momentum after the Council of Trent, which met at intervals between 1545 and 1563, the year before Galileo's birth. Since Antiquity, the

Catholic Church had subscribed to the notion that decisions made by the College of bishops, sitting in an ecumenical council, were binding on the faithful, and especially on theologians who taught the official doctrine of the Church. While the Council of Trent emphasized this belief, it also tried to face up to Protestant criticism that Catholics lacked reverence for Scripture. Catholic theologians became eager, and sometimes over-zealous, in their desire to show Protestants that they took the Word of God seriously. They also became wary of astronomical theories that appeared to criticize Holy Writ. Protestant and Catholic scholars shared these exegetical concerns but Protestants were subject to less control. They had nothing corresponding to the Inquisition, and most Protestant countries did not have the power to enforce judgements of heresy as the Catholics did, although they also believed that heresy was a capital crime because of its harmful effects on society.

An Opportunity Missed

With some luck, Galileo could have convinced the Catholic authorities in Rome that there was no radical incompatibility between what the Bible says and what the new science was beginning to teach. In Koestler's words,

> unless one believes in the dogma of historic inevitability—this form of fatalism in reverse gear—one must regard it as a scandal, which could have been avoided; and it is not difficult to imagine the Catholic Church adopting, after a Tychonic transition, the Copernican cosmology some two hundred years earlier than she eventually did. The Galileo Affair was an isolated, and in fact quite untypical, episode in the history of the relations between science and theology. But its dramatic circumstances, magnified out of all proportion, created a popular belief that science stood for freedom, the Church for oppression of thought.[5]

What prompts Koestler to offer such a radical reinterpretation of the Galileo Affair? The answer is the conceit and arrogance of Galileo that brought him into senseless opposition with the Church. Whereas Draper and White saw Galileo's condemnation as the necessary consequence of clerical pride and stupidity, Koestler lays most of the blame at Galileo's feet, and he protests against the "rationalist mythography" that sees him as the Maid of Orleans of Science, the St George who slew the dragon of the Inquisition. It is, therefore, hardly surprising that the fame of this outstanding genius rests mostly on discoveries he never made, and on feats he never performed. Contrary to statements in even recent outlines of science, Galileo did not invent the telescope; nor the microscope; nor the thermometer; nor the pendulum clock. He did not discover the law of inertia; nor the parallelogram of force or motions, nor the sunspots. He made no contribution to theoretical astronomy; he did not throw down weights from the leaning tower of Pisa, and did not prove the truth of the Copernican system. He was not tortured by the Inquisition, did not languish in its dungeons, did not say "eppur si muove"; and was not a martyr of science. What he did was to found the modern science of dynamics, which makes him rank among the men who shaped human destiny.[6]

In his determination to redress the balance, Koestler leans too heavily on the other side. Although it is true that Galileo did not invent the telescope, he improved it and used it in a novel way to study the Moon, the planets and the stars. For this alone, he deserves a permanent place in the hall of fame. Galileo was also the first to realize the significance of the microscope, the thermometer, and the pendulum. He correctly interpreted the sunspots, and he discovered the law of freely falling bodies and the parabolic shape of projectiles. These two discoveries were to become the pillars of the modern science of motion, and Galileo may be forgiven for having had an exalted opinion of his achievement, even if it is to be regretted that he showed contempt for those who were not as quick as he was at seeing their importance.

Koestler stresses the less pleasant sides of Galileo's personality because he believed that modern science claims too much and delivers too little, especially in moral terms. Koestler did not think that scientific penetration is a substitute for moral insight. "The makers of the scientific revolution," he declares,

> were individuals who in this transformation of the race played the part of the mutating genes. Such genes are *ipso facto* unbalanced and unstable. The personalities of these "mutants" already foreshadowed the discrepancy in the next development of man: the intellectual giants of the scientific revolution were moral dwarfs. They were, of course, neither better nor worse than the average of their contemporaries. They were moral dwarfs only in proportion to their intellectual greatness.[7]

Kepler was Koestler's hero, counterbalanced by Copernicus and Galileo. Gingerich comments:

> *De Revolutionibus* was branded "the book that nobody read" by Arthur Koestler in his best-selling history of early astronomy, *The Sleepwalkers*. Koestler's highly controversial account, published in 1959, greatly stimulated my own interest in the history of science. At the time, none of us could prove or disprove his claim about Copernicus' text. Clearly, however, Koestler, a consummate novelist famous for his gripping *Darkness at Noon*, saw the world in terms of antagonists. Creating a historical vision with Kepler as hero demanded villains, and Koestler placed Copernicus and Galileo into these roles.[8]

There should be no surprise, therefore, if Koestler treats Galileo like a moral dwarf. Koestler was very enthusiastic; his biographer describes him as a volcanic personality, difficult to be understood even by his friends.[9] In addition, Koestler recognizes that Galileo is not sympathetic to him. He considers Galileo as an unpleasant figure whose character was the cause of his misfortunes. He speaks, for instance, of "that cold, sarcastic presumption, by which he managed to spoil his case throughout his life."[10] Nevertheless, Koestler tries to present an image of Galileo faithful to the historical data, and complains that, due to partisan motivations, the figure of Galileo usually appears in a way that does not correspond to the historical facts.

Science and Values

Koestler sees Galileo as a pathologically vain man who thought he had been called by the Almighty to enlighten the Church on the way the world is made. It is interesting to note that this devastating opinion does not come from a disgruntled Catholic, for Koestler was neither a Catholic nor a religious person in the conventional sense. Born into a Jewish family in Budapest in 1905, he attended the University of Vienna, where he was attracted by Zionism and left for Palestine in 1926. He worked in Jerusalem for a German-language periodical before returning to Europe in 1931. After spending a year in Paris, he settled in Berlin at a time when Germany was struggling in the aftermath of the Great Depression. He joined the Communist Party and was sent to the Soviet Union to gather information about the great strides forward that were said to be happening in that country. The Worker's Paradise, as Koestler discovered, was still a distant promise, and he reported as faithfully as he could on the difficulties that he had witnessed. The German Communist Party was not pleased and only published part of his report. Disillusioned, Koestler left the Party in 1938.

During the Spanish civil war, Koestler went to the front as a reporter. He was captured by the army of Franco in Malaga in February 1937, condemned to death, and sent to Seville to face a firing squad. The English secured his release, and allowed him into the U.K., where he worked with British Intelligence during the Second World War. He became a British citizen in 1945 and subsequently played an active role in the Cold War. Catholicism as a personal faith seems at no time to have interested him.

The trials that Stalin orchestrated in the Soviet Union and in which hundreds of innocent men and women accused themselves of deeds they had never committed had sent shock waves though the Communist intelligentsia. In 1940, shortly after these terrible purges, Koestler published his best-selling novel, *Darkness at Noon*. The hero, Rubashov, is a Communist leader who is inculpated on trumped-up charges. He owns to crimes that he never committed in the mistaken and tragic belief that he must surrender himself completely to what the Party expects of him. Koestler captures both the horror and the fascination of dictatorship, and he paints an unforgettable picture of the triumph of propaganda over honesty and moral responsibility. He describes how political power, however well intentioned at first, can become a monster that devours its own children. After the war, when he turned his attention to the history of the Scientific Revolution, Koestler became alarmed that science, once set loose, would crush every human value in order to implement its own narrow program. Copernicus, Galileo and their followers introduced new ways of dealing with nature but their scientific innovations were not matched by a new sense of responsibility.

Koestler's main goal was not so much to write a history of science as to explain how the Scientific Revolution drove a wedge between the quest for knowledge and the search for meaning. As he examined the epigones of the Scientific Revolution, he became increasingly convinced that scientific progress was not the result of systematic enquiry and rational planning but of irrational guesses and blind groping. Hence the title of his book, *The Sleepwalkers*, to describe how scientists went about their work:

The progress of Science is generally regarded as a kind of clean, rational advance along a straight ascending line; in fact it has followed a zigzag course, at time almost more bewildering than the evolution of political thought. The history of cosmic theories, in particular, may without exaggeration be called a history of collective obsessions and controlled schizophrenias; and the manner in which some of the most important individual discoveries were arrived at reminds one more of a sleepwalker's performance than an electronic brain's.[11]

ILLUSTRATION 3   Portrait of Galileo by Francesco Villamena, 1613.

The study of the personality of great scientists is Koestler's way of de-mystifying science. He wants to explode the myth of rationality in order to gain an insight into creativity. "In taking down Copernicus or Galileo from the pedestal on which science-mythography has placed them," he writes,

> my motive was not to "debunk", but to inquire into the obscure work-ings of the creative mind. Yet I shall not be sorry if, as an accidental by-product, the inquiry helps to counteract the legend that Science is a purely rational pursuit, that the Scientist is a more "level-headed" and "dispassionate" type than others (and should therefore be given a leading part in world affairs); or that he is able to provide for him-self and his contemporaries, a rational substitute for ethical insights derived from other sources.[12]

A Demoniac Force

Koestler sees the behavior of Galileo toward Johannes Kepler as an in-stance of the warped, egocentric side of the new science. The first contact between the two men took place in 1597, the year Kepler, who taught mathematics in Austria, had just completed the *Mysterium Cosmo-graphicum* in which he argued that the universe is structured according to a regular sequence of geometrical patterns. He gave two copies to Paul Hamberger to be left with astronomers in Italy. Both copies were given to Galileo who, on 4 August 1597, wrote to thank Kepler in haste, explaining that he had not had time to study it, but that the return of Hamberger to Germany made it imperative for him to write at once. He rejoiced to see that Kepler supported Copernicus, "whose view," Galileo added,

> I adopted many years ago, as from that position I have discovered the causes of many physical effects, which are perhaps inexplicable on the common hypothesis. I have written many reasons and refutations of contrary arguments which up to now I have preferred not to pub-lish, intimidated by the fortune of our teacher Copernicus, who is considered immortal by some but laughed at and hissed off the stage by an infinite number (for such is the multitude of fools).[13]

Galileo was thirty-three years old when he wrote this letter to Kepler. Since he mentions that he had become a Copernican "many years ago," he must have done so in his twenties. But his first explicit public pronounce-ment in favor of the motion of the earth was only made in 1613. Why this long silence when, as early as 13 October 1597, Kepler had written a second time to urge him to declare himself and give Copernicans the comfort and the protection of his authority? "Have faith, Galileo," he exclaimed, "and come forward! If my guess is right there are but few prominent Europeans who would wish to secede from us: for such is the force of Truth."[14] Galileo may have regarded this exhortation as an implied reproach of cowardice, but we shall never know because he made no reply to Kepler.

Between 1600 and 1610, Kepler published two major books, the *Optics* in 1604 and the *New Astronomy* in 1609. In the same period, Galileo carried on his pioneering research on free fall, the motion of projectiles and the oscillation of a pendulum, but he published only one serious work, a brochure containing instructions for the use of a proportional compass that he had invented and put on sale. "Out of this minor publication," writes Koestler, "developed the first of the futile and pernicious feuds which Galileo was to wage all his life."[15] Having thus forewarned his reader, Koestler proceeds to give an account that presents Galileo as over-reacting to the plagiarism of his brochure.

Let us see what actually occurred. Galileo spent the summer of 1605 at Florence as special tutor to the young prince Cosimo de' Medici. He gave him one of his compasses and promised to dedicate to him the brochure that he had drafted on the subject. He did this the following year and had sixty copies printed in his own house. The reason for the private printing was Galileo's desire to maintain his monopoly on the instrument: no illustration of the compass or instruction for calculating its scales were included, and copies went only to those who acquired the compass. Galileo was often short of cash. He was expected to pay the dowries of his two sisters, and he badly needed to supplement his university income by selling his instrument.

In April 1607, almost a year after the brochure appeared, a young mathematician named Baldessar Capra published in Padua a Latin paraphrase including instructions on how to construct the compass. In the prefatory matter, Capra implied that the invention was his own, stolen by others who discussed it. Galileo was justifiably incensed. After all, he had been given no credit, and had even been treated as a thief! He obtained affidavits from reputable persons who declared that he had made a compass as early as 1597. At the time, Capra had been only seventeen years old and had not even begun to study mathematics. Galileo filed a complaint against Capra with the governors of the University at Venice. Hearings were held at which Galileo cross-examined the plagiarist, showing him to be ignorant of matters of which he claimed to be the author. The evidence of fraud was overwhelming. Capra was expelled from the University and the book confiscated.

By that time, however, some thirty copies had been sent abroad and Galileo was concerned about his reputation with foreign mathematicians. Even more sensitive was the implication that in dedicating his brochure to Cosimo de' Medici, Galileo had presented something that was not his to give. To clear his name, he published a full account of the whole affair, the *Defence Against the Calumnies and Impostures of Baldessar Capra*. In his anger, Galileo referred to Capra and his master in unflattering terms, even suggesting that they were sitting on a dunghill. Koestler laments this fuss over "a gadget for military engineers,"[16] but Galileo's contemporaries found it quite normal that a man who was wounded in his pride and his wallet should hit back. Galileo would have done well to use greater restraint, and Koestler reads into his behavior a sign of things to come:

> In his later polemical writings, Galileo's style progressed from coarse invective to satire, which was sometimes cheap, often subtle, always effective. He changed from the cudgel to the rapier; and achieved a rare mastery of it; while in the purely expository passages his lucidity earned him a prominent place in the development of Italian didactic prose. But behind the polished facade, the same passions were at work which had exploded in the affair of the proportional compass; vanity, jealousy, and self-righteousness combined into a demoniac force, which drove him to the brink of self-destruction.[17]

This indictment of Galileo's conduct brings us perilously close to the way Galileo spoke (with more justice, we believe) of Baldessar Capra. It creates the impression that the Galileo Affair hinges almost entirely on Galileo's personality. His arrogance cannot be dismissed but the issue ran deeper, for serious questions emerged in the wake of Galileo's telescopic discoveries. For instance, Was there a convincing proof for the motion of the Earth, regardless of the pride or meekness of those who argued for Copernicanism?

Galileo's Telescopic Observations

Koestler is anxious to have his readers recognize that Galileo did not invent the telescope, but Galileo never said he did. What he claimed was to have improved it and to have had the idea of using it to examine the Moon and other celestial objects. Koestler admits that Galileo discovered that the surface of the Moon is covered with craters, that Jupiter has satellites, and that Venus shows phases, but he does so grudgingly, and when he praises Galileo it is more for his style than for his science. With his *Sidereus Nuncius*, he writes, Galileo "threw his telescopic discoveries like a bomb into the arena of the learned world. It not only contained news of heavenly bodies 'which no mortal had seen before'; it was also written in a new, tersely factual style which no scholar had employed before."[18]

The main reason for the success of the book was "its immense readability,"[19] according to Koestler, but in order to understand why it gave rise to controversy he adds that we must

> take into account the subjective effect of Galileo's personality. Canon Koppernigk had been a kind of invisible man throughout his life; nobody who met the disarming Kepler in the flesh or by correspondence, could seriously dislike him. But Galileo had a rare gift of provoking enmity; not the affection alternating with rage which Tycho aroused, but the cold, unrelenting hostility which genius plus arrogance minus humility creates among mediocrities.[20]

Here again Koestler overstates his case. Galileo encountered the opposition of hard-boiled Aristotelians like Lodovico delle Colombe in Florence, but he was on good terms with his colleague, Cesare Cremonini, the professor of philosophy at Padua. Although Cremonini remained adamant that the heavens were made of a special kind of matter, Galileo lent him money and, in turn, was glad to receive security from him when he had to take a loan himself.

Incensed by Gossip

Koestler describes other manifestations of Galileo's hypersensitivity. One is the seriousness with which he took the rumor of a disparaging remark that an elderly Dominican, Niccolò Lorini, was alleged to have made about his views in the summer of 1612. Galileo wrote to the priest requesting an explanation, and Lorini wrote back:

> I never dreamt of getting involved in such matters. . . . I am at a loss to know what grounds there can be for such a suspicion, as this thing has never occurred to me. It is indeed true that when others started

the discussion, I said a few words just to show I was alive. Without wanting to argue, but merely to avoid giving the impression of a blockhead I said, and I still say, that this opinion of Ipernicus—or whatever his name is—appears to run counter to Sacred Scripture. But it is of little consequence to me, for I have other things to do.[21]

The fact that Lorini was uncertain about the very name of Copernicus is an indication that his criticism should not have been taken seriously, but Galileo, according to Koestler, could not control "his irrepressible urge to get involved in controversy."[22] Irrepressible or not, Galileo's behavior can nonetheless be seen as legitimate self-defense rather than love of controversy. Lorini was no lightweight but a veteran professor of ecclesiastical history in Florence, and he was alleged to have said that Galileo's views were contrary to Scripture, no jesting matter. Indeed, we shall see that Lorini was later to lodge a complaint against Galileo. Koestler underestimates Galileo's problem:

> Up to the fateful year 1616, discussion of the Copernican system was not only permitted, but encouraged, under one proviso, that it should be confined to the language of science, and should not impinge on theological matters. The situation was summed up clearly in a letter from Cardinal Dini to Galileo in 1615: "One may write freely as long as one keeps out of the sacristy." This was precisely what the disputants failed to do, and it was at this point that the conflict began.[23]

Let us note in passing that Dini was not a Cardinal but a minor official with the title of Monsignor. Here as elsewhere, Koestler quotes from secondary sources, in this case from a work by Sherwood Taylor. What is more serious is his erroneous claim that although scientific discussion of Copernicanism was encouraged, Galileo welcomed theological discussions. The truth of the matter is that Galileo did not venture into theology until his opponents provoked him by declaring that the motion of the Earth ran counter to the Bible. It was in order to vindicate himself that he took up the cudgels.

The letter from Dini that Koestler quotes is presented as though it had been written by a Cardinal, who stated, as a matter of general knowledge, that astronomers had nothing to fear as long as they avoided talking about religion. But when this letter was written, on 2 May 1615, Galileo had already been dragged, against his will, into theological hot water. As we have seen in Chapter One, Benedetto Castelli, a former student who taught at the University of Pisa, had informed Galileo on 14 December 1613 that he had dined with the Grand Duke Cosimo II. The distinguished company included the Dowager Grand Duchess Christina, several other guests, and a professor of philosophy named Boscaglia, who had the ear of the Grand Duchess. He told her that the things that Galileo had discovered in the sky were all true but "that the motion of the earth had something incredible in it, and could not take place, in particular because Holy Scripture was obviously contrary to this view."[24] After the meal, Castelli was detained for further discussion by the Grand Duchess, who "began," he writes, "to argue Holy Scripture against me. Thereupon, after having made suitable disclaimers, I commenced to play the theologian and carried things off like a paladine." Everyone sided with Castelli and Galileo, "only Madame Christina remained against me, but from her manner I judged that she did this only to hear my replies. Professor Boscaglia never said a word."[25]

According to Koestler,

> Galileo reacted to the incident with his usual touchiness, and was at once up in arms. His counter-blast to the dinner-table chirpings of the obscure Dr. Boscaglia (who is never heard of again) was a kind of theological atom bomb, whose radioactive fall-out is still being felt. It took the form of a *Letter to Castelli*, enlarged a year later into a *Letter to the Grand Duchess Christina*. . . . Its purpose was to silence all theological objections to Copernicus. Its result was precisely the opposite: it became the principal cause of the prohibition of Copernicus, and of Galileo's downfall.[26]

Although Castelli was quite happy with his performance, Galileo was uneasy at the thought that the soundness of Copernicanism had been queried at court, even if it was only in a friendly discussion. To remove any doubt concerning the orthodoxy of his views, he wrote a long letter to Castelli on 21 December in which he explained why the motion of the Earth was compatible with Scripture, and he offered a Copernican interpretation of the miracle of Joshua. The Grand Duchess was reassured, but some friars saw copies of the *Letter to Castelli* and took offence. A year later, on 21 December 1614, from the pulpit of the Dominican church of Santa Maria Novella in Florence, Tommaso Caccini launched an attack. He denounced as inimical to religion and the state not only Copernicanism but mathematical sciences in general. A few weeks later, Niccolò Lorini, with whom Galileo had corresponded in 1612, sent a copy of Galileo's *Letter to Castelli* to Cardinal Paolo Sfondrati, the Head of the Congregation of the Index of Prohibited Books in Rome. In his covering letter, dated 7 February 1615, Lorini called for an investigation of what appeared to him a dangerous position, although he had no doubt that the "Galileists," as he called them, were "good people and good Christians, if just a shade too arrogant."[27]

Galileo heard that Lorini had secured a copy of his *Letter to Castelli* and he guessed that it would promptly be forwarded to Rome. Lest some of the expressions he had used be misunderstood, he recovered the original from Castelli, revised it, and forwarded it to Monsignor Piero Dini in Rome. He asked that the letter be shown to the Jesuit Christopher Grienberger, who taught mathematics and astronomy at the Roman College, in the hope that he might pass it on to Cardinal Bellarmine, who was quite influential in the Holy Office. In his letter of transmittal, dated 16 February 1615, Galileo explained that the original letter had been written in haste and that he now wanted to expand and improve it. This new version, the *Letter to the Grand Duchess Christina*, is the fullest statement of Galileo's views on science and religion. Dini received the authorized copy on 21 February but he dilly-dallied about showing it to Cardinal Bellarmine and, on 2 May 1615, finally told Galileo that Prince Cesi, the Head of the Academy of the Lynxes, had advised him against doing so. It seemed to Cesi that since Bellarmine was willing to allow a discussion of Copernicanism as a hypothesis, it would be unwise to ask for more.

It is from this letter that comes the remark by Dini that Koestler quoted. We now give the passage in full to allow the reader to see in what context it was meant to be read. "The Cardinal and other persons of authority," says Dini,

> are typical Aristotelians, and they might be annoyed if someone raised a point that has already been won, namely that it is allowed to write in the way mathematicians deal with hypotheses. This is what they think Copernicus did and, although this may be denied by his followers, they think that the result is the same, namely that one may write freely as long as one, as was said on other occasions, keeps out of the sacristy.[28]

As we can see, this letter is not a perfectly serene letter written by a high prelate who states the obvious truth that astronomers can argue as much as they like about the motion of the Earth as long as they do not play the theologian. Dini was concerned that the right to speak about the motion of the Earth might be questioned if the Holy Office was pressed too hard, but Koestler ascribes Galileo's worries to nothing more than fear of ridicule:

> Thus legend and hindsight combined to distort the picture, and gave rise to the erroneous belief that to defend the Copernican system as a working hypothesis entailed the risk of ecclesiastical disfavour or persecution. During the first fifty years of Galileo's lifetime, no such risk existed; and the thought did not even occur to Galileo. What he feared is clearly stated in his letter: to share the fate of Copernicus, to be mocked and derided. And this fear, as will be seen, was fully justified.[29]

ILLUSTRATION 4   Grand Duchess Christina of Lorraine by Adrian Haelweg, 17th century.

The Letter to the Grand Duchess Christina

Galileo was a proud man and the last thing he wanted was to become a laughingstock. He had no intention of inviting derision by defending a theory for which he had no evidence, but he honestly believed that he had. He leaves no doubt about this in his *Letter to the Grand Duchess Christina*. His critics "are aware," he says,

> that on the question of the constitution of the world, I hold that the Sun is located at the centre of the revolutions of the heavenly orbs and does not change place, that the Earth rotates on itself, and moves around the Sun. Moreover, they know that I confirm this view not only by refuting the arguments of Ptolemy and Aristotle, but also by producing many for the other side. Some pertain to physical effects, whose causes probably cannot be found in any other way, and others to astronomical ones and depend on many features of the new celestial discoveries. These discoveries clearly confute the Ptolemaic system, and agree admirably with the other position, which they confirm.[30]

The "physical effects" that Galileo mentions are the to and fro motion of the tides. It was his misfortune that his argument, however ingenious, is completely wrong. Convinced that he had the truth, Galileo saw himself as making a case for the right of scientists to enlighten society, including its clerical members. This was not mere pride or senseless ambition. It was a genuine quest for the truth about the natural world. Galileo rightly proclaimed that the Bible is not a scientific text. It is a moral and spiritual document, and it was not written to provide information about physics and astronomy. Quoting from St. Augustine, Galileo stressed that Scripture is sometimes allegorical and often needs interpretation to draw out its true meaning (for instance, when it attributes human features to God). That being the case, it does not make sense to insist that the Earth is stationary because a handful of scriptural references seem to imply it.

Galileo was concerned about his reputation but he was also deeply convinced that he had excellent grounds to advocate heliocentrism. He was also anxious lest the Church should render itself open to criticism, and he made an eloquent plea for a clear distinction between science and theology. Koestler does him injustice when he declares, "In the letter to the Grand Duchess Christina the whole tragedy of Galileo is epitomized. Passages which are classics of didactic prose, superb formulations in defense of freedom of thought, alternate with sophistry, evasion, and plain dishonesty."[31]

Too Bold by Far

While Galileo was completing the revised version of his *Letter to the Grand Duchess Christina*, he began to fear that Copernicus's book might be banned, and he wrote to Piero Dini about it. His Roman friend saw Cardinal Bellarmine and then reported to Galileo that the Cardinal felt that there was no question of Copernicus's book being prohibited. "The worst that might happen," he said,

> would be the addition of some material in the margins of the book to the effect that Copernicus had introduced his theory in order to save the appearances. . . . And acting with the same caution you may at any time deal with these matters. If things are explained according to the new system, for the time being it does not appear that there is any greater obstacle in the Bible than [speaking of the Sun] to say that it "exults as a giant to run his course (*Psalm* 19:5)," etc., which all expositors up to now have interpreted as attributing motion to the Sun. And although I replied that this could be explained as a concession to ordinary ways of speaking, I was told that this was not a thing to be done in haste.[32]

The Cardinal developed his position in a letter that he wrote in April 1625 to Paolo Antonio Foscarini, a priest who had sent him a brochure in which he argued that the motion of the Earth is not incompatible with Scripture. Bellarmine granted that the celestial phenomena could be described by assuming that the Earth moves. "But to wish to affirm," he added,

> that the Sun is really fixed in the centre of the heavens and merely turns upon itself without travelling from east to west, and that the Earth in situated in the third sphere and revolves very swiftly around the Sun is a very dangerous thing. It not only provokes theologians and scholastic philosophers, it also causes injury to our holy faith, and makes Sacred Scripture false.[33]

Bellarmine added that the Council of Trent prohibited expounding the Bible in a way that was contrary to the common agreement of the ancient

Church Fathers. Should the motion of the Earth be proved, he added, then Scriptures would have to be reinterpreted,

> and we should have to say that we do not understand them rather than to say something that had been proven to be false. But I do not think that there is any such proof, since none has been shown to me. To show that appearances are saved by assuming the Sun at the center and the Earth in the heavens is not the same thing as to demonstrate that the Sun is really at the center and the Earth is in the heavens. . . . In case of doubt, one should not abandon the Holy Scriptures as expounded by the Holy Fathers.[34]

The message from the highest theological authority could not have been plainer: unless and until astronomers are in a position to clearly and definitively demonstrate the motion of the Earth and the stability of the Sun, they should keep their own counsel. Warning signals had also come from another friend, Giovanni Ciampoli, who provided Galileo with this summary of a conversation he had with Cardinal Barberini (later Urban VIII) concerning Galileo:

> As you know from experience, Cardinal Barberini has always admired your worth. He told me only yesterday evening that he would like greater caution in not going beyond the arguments used by Ptolemy and Copernicus, and not exceeding the limitations of physics and mathematics. Theologians claim that the explanation of Scripture is their field, and if new things are suggested, even by a first-rate mind, not everyone is objective enough to take them as they are said. One person enlarges, the next alters, and what came from the author's own mouth becomes so distorted in spreading that he would no longer recognize it as his own. And I know what he means. Your interpretation of light and shadow in the bright and dark spots of the moon assumes some similarity between the lunar globe and the Earth; somebody expands on this and says you place human inhabitants on the Moon; the next fellow starts to dispute how these can be descended from Adam, or how they came off Noah's Ark; and many other extravagant ideas that you never dreamed of. Hence, to declare frequently that you place yourself under the authority of those who have jurisdiction over the minds of men in the interpretation of Scripture is to remove this pretext for other people's malice. Perhaps you think I go too far in playing the sage with you; please forgive me, and kindly acknowledge the infinite esteem that makes me speak thus.[35]

When Galileo heard that he had been denounced to the Holy Office, he went to Rome to argue in favor of Copernicanism. His task was not easy. The procedures of the Holy Office were secret, as Galileo complained in a report to the Grand Duke, Cosimo II:

My business is far more difficult, and takes much longer owing to outward circumstances, than its nature would require because I cannot communicate directly with those with whom I have to negotiate. This is partly to avoid embarrassing my friends, and partly because they cannot communicate anything to me without running the risk of grave censure. And so I am obliged to be careful and cautiously seek out third persons, who, without even knowing my intent, can serve as mediators with the principals, so that I may have the opportunity of setting forth, incidentally as it were, and at their request, the particulars of my case.[36]

The Florentine Ambassador, Piero Guicciardini, found Galileo's behavior not only alarming but dangerous. "Galileo," he declared to the Grand Duke,

states his position with great passion, but with little prudence or self-control. The Roman climate is becoming very dangerous for him, especially at this time. The present Ruler [Paul V], who abhors the liberal arts and this cast of mind, does not want to hear about new or subtle ideas. . . . Some monks and other people dislike Galileo and persecute him, and, as I said, this is not the place for him. He can get himself and others into serious trouble. . . . I do not see why anyone should run, without serious motive, risks from which we can expect nothing useful but rather serious damage, the more so when this is only to satisfy Galileo. He is passionately involved in this quarrel, as if it were his own business, and he does not see or sense what the consequences might be. He is deceiving himself, and will get into trouble with those who support him. . . . This is no joke and could become very serious for this man is here under our protection and responsibility.[37]

In the same letter the ambassador wrote:

Galileo has relied more on his own counsel than on that of his friends. Cardinal del Monte and myself, as well as several cardinals of the Holy Office, have tried to persuade him to be quiet and not to go on irritating this issue. If he wants to hold this Copernican opinion, he was told, let it be quietly, without spending so much time in trying to have others share it. Everyone fears that his coming here may be very prejudicial and that, instead of justifying himself and succeeding, he may end up with scars.[38]

The outcome of Galileo's efforts in Rome is well known. The Vatican told him that he should abandon the heliocentric system. "For almost fifty years of his life," writes Koestler,

> he had held his tongue about Copernicus, not out of fear to be burnt at the stake, but to avoid academic unpopularity. When carried away by sudden fame, he had at last committed himself, it became at once a matter of prestige to him. He had said that Copernicus was right, and whosoever said otherwise was belittling his authority as the foremost scholar of his time. That this was the central motivation of Galileo's fight will become increasingly evident. It does not exonerate his opponents; but it is relevant to the problem whether the conflict was historically inevitable or not.[39]

On 5 March 1616, a decree of the Congregation of the Index included Copernicus's book among proscribed works. Koestler feels that this is often misrepresented by biographers "anxious," as he puts it, "to give the impression that the Decree of 5 March was not caused by Galileo's persistent provocations, but the result of a coldly inquisitorial campaign to stifle the voice of science."[40] Koestler indulges in overstatement. The Decree of 5 March 1616 cannot be blamed entirely on Galileo's harassment of his critics or the bad will of his opponents. There were more serious reasons, as Koestler himself acknowledges:

> The real danger of removing the earth from the centre of the universe went much deeper; it undermined the whole structure of medieval cosmology. The people of Rome were indeed beginning to discuss questions such as whether other planets were inhabited; and if so, could their inhabitants descend from Adam?[41]

It was normal for theologians to raise such questions, but they might have done so in a more leisurely and academic fashion if they had not felt challenged from someone who was a prestigious scientist but not an expert in their field. In retrospect, we can see that the theologians were out of step. Matters were less clear in 1616.

Real and Virtual Jesuits

Koestler's indictment of Galileo's behavior after 1616 is equally harsh. Galileo had befriended the Jesuits when he was teaching mathematics at the University of Pisa (1589–1592) and the University of Padua (1592–1610), but he became embroiled in bitter controversies with two of them after his return to Florence in 1610. One was Christoph Scheiner, who taught at the University of Ingolstadt in Germany, the other was Orazio Grassi, a professor at the Roman College. Galileo was critical of Scheiner's interpretations of the sunspots that both had observed in 1611, and he was scathing in his appraisal of Grassi's study of the comet of 1618. Koestler is right in stressing that Galileo was overbearing in the case of Scheiner, and that in his polemic with Grassi he gave an account of the comet that was completely misleading. What Koestler underplays is Galileo's convincing mathematical demonstration that sunspots are on the surface of the Sun, and his brilliant illustration of the scientific method in the debate that he carried on with Grassi.

Koestler is so intent in decrying Galileo's attitude that he even invents another Jesuit: "A third Jesuit whom he had attacked without necessity (on a question of military engineering, of all things) was Father Firenzuola, who built the fortifications of the Castle St. Angelo. Twenty-five years later, Firenzuola was the Inquisition's Commissary General at Galileo's trial. The result of all this was that the Jesuits as a body turned against Galileo."[42] Father Firenzuola (actually Father Vincenzo Maculano, born in Firenzuola in 1578) was not a Jesuit but a prominent member of the Dominicans, whom Pope Urban VIII appointed Commissary General of the Holy Office in December 1632. Galileo did not meet him in 1608, twenty-five years before the trial, and Maculano could not have worked on improving the fortifications of Castel Sant'Angelo in Rome prior to the election of Urban VIII in 1623. There is not a shred of evidence that Galileo ever commented on his work before or after.

Sleepwalker Awake!

Galileo published his *Dialogue on the Two Chief World Systems* in 1632. It is a defense of the Copernican system disguised as an impartial weighing up of the pros and cons of the theory. At the request of the Holy Office, it was examined by three theologians who rightly concluded that it was a defense of Copernicanism. The Roman Inquisition summoned Galileo to Rome and charged him with disobeying the orders received in 1616. The *Dialogue* is divided into four days, and Koestler's assessment of the third day, which is concerned with the astronomical arguments for and against Copernicus, is wholly negative:

> Here Galileo is downright dishonest. . . . It is true that Galileo was writing for a lay audience, and in Italian; his account however, was not a simplification but a distortion of the facts, not popular science, but misleading propaganda. . . . Even so, the arguments are again inconclusive.[43]

In order to rehabilitate Galileo's adversaries, Koestler goes overboard and brands virtually all of Galileo's arguments as impostures:

> There can be no doubt that Galileo's theory of the tides was based on unconscious self-deception; but in the light of the above there can also be little doubt that the sunspot argument was a deliberate attempt to confuse and mislead . . . was part of a deliberate strategy, based on Galileo's contempt for the intelligence of his contemporaries. We have seen that scholars have always been prone to manias and obsessions, and inclined to cheat about details; but impostures like Galileo's are rare in the annals of science.[44]

Koestler is so intent on using Galileo as a symbol of the danger of allowing scientists to tell us how to think that he tars and feathers him regardless of the complexity of the evidence. He wants his reader to wake up to the fact that much of what was written about Galileo is anti-clerical propaganda. He succeeds in showing that Galileo was not a lay saint and that worshipping him is not the best way of doing justice to history or understanding how he contributed to the birth of modern science. Koestler makes some telling points. For instance, he shows that the ban on Copernicanism in 1616 was an administrative act that did not involve papal infallibility, and that the decrees of 1616 and 1633 were both open to recall. He explains how the license to print the *Dialogue on the Two Chief World Systems* was obtained through the political pressure that Galileo was able to bring to bear on the Master of the Sacred Palace, the Dominican Niccolò Riccardi. Koestler also dispels the notion that Galileo was tortured or incarcerated.

Galileo had a high regard of his capabilities, and he was often condescending, if not downright contemptuous, in his assessment of the work of others. But his campaign in favor of Copernicanism cannot be entirely ascribed to pride or pique. He had an arsenal of powerful arguments and he understood that the modern science of motion that was coming into being would alter significantly the traditional cosmology inherited from Aristotle. His own law of freely falling bodies was to send shockwaves throughout physics, and eventually topple the wisdom of the Ancients. The error of Galileo, if we can call it that, was that he underestimated the objections of his opponents, and overestimated his rhetorical abilities. Had he been more diplomatic, he would have achieved infinitely more, and theologians would have learned earlier that they must not only recognize the value of science but be willing to be guided by it when interpreting the meaning of natural phenomena in Scripture.

Koestler's History

"It is perhaps no exaggeration to say," writes Maurice A. Finocchiaro, "that Koestler's criticism is the most serious indictment of Galileo since the original trial," and it should be taken to task because it appears in a book

> that has all the trappings of scholarship (references, footnotes, etc.); and that is well written, highly readable, and widely accessible. Moreover, Koestler's book is full of arguments that have the appearance of strength; I do not say that his account is well argued, for in this case the appearance does not correspond to reality. In short, Koestler was a sophisticated sophist.[45]

Finocchiaro considers Koestler's account of what occurred in 1616 as "mostly a fabrication that can give the appearance of being historically accurate by constantly perpetrating the straw-man fallacy; that is, attributing to the individual under scrutiny silly and untenable views by interpreting relevant texts in the most uncharitable manner and most unfavorable light."[46] But Finocchiaro realizes that Koestler's purpose in writing *The Sleepwalkers* went beyond Galileo:

> Koestler's purpose was not primarily to debunk Galileo but rather to explain the existence of the modern cultural gap between science and

religion as originating largely with him. And the connection is that his condemnation could and would have been avoided if he had not insulted the intelligence of his contemporaries with the fallacies, sophistries, confusions and errors of the *Dialogue*, and had not offended their sensibilities with his insults, lies, deception, dishonesty, hypocrisy, false promises, and so on.[47]

Finocchiaro is right in stressing that Koestler is unfair to Galileo, but the intense dislike that Galileo sometimes provoked among his contemporaries rested on more than prejudice. His behavior could be seen as either arrogance or as courage. He was instructed to present heliocentrism as a mathematical fiction, useful for calculating the heavenly phenomena, not as something real. He could have accepted, but he believed that the science was a quest for truth, and that heliocentrism was more than a useful device. He saw himself as a pioneer of a new science that would help to establish criteria of rigor in the search for a true knowledge of the natural world.

The main idea advanced by Koestler is that the conflict between science and religion could have been avoided. In this he is right. The Galileo Affair was influenced by a number of fortuitous circumstances. Koestler focuses on Galileo's difficult temper, and the fact that if Galileo had not gone to Rome to argue for Copernicanism, the Vatican would probably have taken a softer line. But Galileo knew that he had been denounced to the Roman authorities, and that there was a real risk that Copernicanism would be condemned. In trying to avoid that condemnation, Galileo was seeking not only his own benefit, but also that of the Church.

NOTES

1. The web site of NASA singles out Arthur Koestler's *The Sleepwalkers* as one of the most interesting works on Galileo and the Copernican Revolution: see David P. Stern (author and curator) at: http://www-spof.gsfc.nasa.gov/stargaze/Ssolsys.htm.
2. Arthur Koestler, *The Sleepwalkers* (London: Penguin Books, 1988), p. 432. Out of 623 pages, roughly 200 deal with Galileo.
3. A marginal note by Galileo in his *Letter to the Grand Duchess Christina* assigns this epigram to Cardinal Cesare Baronio, whom Galileo may have met in 1598 when Baronio and Cardinal Bellarmine visited a friend of Galileo in Padua. See *Le Opere di Galileo Galilei*, edizione nazionale, ed. Antonio Favaro (Firenze: Barbèra, 1968), vol. V, p. 319.

4. See the excellent account by Kenneth J. Howell, *God's Two Books: Copernican Cosmology and Biblical Interpretation in Early Modern Science* (Notre Dame, Indiana: University of Notre Dame Press, 2005).
5. Koestler, *The Sleepwalkers*, p. 533.
6. *Ibid.*, p. 358.
7. *Ibid.*, p. 356.
8. Owen Gingerich, *The Book Nobody Read* (New York: Walker & Company), pp. vii–viii.
9. "Koestler's volcanic personality casts such a shadow over his life that it is hard to reach a balanced assessment of the kind of man he was. Opinions of him were sharply polarized: even his friends equivocated about his character." David Cesarani, *Arthur Koestler: The Homeless Mind* (The Free Press: New York, 1999), p. 559.
10. Koestler, *The Sleepwalkers*, p. 360.
11. *Ibid.*, p. 11.
12. *Ibid.*
13. Galileo Galilei to Johannes Kepler, 4 August 1597, *Opere di Galileo*, vol. X, p. 68.
14. Johannes Kepler to Galileo Galilei, 13 October 1597, *Opere di Galileo*, vol. X, p. 70.
15. Koestler, *The Sleepwalkers*, p. 367.
16. *Ibid.*, p. 368.
17. *Ibid.*
18. *Ibid.*, p. 370.
19. *Ibid.*, p. 372.
20. *Ibid.*, p. 373.
21. Niccolò Lorini to Galileo Galilei, 5 November 1612, *Opere di Galileo*, vol. XI, p. 427.
22. Koestler, *The Sleepwalkers*, p. 438.
23. *Ibid.*, p. 363.
24. Benedetto Castelli to Galileo Galilei, 14 December 1613, *Opere di Galileo*, vol. XI, p. 606.
25. *Ibid.*
26. Koestler, *The Sleepwalkers*, p. 440.
27. Niccolò Lorini to Cardinal Sfondrati, February 1615, *Opere di Galileo*, vol. XIX, p. 298.
28. Piero Dini to Galileo Galilei, 2 May 1615, *Opere di Galileo*, vol. XII, p. 175.
29. Koestler, *The Sleepwalkers*, p. 363.
30. Galileo Galilei, *Letter to the Grand Duchess Christina*, *Opere di Galileo*, vol. V, p. 311; translated by Stillman Drake in *Discoveries and Opinions of Galileo* (New York: Doubleday, 1957), p. 177.
31. Koestler, *The Sleepwalkers*, p. 445.
32. Piero Dini to Galileo Galilei, 7 March 1615, *Opere di Galileo*, vol. XII, p. 151.
33. Robert Bellarmine to Paolo Antonio Foscarini, 12 April 1615, *Opere di Galileo*, vol. XII, p. 171.

34. *Ibid.*, p. 172.
35. Giovanni Ciampoli to Galileo Galilei, 28 February 1615, *Opere di Galileo*, vol. XII, p. 146.
36. Galileo Galilei to Curzio Picchena, 23 January 1616, *Opere di Galileo*, vol. XII, p. 227.
37. Piero Guicciardini to Cosimo II, 4 March 1616, *Opere di Galileo*, XII, pp. 242–243.
38. *Ibid.*, pp. 241–242.
39. Koestler, *The Sleepwalkers*, pp. 444–445.
40. *Ibid.*, pp. 600–601.
41. *Ibid.*, pp. 465–466.
42. *Ibid.*, p. 477.
43. *Ibid.*, pp. 483–484.
44. *Ibid.*, p. 486.
45. Maurice A. Finocchiaro, *Retrying Galileo, 1633–1992* (Berkeley: University of California Press, 2005), p. 308.
46. *Ibid.*, p. 311.
47. *Ibid.*, p. 315.

CHAPTER THREE

Brecht and the Revolutionary Who Moved the Earth

Many readers of this book will have become acquainted with Galileo through Brecht's *Life of Galileo*, a play that continues to be performed and draw large audiences. But how faithful is Brecht's depiction of Galileo? The answer is that he takes considerable liberties with history, and that the play stems more from his creative imagination than from any research into what really happened.

Before examining the most glaring errors, we must ask ourselves whether historical accuracy is to be expected (let alone required) from a playwright. Is it legitimate to speak of misrepresentation in a work of fiction? We believe that although a great name can be used as a peg upon which to hang a tale, it should be made clear to the reader (say in the preface of the published version) that what is offered is not a factual account. Someone might of course reply that Brecht grasped what is essential about the life of Galileo, namely the head-on collision between scientific freedom and censorship. Who cares about petty details when what is at stake is perfectly clear? Should we not rather be grateful to Brecht for a timely reminder of the danger of allowing authority, any authority, to interfere with freedom of research?

We should indeed be more than willing to recognize that the abuse of clerical, political or academic power is to be condemned and resisted. But in order to avoid slipping into license, freedom must be mindful of truth, and historical facts are part of the truth. Spectators, who are not apprised of Brecht's distortion of facts, often leave the theater believing that they have learned a lesson from history.

The Genesis of the Life of Galileo

Before attempting to set the facts straight, let us trace the long and involved story of Brecht's *Life of Galileo*, of which there are three versions linked to three crucial moments in the history of the twentieth century: Hitler's triumph in 1938, the dropping of the first nuclear bomb in 1945, and the death of Stalin in 1953. These events gave the play continued relevance, and each found Brecht rewriting parts of the dialogue. The first version, which was called *The Earth Moves*, was written in three weeks in 1938, not long after the Munich agreement set a seal of approval on the Nazi annexation of Austria and the German-speaking areas of Czechoslovakia. Brecht, who was living in exile in Denmark, was shaken by the relentless spread of the "dark times," and he began to back away from the close political engagement that had characterized his plays and poems since the end of World War I when he moved in Marxist circles. Although the Communists had made him nominal editor of *Das Wort*, a German Journal that was published in Moscow, Brecht was wary of the imposition of Socialist Realist aesthetics. When Walter Benjamin (himself an exile in Paris) visited him in Denmark in 1938, Brecht confided: "They want to play the *apparatchik* and exercise control over the people. Everyone of their criticisms contains a threat." In January 1939, Mikhail Koltsov, who had backed *Das Wort*, was arrested. In the *Arbeitsjournal* ("working diary") that he was now keeping, Brecht describes Koltsov as "my last link with that place," and declares that the right Marxist attitude to Stalinism should be that of Marx towards German social-democracy, namely "constructively critical."[1]

The first version of the play, written in a measured, down-to-earth style, was given its première in Zurich in September 1943. Directed by Leonard Steckel, who also played Galileo, it was greatly applauded despite its lack of dramatic effects. Spectators were left puzzling whether Galileo recanted out of cowardice or as part of a deliberate plan to complete his life's work on behalf of human reason, and smuggle it out to the free world. This ambiguity is, indeed, built into the play.

Brecht and his wife left for America in the summer of 1941, and he settled in California in the hope of finding work in the film industry. A translation of the play was undertaken and Brecht showed it to the physicist and philosopher of science Hans Reichenbach, who was teaching at the University of California in Los Angeles. A pupil of Einstein, but no historian, Reichenbach is reputed to have congratulated Brecht on the accuracy of the scientific and historical aspects of the play.[2] Sometime in 1944 Brecht made the acquaintance of the famous actor, Charles Laughton, and they got on like wildfire. Laughton cast himself enthusiastically into the role of Galileo and suggested that Galileo's self-abasement at the end of the play be made more of a piece with Galileo's concern for his own comforts. In the notes that he wrote on this second version of the *Life of Galileo*, Brecht describes how Laughton brought Galileo to life on the stage:

> Galileo is a powerful physicist with a tummy on him, a face like Socrates, a vociferous, full-blooded man with a sense of humor, the new type of physicist, earthly, a great teacher. Favorite attitude: stomach thrust forward, both hands on the buttocks, head back, using one meaty hand all the time to gesticulate with, but with precision; comfortable trousers for working in, shirtsleeves or (particularly at the end) a long whitish-yellow robe with broad sleeves, tied with a cord round his stomach.[3]

In another note, Brecht explains that Galileo is not merely a *bon vivant*, but a man who

> insists on his physical pleasures because of his materialist convictions. He wouldn't, for instance, drink at his work; the point is that he *works* in a sensual way. He gets pleasure from handling his instruments with elegance. A great part of his sensuality is of an intellectual kind: for instance, the "beauty" of an experiment.[4]

Nonetheless, Brecht could not resist intellectualizing Laughton's embodiment of Galileo's personality:

> It is less a matter of the artist's temperament than of the notions of reality which he has *and communicates*; less a matter of his vitality than of the observations that underlie his portraits and can be derived from them. This means neglecting much that seemed to us to be "inimitable" in Laughton's achievement, and going on rather to what can be learned from it. For we cannot create talent; we can only set it tasks.[5]

Asked why he acted, Laughton answered, "Because people don't know what they are like, and I think I can show them."[6] This prompted Brecht to make the following remark:

His collaboration in the rewriting of the play showed that he had all sorts of ideas which were begging to be disseminated, about how people *really* live together, about the motive forces that need to be taken into account here. L.'s attitude seemed to the playwright to be that of a realistic artist of our time. For whereas in relatively stationary ("quiet") periods artists may find it possible to merge wholly with their public and to be a faithful "embodiment" of the general conception, our profoundly unsettled time forces them to take special measures to penetrate to the truth. Our society will not admit of its own accord what makes it move. It can even be said to exist purely through the secrecy with which it surrounds itself.[7]

The Battle Against Authority

What Brecht saw as the crucial issue was not the specific nature of the Roman Catholic Church but the threat of totalitarianism that is inherent in any group that bows down before authority. "In the present play," he writes,

the church functions even when it opposes free investigation, simply as authority. . . . The play shows the temporary victory of authority, not the victory of the priesthood. It corresponds to the historical truth in that the Galileo of the play never turns directly against the church. There is not a sentence uttered by Galileo in that sense. If there had been, such a thorough Commission of Investigation as the Inquisition would undoubtedly have brought it to light. And it equally corresponds to the historical truth that the greatest astronomer of the Papal Roman College, Christopher Clavius, confirmed Galileo's discoveries.[8]

According to Brecht, power surrounds itself with secrecy to better dupe its victims:

It is important to realize that our performance took place at the time and in the country of the atom bomb's recent production and military application: a country where nuclear physics was then shrouded in

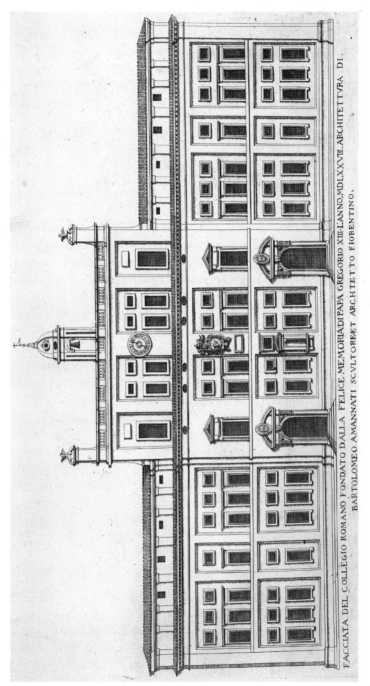

FACCIATA DEL COLLEGIO ROMANO FONDATO DALLA FELICE MEMORIA DI PAPA GREGORIO XIII·L'ANNO·MDLXXVII· ARCHITETTVRA· DI·
BARTOLOMEO AMANNATI SCVLTORE ET ARCHTET TO FIORENTINO.

ILLUSTRATION 5   The Roman College.

deepest secrecy. The day the bomb was dropped will not easily be forgotten by anyone who spent it in the United States. . . . It was victory,
but it was the shame of defeat. Next came the suppression of the
tremendous energy source by the military and politicians, and this
upset the intellectuals. Freedom of investigation, the exchange of scientific discoveries, the international community of scholars: all were
jettisoned by authorities that were strongly distrusted. Great physi-
cists left the service of their bellicose government in headlong flight;
one of the best known took an academic position where he was forced
to waste his working time in teaching rudimentary essentials solely
to escape working for the government. It had become ignominious to
make new discoveries.[9]

Brecht thought that America was reliving what had been the conditions of Italy in Galileo's time. In his diary, he notes: "the church (i.e. the
authorities) defended the teachings of the bible purely as a way of defending itself, its authority and its power of oppression and exploitation."[10]
This comment stems from Brecht's Marxist view that science became a
means of exploitation when it fell into the hands of the bourgeoisie, of
which he saw the Church as an embodiment.

The second version of the play, written in America, was simply entitled *Galileo*. With Laughton as the main actor, it was practically ready on
1 December 1945. Brecht would have liked to see it turned into the script
of a film, but he got little encouragement and it was kept as a play. Premièred in Los Angeles in July 1947, it was performed shortly thereafter
in New York. In both cities it received little acclaim, and Brecht sadly
commented:

> Though it resulted from several years of preparation and was brought
> about by sacrifices on the part of all concerned, the production of
> *Galileo* was seen by a bare ten thousand people. It was put on in two
> small theatres, a dozen times in each: first in Beverly Hills, Los An-
> geles, and then with a completely new cast in New York. Though all
> the performances were sold out the notices in the main papers were
> bad. Against that could be set the favorable remarks of such people
> as Charles Chaplin and Erwin Piscator, as well as the interest of the
> public, which looked like being enough to fill the theatre for some
> considerable time. But the size of the cast meant that the potential
> earnings were low even if business was really good, and when an ar-
> tistically interested producer made an offer it had to be rejected be-
> cause L. [Laughton], having already turned down a number of film

engagements and made considerable sacrifices, could not afford to turn down another.[11]

Brecht's comment on Laughton's behavior hardly reflects the complexity of the situation in the second half of 1947 when the United States and the Soviet Union had already entered the Cold War. In Hollywood, possible Communist agents were being ferreted out by U.S. agents, and Brecht himself had to appear before the House Committee on Un-American Activities on 30 October 1947, along with Hans Eisler, who had written the musical parts of *Galileo*, and was the brother of Gerhard Eisler, a notorious Communist. Brecht declared that he had never been a member of the Communist party, which was literally the case, and he was given a clean bill of health. But by then he had already taken steps to return to Europe. He left for Switzerland in 1947 and a year later settled in the Eastern zone of Berlin, where he remained until his death on 14 August 1956. This zone was under Russian occupation and the Communists provided him with a playhouse, the Deutscher Theater, and a company, the Berliner Ensemble, which was directed by his second wife. Brecht was showered with prizes and supplied with funds, but his work was scrutinized by state censors. To avoid unpleasantness, Brecht adopted a more oblique style in the hope of creating a certain distance between the spectators and the actors, so that he could not be said to invite a close identification with what the hero said. He also revised and expanded his *Galileo*. A few days before the heart attack that took his life, he attended a rehearsal of the play. The new third version was completed by Erich Engel and premièred in Berlin on 15 January 1957.

History on Stage

Brecht respects the rough chronology of events. Galileo did use his improved version of the telescope to make a number of important celestial discoveries between 1609 and 1610, and his success enabled him to leave the University of Padua, where he had been teaching since 1592, in order to return to his native Tuscany as Mathematician and Philosopher of the Grand Duke. He embraced Copernicanism, which was condemned by the Church in 1616, and he was admonished by Cardinal Robert Bellarmine to abandon the theory in the same year. In 1623, when his friend Maffeo Barberini was elected Pope, Galileo resumed his work on heliocentrism and published his masterpiece, the *Dialogue on the Two Chief World Systems*, in 1632. The next year he was tried in Rome and condemned to imprisonment, a sentence that was commuted to house arrest in his home in Arcetri, on the outskirts of Florence. He returned to physics and wrote his *Discourse on Two New Sciences*, which was smuggled out of Italy and published in the Protestant Low-Countries.

Brecht uses an interesting device to convey a feeling of historical accuracy. He supplies precise dates at the beginning of some scenes, for instance, "March 5th, 1616," before scene 7, which is entitled, "But the Inquisition puts Copernicus' teaching on the Index." The spectator, and even more the reader of the play, is led to believe that he is being presented with hard facts although not all the actors stand for historical figures. The cast includes Venetian senators (unidentified), two nuns, two soldiers, an old woman, a farmer and an unspecified number of men, women and children. Some personages have fictitious names such as Andrea Sarti, Galileo's young assistant and disciple, and Lodovico Marsili, a rich landowner who is engaged to Galileo's daughter. Eight historical figures are designated by their own name. These are Galileo; Giovanfrancesco Sagredo, a Venetian friend; Virginia, Galileo's daughter; Cosimo de' Medici, the Grand Duke of Tuscany; Christopher Clavius, a Jesuit astronomer; Cardinal Maffeo Barberini, who became Pope Urban VIII; Cardinal Robert Bellarmine; and Antonio Priuli, a Procurator and future Doge of Venice. We shall describe them in turn and see how they fare in Brecht's play.

Sagredo, Galileo's Friend

Giovanfrancesco Sagredo (1571–1620), who was seven years younger than Galileo, belonged to the Venetian patrician class. He became a close friend of Galileo after he arrived in Padua, and he corresponded with him after his return to Florence, although they were never to meet again. Galileo immortalized him in his *Dialogue on the Two Chief World Systems* along with another friend, the Florentine Filippo Salviati, who had also died by the time the book appeared. Whereas Salviati is Galileo's mouthpiece and argues in favor of the motion of the Earth, Sagredo plays the role of the open-minded person, who welcomes Salviati's hypothesis, but knows how to raise pertinent questions, in stark contrast to the third interlocutor with the fanciful name of Simplicio, who never seems to grasp the point that is being made. Both Sagredo and Salviati reappear as the main protagonists in Galileo's *Discourse on Two New Sciences*.

In Brecht's play, Sagredo is portrayed as the confidant with whom Galileo, while still in Padua, can speak freely. In scene two, when Galileo presents his telescope to the Venetian authorities, Sagredo says little, but in scene three they have a lengthy discussion, and watch the night-sky through a telescope from Galileo's house in Padua. The location is unlikely because Galileo usually met Sagredo in Venice, but it is a legitimate license since the issue is not whether they made observations in Venice or Padua but what they said to each other. Galileo offers a running commentary on his discoveries. The Moon, he says, has mountains and valleys like the Earth. Sagredo expostulates, "Ten years ago in Rome they burnt a man at the stake for that. His name was Giordano Bruno, and that is what he said." To which Galileo replies, "Exactly. And that's what we can see. Keep your eye glued to the telescope, Sagredo, my friend. What you're seeing is the fact that there is no difference between heaven and earth. Today is 10 January 1610. Today mankind can write in its diary: Got rid of Heaven."[12] The date, 10 January 1610, which gives an appearance of historical exactitude, is not substantiated by any document.

Giordano Bruno (1548–1600) is one of the tragic figures of the Late Italian Renaissance. Theologian, natural philosopher, playwright and hermeticist, he believed in the plurality of worlds, relativized the importance of Christianity, and rejected the traditional geocentric astronomy. After lecturing for several years in France, England and Germany, he returned to his native Italy as the guest of the Venetian patrician Giovanni Mocenigo. He hoped to be appointed to the Chair of Mathematics at the University of Padua but it was offered to Galileo instead in 1592. In that year Bruno was denounced to the Venetian Inquisition for his conception of God and creation (he had already been excommunicated by the Lutheran Church) and, in 1593, he was turned over to the Roman Inquisition. His trial lasted for seven years and when he refused to recant he was sentenced to death and burned in Rome on 17 February 1600.

Galileo and Sagredo probably never met Bruno, but they could not have been ignorant of his fate. Among the judges were two cardinals who would play a decisive role in Galileo's subsequent career: Robert Bellarmine, who became one of the most influential theologians in the Roman Catholic Church, and Camillo Borghese, who became Pope Paul V. The figure of Bruno cast a shadow on Galileo's trial and Brecht uses it effectively, albeit anachronistically. In scene three, after the passage we have quoted above, Galileo and Sagredo observe the motion of four hitherto unknown satellites of Jupiter. Galileo cries out, "They were right." "Who," asks Sagredo, "Copernicus and his lot?" Galileo replies, "And the other fellow. The whole world was against them, and they were right." After this clear reference to Bruno, the exchange goes on:

SAGREDO: Don't get worked up, Galileo!

GALILEO: Get worked up, Sagredo! Mrs. Sarti!

SAGREDO *turns the telescope away*: Stop bellowing like an idiot.

GALILEO: Stop standing there like a stuffed dummy when the truth has been found.

SAGREDO: I'm not standing like a stuffed dummy; I'm trembling with fear that it may be the truth.

GALILEO: Uh?

SAGREDO: Have you completely lost your head? Don't you realize what you'll be getting into if what you see there is true? And if you go round telling all and sundry that the earth is a planet and not the centre of the universe?

GALILEO: Right, and that the entire universe full of stars isn't turning around our tiny little earth, anyone could guess.

SAGREDO: In other words that it's just a lot of stars. Then where's God?

GALILEO: What d'you mean?

SAGREDO: God! Where is God?

GALILEO *angrily*: Not there anyway. Any more than he'd be here on earth, suppose there were creatures out there wanting to come and look for him.

SAGREDO: So where is God?

GALILEO: I'm not a theologian. I'm a mathematician.

SAGREDO: First and foremost you're a human being. And I'm asking: where is God in your cosmography?

GALILEO: Within ourselves or nowhere.

SAGREDO *shouting*: Like the man they burned said?

GALILEO: Like the man they burned said.

SAGREDO: That's what they burned him for. Less than ten years back.[13]

This powerful scene shows Brecht at his best as a dramaturge, but it is not historically correct. The theory that the Earth moves was not the reason why Bruno ran afoul of the Inquisition, and Galileo's telescopic observations earned him only praise when he went to Rome in 1611, a triumphal trip that Brecht does not mention. On 30 March 1611, the day after his arrival, Galileo went to the Roman College to call on the Jesuit astronomers who were already acquainted with his celestial discoveries. Galileo then spent several evenings in different houses to allow as many people as possible to have a peak through his telescope. On 22 April, he was granted an audience by Pope Paul V. On 24 April, the Jesuits confirmed his findings in a letter to Cardinal Bellarmine. On 13 May, the Roman College gave him the equivalent of an honorary doctorate in the presence of important dignitaries. About all of this, Brecht is silent. The only indirect reference is the mention, later on in the play, that Clavius acknowledged Galileo's discoveries.

At the end of scene three, Sagredo attempts to persuade Galileo not to leave the Republic of Venice for Florence, "because it's run by monks." To which Galileo replies, "I'll take them by the scruff of the neck and I'll drag them to the telescope."[14] A fine rhetorical flourish but ridiculous in historical terms since in 1610 friars, as well as laymen, were just delighted to welcome Galileo back to Florence. In retrospect, it might be argued that Galileo would have had a better chance of avoiding an open clash with the Pope if he had remained in Venice, which protected its professors from ecclesiastical meddling. In scene one, Brecht has Galileo point out to the Venetian Procurator Priuli that his government had handed Bruno over to Rome "because he was propagating the ideas of Copernicus." Priuli corrects him:

> Not because he was propagating the ideas of Mr. Copernicus, which anyway are wrong, but because he was not a Venetian citizen and had no regular position here. So you needn't drag in the man they burned. Incidentally, however free we are, I wouldn't go around openly citing a name like his, which is subject to the express anathema of the church: not even here, not even here.[15]

Priuli might have made some such comment had he spoken to Galileo at the time, but Galileo was not, and could not aspire to become, a Venetian citizen even though he held an official post and could count on the protection of the Republic. In 1610 he was basking in the glory of his heavenly discoveries, and there were no clouds on the Venetian or the Tuscan horizon.

Virginia, Galileo's Daughter

Virginia appears in eight of the fifteen scenes of the play. Although she is called after Galileo's daughter, she is a completely fictional character, said to be fifteen when she makes her first appearance in scene two, which is set in 1609. At the time, the real Virginia was nine years old. Brecht's reason for making her older is disclosed in the next scene, dated 10 January 1610 by Brecht, where we are told that Virginia will soon need her dowry to marry Lodovico Marsili, a fictitious character.

The story of Galileo's two daughters, Virginia and Livia, who was one year her junior, is not flattering for Galileo, and is a sad indictment of the way children were treated in the seventeenth century. When Galileo left Venice to take up his new appointment at the court of the Grand Duke of Tuscany, he had to decide what to do with the three children (a boy and two girls) he had had from his common-law wife, Marina Gamba, a woman that he had met in one of the jaunts he took to Venice. There was no question of marrying a woman with her background, and Galileo had no desire of taking her to Florence. He decided to put the girls in a convent, a practice that the Church was trying to curtail. Galileo asked his friend Cardinal Del Monte to use his influence, but the Cardinal replied that he could not comply for three reasons mentioned in Canon Law: first, two siblings could not be admitted to the same convent; secondly, when the number of nuns was already complete (as was the case of the convent Galileo had in mind), the dowry had to be doubled for each; and third, and most importantly, admittance was conditional upon applicants reaching the canonical age of sixteen. Now the oldest, Virginia, was only twelve. Under these circumstances, no dispensation was possible. Undeterred, Galileo approached the more pliant Cardinal Ottavio Bandini and, through his good office, obtained the dispensation of age. In October 1613, Galileo placed his two daughters in the Convent of San Matteo in Arcetri near Florence. The nuns belonged to the cloistered order known as the Clarisses, or the poor Clares. They fasted all year long, and filled the hours between the daily offices with spinning and embroidery. They were never allowed outside the walls of the convent, even in the case of the death of a parent or near relative.

Virginia took the religious name of Sister Maria Celeste, and her sister Livia that of Sister Arcangela. Virginia became a remarkable nun who led a deeply spiritual life, and was a constant source of comfort to her father. Livia broke down under the stress and suffered from constant depression. The times were indeed out of joint. Brecht would have nothing to do with this aspect of Galileo's behavior, and he chose to invent the engagement of Virginia and Lodovico to score a number of points against capitalism. In scene nine, which takes place in 1623, Virginia fiancé, Lodovico, a young man of the landed gentry, expresses concern over Galileo's determination to resume his work on the heliocentric theory. The "peasants," he declares,

> could be upset if they heard that frivolous attacks on the Church's sacred doctrines were in future to go unpunished. Don't forget that the poor things are little better than animals and get everything muddled up. They truly are like beasts, you can hardly imagine it. If rumor says a pear has been seen on an apple tree they will drop their work and hurry off to gossip about it.
>
> GALILEO *interested*: Really?
>
> LODOVICO: Beasts. If they come up to the house to make some minor complaint or other, my mother is forced to have a dog whipped before their eyes, as the only way to recall them to discipline and order and a proper respect. You, Mr. Galileo, may see rich cornfields from your coach as you pass, you eat our olives and our cheese, without a thought, and you have no idea how much trouble it takes to produce them, how much supervision.

Galileo admits that he might "stir up his peasants to think new thoughts," and willingly declares that he writes,

> in the language of the people, for the many, rather than in Latin for the few. Our new thoughts call for people who work with their hands. Who else cares about knowing the causes of things? People who only see bread on their table don't want to know how it got baked; that lot would sooner thank God than thank the baker. But the people who make the bread will understand that nothing moves unless it has been made to move.[16]

Brecht's Galileo speaks like a Marxist for whom a man of wealth is a tight-fisted, patronizing lout whereas the scientist is a man of the people, who works with his hands and speaks their language. The stupid and disagreeable Lodovico stomps out of the house never to return. The epitaph to the tryst between him and Virginia is aptly (from Brecht's point of view) pronounced by Andrea, Galileo's servant-disciple, who observes that all the ruling families "are prepared to kiss the Pope's toe only if he uses it to kick the people with!" So much for the upper classes to which the historical Galileo was always eager to proclaim that he belonged!

Brecht's rewriting of history is intelligible in the light of his deep-seated commitment to class struggle as the motor of progress. What is more difficult to grasp is why he makes Galileo treat his daughter so harshly that she becomes an informer for the Inquisition, something that is preposterous. Dava Sobel, the author of the best-selling book, *Galileo's Daughter*,[17] shows that she was warm-hearted, considerate and loyal. For instance, here is what she told her father after meeting Sestilia Bocchineri, the newly wed bride of her brother Vincenzo. Writing on behalf of her sister and herself, she begins as follows:

> We are delighted with the bride, who is most affable and gracious. But above all else what makes us happy is the love she bears you, and we suppose that she will be eager to perform all those services for you that we would undertake if we were allowed to. We will never stop doing our part by which I mean that we will continually commend you to the Lord our God. This is our duty, not only as daughters, but as the abandoned orphans we would become if you were not there. Oh, if only I were capable of expressing to you my innermost thoughts! Then I would be certain that you could not doubt whether I loved you every bit as tenderly as ever a daughter loved a father. But I do not know how to convey these feelings to you in other words, if not by telling you that I love you more than myself since, after God, I owe to you my life and innumerable other good things. I stand ever obliged to you and would be most willing, should the need arise, to risk my life for your sake.[18]

Virginia never had to risk her life but she abetted a plan to suppress evidence that could have incriminated her father. On 9 July 1633, her brother-in-law, Geri Bocchineri, wrote from Florence to Galileo, who had gone to Siena after his trial. The letter contained an enclosure in cipher, and the mention that it could only be decoded if Galileo had already received another letter with names in cipher sent to Rome a week earlier in the diplomatic pouch. This letter was to have been handed over to Galileo personally by the Florentine ambassador, but Galileo had already left Rome when the letter arrived, and it had been returned to Bocchineri, who forwarded it to Galileo on 13 July with the remark that Galileo "had guessed the gist of it."[19] What was at stake can be understood from a letter that Virginia sent to her father on the same day:

> Signor Geri was here one morning at the time when we guessed that you were in distress. With Signor Aggiunti he did in your house what he later informed me he had told you. It seemed to me appropriate and necessary to avoid consequences that might have ensued. Thus I could not refuse him the keys and the means to do what he intended, seeing his concern for your interests.[20]

It is clear that Maria Celeste, who had the keys to Galileo's house, handed them over to Geri Bocchineri knowing full well that he wanted to remove any document that might harm her father should they fall into the hands of the Inquisition. Maria Celeste was anxious to see a copy of Galileo's sentence, and she informed him when she managed to do so:

> On the one hand, what I read distressed me, but on the other hand I was glad to have seen it, and I realized that I could help you a bit by taking upon myself the obligation you have to recite once a week the seven psalms, and I have already begun to fulfill this requirement. I do so with pleasure, first because I believe that prayer, made in obedience to the Holy Church, is very effective, and then to relieve you of this care. Were I able to shoulder the rest of your punishment, most willingly would I elect a prison even straighter than the one in which I dwell, if by so doing I could set you free.[21]

Less than three weeks later, she wrote again to her father in a touching blend of affection and literary affectation:

> I do not know how to convey the happiness I derived from learning that you continue in good health in spite of everything, except to say that I enjoy your well-being more than my own, not only because I love you as myself, but also because I can imagine that if I were ill or taken from this world it would matter little or nothing to anyone, since I am good for little or nothing. Whereas in your case, the opposite holds true for a host of reasons, but especially (beyond the fact that you do so much good and are able to help so many others) because the great intellect and knowledge that the Lord God has given you enables you to serve Him and honor Him far more than I ever could. So that with this consideration I take greater pleasure in your well-being than in my own.[22]

Galileo was allowed to return to Florence in December 1633, but the happiness of his homecoming was short-lived. Maria Celeste fell ill with dysentery toward the end of March 1634. From the moment she took sick, Galileo walked from his house to the convent every day, trying to hold on to her with love and prayer. The medical skills of the time could do little, and she passed away on the night of 2 April. Galileo was heart-broken. Geri Boccherini understood his plight, and attempted to console him. "A father," he wrote,

> cannot but grieve. But Your Lordship can cherish the hope that a maiden so good and holy will make her way straight to the Lord God, and pray for you . . . for I believe we will need her prayers far more than she will need ours. I have always admired and esteemed her, and never once did I leave her without feeling edified, moved, and contrite. Surely, the Blessed Lord has already gathered her into His arms.[23]

In the interest of dramatic effect, Brecht distorts these facts and turns Virginia into a mixed-up and unreliable woman. In scene 7, she tells the Cardinal Inquisitor that she is about to return with her father to Florence to make the preparations for her marriage. The Cardinal replies, "Ah yes, I am glad that you will be going with your father. He will need you; perhaps you cannot imagine this, but the time will come."[24] This reference to future events is meant to suggest that the Church was already planning to bring Galileo to trial. This is pure invention. In 1616, Galileo enjoyed the protection of Paul V, who told him personally that he had nothing to fear from his enemies as long as he was Pope. The problems that Galileo faced several years later were not foreseeable in 1616. To suggest that Galileo's trial was a sinister plot that had been prepared long beforehand is perhaps good drama but it is bad history.

In scene 9, Virginia is sewing her trousseau with Mrs. Sarti, to whom she confides that the mother of her fiancé does not like her father's book. "He hasn't written a book for years," says Mrs. Sarti. To which Virginia replies, "I think he realizes he was wrong. A very high church person in Rome told me a lot about astronomy. The distances are too great."[25] Nothing could be further from the truth. No one sought to discredit Galileo in the eyes of his daughter.

In scene 13, Galileo's friends are waiting in the residence of the Tuscan ambassador for news of the outcome of the trial. In one corner Virginia kneels and prays that her father will recant. The reason for this is that she is confused "ever since they spoke to her,"[26] one of these persons being her father's confessor who was brought from Florence to Rome. The suggestion that Virginia was brainwashed is coherent with Brecht's fictional character but completely at variance with historical facts. In the next scene, Virginia is living with her father during the period that extends from 1633 until his death in 1642. As we have seen, the historical Virginia could not leave her convent. Furthermore, she had died less than four months after her father's return to Florence at the end of 1633. Brecht indulges in make-believe of a kind that says more about his own convoluted mind than about that of either Galileo or his daughter. Here is his comment on the perverse father-daughter relation that he fabricated:

> Galileo spends the last years of his life on an estate near Florence as a prisoner of the Inquisition. His daughter Virginia, whom he has neglected to instruct, has become a spy for the Inquisition. He dictates his *Discorsi* to her, in which he lays down his main teachings. But to conceal the fact that he is making a copy of the book he exaggerates the extent of his failing eyesight. Now he pretends not to recognize a goose which she shows him, the gift of a traveler. His wisdom has been degraded to cunning. But his zest for food is undiminished: he instructs his daughter carefully how he wants the liver prepared. His daughter conceals neither her disbelief in his inability to see nor her contempt for his gluttony. And Galileo, aware that she defends him vis-à-vis the Inquisition's guards, sharpens the conflicts of her troubled conscience by hinting that he may be deceiving the Inquisition. Thus in the basest manner he experiments with her filial love and her devotion to the Church.[27]

Brecht represents the relationship between Galileo and his daughter as perverse feelings when they really loved each other with great tenderness.

Cosimo De' Medici, Grand Duke of Tuscany

Cosimo II (1590–1621) suffers the same fate as Virginia at the hands of Brecht. In scene four, Cosimo, still a boy of about nine years old, arrives at the home of Galileo, who is about to return from the University. The boy wants to be shown the telescope with which Galileo discovered the satellites of Jupiter that he christened Medicean stars. He rushes up the staircase and enters Galileo's study where he finds the housekeeper's son,

ILLUSTRATION 6   Pope Urban VIII by Gian Lorenzo Bernini, about 1632.

Andrea, who is about his own age. Andrea does not know who the visitor is and treats him as an ignoramus who hasn't a clue about the difference between Ptolemy and Copernicus. They quarrel and wrestle like street urchins over a model of the heliocentric system. They stop when they hear Galileo arriving with some company, including a philosopher and a mathematician who declare that all celestial bodies must revolve around the Earth. Galileo suggests that they take a look through the telescope, but the mathematician declines until it has been settled whether objects, hitherto unknown, can, in principle, ever be seen. Cosimo asks whether there is anything wrong with "his" stars, meaning Jupiter's satellites, and Galileo urges them again to try the telescope: "Well, are you gentlemen to look through it or not?"[28] The mathematician and the philosopher prefer to pursue their learned disquisition about crystalline spheres while Galileo puts in a plea for "the evidence of their five senses,"[29] the criterion of the truth that the workers in the Venetian dockyards taught him to rely upon. To no avail, for they have to rush to a court ball, and all its implied world of frivolity and make-believe.

Brecht pokes fun at professors, aristocratic hangers-on, and even the nine-year-old Grand Duke. Good entertainment but completely at variance with the facts. The real Cosimo was born in 1590 and succeeded his father, Ferdinando I, in 1609. He married Maria Maddalena of Austria, who gave him a child, the future Ferdinando II, in 1610, the year Galileo returned to Florence. So when scene four takes place Cosimo was twenty-years old. He had been tutored by Galileo since the age of fifteen during the summer holidays, and he was to show him great consideration during his reign until his premature death in 1621. He granted him the prestigious title of "Mathematician and Astronomer to the Grand Duke," and one of the highest salaries among civil servants in Tuscany. He encouraged Galileo to present his telescopic discoveries in Rome, told the Florentine Ambassador to welcome him as an official guest, and provided him with letters of recommendation for high-ranking cardinals. Brecht's title for scene four, "Galileo has exchanged the Venetian Republic for the Court of Florence. His discoveries with the telescope are not believed by the court scholars,"[30] is pure fantasy. Galileo telescopic discoveries met with praise at court and elsewhere.

In scene eleven, which Brecht dates 1633, Galileo attempts to give a copy of his *Dialogue on the Two Chief World Systems* to Cosimo, who refuses to accept the book and snubs him with the ungracious remark, "The state of your eyes worries me. It worries me, truly. It shows me that you've been a little too eager to use that admirable tube of yours, haven't you?"[31] Since Cosimo had died in 1621, he could not have made the comment. In 1633, the Grand Duke was his son, Ferdinando II, to whom Galileo presented the first bound copy of his book at a formal audience on 22 February 1632, the day after the work issued from the press. On the same occasion, copies were distributed to other princes and notabilities present.

When the Inquisition in Rome claimed that there had been irregularities in the way the license to print had been secured, the Grand Duke did his best to protect Galileo, and he kept him in Florence until the Pope wrote to say that he would issue a warrant for his arrest unless he left for Rome forthwith. At this point, the Grand Duke agreed that Galileo would do well to comply, but he arranged for him to be his guest at the Florentine Embassy in Rome and not placed in prison in the Vatican. The Grand Duke and his Court were never contemptuous, cynical or cold in their behavior towards Galileo. When Galileo returned to Florence after his trial, the Grand Duke promptly went to visit him in his house in Arcetri where they had a long and friendly conversation. After Galileo died in 1642, the Grand Duke wanted to erect a mausoleum to Galileo in the church of Santa Croce in Florence, and he was only deterred by the Pope's express wish that this plan not be carried out.

Christopher Clavius, Jesuit and Astronomer

Another historical figure who appears in the play is Christopher Clavius (1538–1612), who taught mathematics and astronomy at the Roman College. Galileo called on him in 1587 when he made his first trip to Rome, and Clavius commented favorably on his work on the center of gravity of solids, a fashionable mathematical topic at the time. They later corresponded and Clavius's good opinion of Galileo contributed to his appointment to the University of Pisa in 1589, and his promotion to the University of Padua, three years later. Galileo admired Clavius and used material of his when he gave his first course on celestial matter in Pisa.

Galileo's *Sidereus Nuncius* was published on 13 March 1610, and the 550 copies were sold out within a week. The sensational news soon reached Rome, but the Jesuits experienced some difficulty in making telescopes as good as Galileo's. Nonetheless, by the end of the year they had confirmed Galileo's discoveries. Clavius, who was seventy-two at the time, had trouble handling the telescope, which was hard to focus, but he wrote to Galileo to congratulate him and to say that his new instrument would dramatically alter our understanding of the heavens. Brecht brings Clavius into the play in scene six, which is entitled: "1616. The Vatican research institute, the Collegium Romanum, confirms Galileo's findings."[32] The action takes place in the hall of the Roman College where a fat prelate and a frivolous monk poke fun at Copernicanism:

> A FAT PRELATE: They'd believe it; they'd believe it. Things have to make sense to be disbelieved. That Satan exists: that's something they doubt. But that the earth spins round like a marble in the gutter; that's believed all right. O sancta simplicitas!
>
> A MONK *play-acting*: I'm getting giddy. The earth's spinning round too fast. Permit me to hold on to you, professor. *He pretends to lurch and clutches one of the scholars.*[33]

The two silly members of the clergy are joined by two equally inane astronomers, one of which says, "It all started when we began reckoning so many things—the length of the solar year, the dates of solar and lunar eclipses, the position of the heavenly bodies—according to the tables established by Copernicus, who was a heretic."[34] A feeble-minded, superannuated cardinal adds to the foolishness by declaring that he is at the center of the world. Finally, the back door opens and Clavius enters followed by his staff. He hastens across the hall without uttering a word until he reaches the other side, where he tosses out the two words, "He's right," before disappearing. A monk whispers confidentially to Galileo: "Mr. Galilei, before he left Father Clavius said: Now it's up to the theologians to see how they can straighten out the movements of the heavens once more. You've won." To which Galileo replies, "*It* has won. Not me: reason has won."[35]

The scene is said to take place in 1616, but by that time Clavius had been dead for four years. Brecht chose that date because he wanted his audience to believe that the condemnation of Copernicus's book in that year had been made despite Clavius's approval of the heliocentric system. Brecht does not breathe a word of what really happened in 1611 when Clavius and his colleagues gave Galileo a triumphal welcome and organized a special session to celebrate his telescopic discoveries.

Robert Bellarmine, Inquisitor

In scene seven, dated 5 March 1616, Cardinal Robert Bellarmine is introduced as the host of a ball that is attended by the great families not only of Rome but of the whole of Italy. Cardinal Bellarmine and Cardinal Barberini, the future Pope Urban VIII, walk in holding over their faces the masks of a lamb and a dove. They exchange trivial quotations from the Bible with Galileo, who becomes annoyed and tries to make them grasp that he follows "men's reason." As the festivities proceed, Cardinal Bellarmine says, "Mr. Galilei, tonight the Holy Office decided that the doctrine of Copernicus, according to which the sun is motionless and at the centre of the cosmos, while the earth moves and is not at the centre of the cosmos, is foolish, absurd, heretical and contrary to our faith. I have been charged to warn you that you must abandon this view." "And the facts?" Galileo replies. "I understand that the Collegium Romanum has approved my observations." Bellarmine admits that the Jesuits "expressed their complete satisfaction, in terms very flattering to you," but he immediately adds that the Inquisition "took its decision without going into such details."[36]

Brecht is eager to have us believe that the Holy Office simply disregarded the opinion of Clavius and the Roman College. If this were true, the condemnation of Copernicus's book would have to be judged not only as misguided but as done in bad faith. Nothing could be further from the truth. The Holy Office had appointed a committee of eleven experts who, on 24 February 1616, submitted a report to the Holy Office in which they expressed the view that denying the motion of the Sun was heretical because it went against the literal meaning of some passages of the Bible. The next day, Pope Paul V told Cardinal Bellarmine to inform Galileo that he should abandon this view. On 26 February, Bellarmine carried out his assignment. What happened on 5 March (the day of Brecht's ball) is that the Congregation of the Index, not the Holy Office, banned Copernicus's book as contrary to Scripture, but without damning the book as heretical. It should also be noted that Bellarmine, who was a Jesuit and an unworldly prelate, never gave a ball at his house, never attended one, and never would have worn a mask.

Maffeo Barberini, the Future Urban VIII

Maffeo Barberini wears the mask of a lamb at Bellarmine's ball. He takes Galileo by the arm and says, "You too, my dear fellow, ought really to have come disguised as a good orthodox thinker. It's my own mask that permits me certain freedoms today. Dressed like this I might be heard to murmur: If God didn't exist we should have to invent him. Right, let's put on our masks once more. Poor old Galileo hasn't got one."[37] Such behavior is not in keeping with what we know of Barberini, who was not given to jesting about religious matters. Brecht gets it all wrong when he ascribes to him Voltaire's famous saying, "If God didn't exist we would have to invent him." Barberini was well acquainted with Bellarmine but he did not belong to the Holy Office as Bellarmine did; he was a member of the Congregation of the Index, which censured books. Now members of these two pontifical organizations observed the greatest discretion, and Barberini was never apprised of what Bellarmine had told Galileo on 26 February 1616. He only discovered that Galileo had been admonished not to teach or write about Copernicanism after the publication of Galileo's *Dialogue on the Two Chief World Systems*, and he was indignant that Galileo should not have told him or the official censor about the orders received in 1616 when he applied for a license to print his *Dialogue*. Brecht knew about this problem as he admits in a note dated 1939: "There is no doubt that Urban VIII was personally incensed at Galileo and, in the most detestable manner, played a personal part in the proceedings against him. The play passes this over." Brecht's justification for disregarding history is his determination to make the trial a symbol of modern abuses of authority:

Casting the Church as the embodiment of authority in this theatrical trial of the persecutors of the champions of free research certainly does not help to get the church acquitted. But it would be highly dangerous, particularly nowadays, to treat a matter like Galileo's fight for freedom of research as a religious one; for thereby attention would be most unhappily deflected from present-day reactionary authorities of a totally unecclesiastical kind.[38]

Barberini reappears a second time, in scene twelve, when he has become Pope Urban VIII. The Cardinal Inquisitor urges him not to risk upsetting the naive faith of those who believe that the Bible is literally true by allowing Galileo to assert that astronomy teaches otherwise. The Pope wants to back reason and science, but the Inquisitor argues that the issue is dangerous as it favors the spirit of doubt and insubordination: if Galileo only believes in reason, then God is no longer necessary. The following exchange takes place between them:

THE POPE: But I won't have any condemnation of the physical facts, no war cries of "Up the Church!", " Up Reason!". I let him write his book on condition that he finished it by saying that the last word lay with faith, not science. He met that condition.

THE INQUISITOR: But how? His book shows a stupid man, representing the view of Aristotle of course, arguing with a clever one who of course represents Mr. Galilei's own; and which do you think, your Holiness, delivers the final remark?

THE POPE: What did you say? Well, which of them expresses our view?

THE INQUISITOR: Not the clever one.

THE POPE: Yes, that is an impertinence.[39]

In the end, the Pope gives in to the Inquisitor, but he stresses that Galileo is not to be tortured. At the most, the instruments are to be shown. "That will be enough your Holiness," replies the Inquisitor, who adds the poor joke, "Instruments are Mr. Galilei's specialty."[40] Here again Brecht mixes fact and fiction. Galileo did not oppose reason and faith, and his trial was not the logical outcome of warfare between science and religion. Urban VIII was incensed that his argument about the infinite number of ways God could fashion the universe should have been placed in the mouth of Simplicio, the Aristotelian pedant who gets kicked in the pants during the four days of Galileo's *Dialogue*. The Pope had befriended Galileo, and had spoken well of him many years before the trial. A proud man, Urban VIII could not brook what he considered an act of *lèse-majesté*. An equally proud man, Galileo could not bring himself to believe that an intelligent person would not necessarily agree with him.

Galileo Galilei, the Scientist

Brecht left a series of notes that give an idea of how he proceeded in re-molding Galileo's character to suit his purposes. In the draft of a preamble to the American version dated 1946, Brecht wrote, "Already in the original version the church was portrayed as a secular authority, its ideology as fundamentally interchangeable with many others. From the first, the keystone of the gigantic figure of Galileo was his conception of a science for the people."[41] As we have mentioned above, Brecht saw the Church as a symbol of contemporary reactionary authorities. "In this play," he explains in an extended note, "the church mainly represents authority; as types the dignitaries should resemble our present-day bankers and senators."[42] In other words, the Church embodied the ills of capitalism when the Marxist struggle was just beginning. "Time did not stand still," he writes,

> a new class, the bourgeoisie with its new industries, had assertively entered the scene; no longer was it only scientific achievements that were at stake, but battles for their large-scale general exploitation. This exploitation had many aspects because the new class, in order to pursue its interests, had to come to power and smashed the prevailing ideology that obstructed it. The church, which defended the privileges of princes and landowners as God-given and therefore

natural, did not rule by means of astronomy, but it ruled within astronomy, as in everything else. And in no field could it allow its rule to be smashed. The new class, clearly, could exploit a victory in any field including that of astronomy.[43]

In order to get his message across, Brecht distorts facts of which he is perfectly aware. In scene two, he states that Galileo was both professor of mathematics at the University of Padua and director of the arsenal of Venice, a position he never held. This serves to link science with manual work and practical applications. Galileo is made to say, in what is a mixture of arrogance, falsehood and cynicism, "It is with deep joy and all due deference that I find myself able to demonstrate and hand over to you a completely new instrument, namely my spyglass or telescope, fabricated in your world-famous Great Arsenal on the loftiest Christian and scientific principles, the product of seventeen years of patient research by your humble servant."[44]

Galileo did not spend seventeen years working out the principles of the telescope. He only heard about the instrument on a trip to Venice in the summer of 1609, but within a few days he put together a combination of two lenses that enlarged objects. About the optical laws, he was to remain in the dark. His "spyglass" had nothing to do with the Arsenal, and Galileo would never have had the gall to declare that it was the outcome of research based on "the loftiest Christian and scientific principles." All Galileo claimed was that his telescope was a vast improvement on the ones that were already on sale in the market place in Venice.

Scene three is entitled, "10 January 1610. Using the telescope, Galileo discovers celestial phenomena that confirm the Copernican system. Warned by his friend of the possible consequences of his research, Galileo proclaims his belief in human reason."[45] Galileo's discoveries raised fundamental questions about the structure of the solar system but they did not, by themselves, prove that the Earth revolved around the Sun. Brecht wanted to show that Galileo clashed with the Church over matters of fact, not over an unproved hypothesis. Hence he has Sagredo declare:

Galileo, I see you embarking on a frightful road. It is a disastrous night when mankind sees the truth. And a delusive hour when it believes in human reason. What kind of person is said to go into things with his eyes open? One who is going to his doom. How could the people in power give free rein to somebody who knows the truth, even if it concerns the remotest stars? Do you imagine the Pope will hear the truth when you tell him he's wrong, and not just hear that he's wrong? Do you imagine he will merely note in his diary: January 10th 1610—got rid of heaven?[46]

Here are Brecht's comments on the way Charles Laughton acted out the scene:

> Looking up from their calculations of the movements of Jupiter's moons, Sagredo voices his concern for the man about to publish a discovery so embarrassing to the church. Galileo mentions the seductive power of evidence. He fishes a pebble from his pocket and lets it fall from palm to palm, following gravity: "Sooner or later everybody must succumb to it" [the evidence]. As he argued along these lines, L. never forgot for a moment to do it in such a way that the audience would remember it later when he announced his decision to hand over his dangerous discoveries to the Catholic court of Florence.[47]

This makes no sense. The discoveries, applauded in Rome as well as in Florence, were not considered a threat to anyone. In the same scene, Brecht makes an apparently trivial alteration in the actual dates of Galileo's observation of the satellites of Jupiter to show that Galileo had proof that Copernicus was right. The facts are as follows. On the evening of 7 January, Galileo saw three small but very bright stars in the immediate vicinity of Jupiter. The idea that they might be satellites did not occur to him. What struck him was the fact that they were in the unusual configuration of a short straight line along the ecliptic. Looking at Jupiter on the next night, he noticed that whereas two had been to the east and one to the west of Jupiter on the previous evening, they were now all to the west of the planet. Again he did not suspect that they might be in motion but wondered whether Jupiter might not be moving eastwards contrary to what the standard astronomical tables predicted. On the 9th, the sky was overcast. On the 10th, he observed two stars to the east of Jupiter. This seemed to dispose of the conjecture that Jupiter might be moving in the wrong direction. On the 11th, he again saw two stars to the east of Jupiter, but the furthest from the planet was now much brighter. On the 12th, the third star reappeared to the west of Jupiter. On the 13th, a fourth star became visible; three stars were now to the west and one to the east of Jupiter. On the 14th, all four were to the west, and on the 15th, only three remained to the west.

In the play, Brecht has Galileo say, on 10 January, "Yesterday, I looked again. I could swear the position of all four had changed,"[48] but "yesterday," namely 9 January, was a day when the sky was overcast and Galileo could not make any observation. Brecht's collapsing of events may be considered a legitimate use of theatrical license, but he is completely wrong when he assumes that the discovery of the satellites of Jupiter ruled out the geocentric system. What the discovery showed was that not all celestial bodies revolve around the same central body, be it the Earth or the Sun, since four satellites clearly go around Jupiter. It did not prove the motion of the Earth.

Brecht's determination to give Galileo a proto-Marxist tone of voice leads him to invent an unlikely story in scene eight. Galileo is asked by a young monk, whose family is of peasant stock and ekes out a pitiable existence from the fields, how he could tell them that they cling to "a small knob of stone twisting endlessly though the void round a second-rate star, just one among myriads." For a reply, the monk gets the sarcastic answer that the peasants

> are paying for wars which the representative of gentle Jesus [the Pope] is waging in Germany and Spain. Why does he make the earth the centre of the universe? So that the See of St Peter can be the centre of the earth! That's what it is all about. You're right, it's not about the planets, it's about the peasants.[49]

It would never have occurred to the real Galileo to use such language because he never held such ideas. In scene nine, Brecht indulges in the same kind of extravaganza when he declares in the title that Galileo is about "to resume his researches into the forbidden area: the sunspots."[50] The spots on the Sun were never a religious issue, and Galileo had easily obtained permission to publish his *Letters on the Sunspots* in Rome in 1612. The rotation of the spots on the Sun were a powerful argument in favor of the revolution of the Sun on its axis, but it was not a decisive proof that the Earth goes around the Sun.

Brecht is dishonest when he creates the impression that Galileo based his heliocentrism on careful observation or that he attempted to falsify the Copernican hypothesis in order to show that it was incontrovertible:

> So we shall approach the observation of the sun with an irrevocable determination to establish that the earth does *not* move. Only when we have failed, have been utterly and hopelessly beaten and are

licking our wounds in the profoundest depression, shall we start asking if we weren't right after all, and the earth does go round. *With a
twinkle*: But once every other hypothesis has crumbled in our hands
then there will be no mercy for those who failed to research, and who
go on talking all the same. Take the cloth off the telescope and point
it at the sun![51]

In scene thirteen, Brecht again presents matters as though the telescope had enabled Galileo to prove that the Sun is at the center of the
world, so that "no force will help them [the Inquisitors] to make what has
been seen unseen." Andrea, Galileo's servant-pupil declares, "They're be-
heading the truth."[52] But what happened at the trial, which took place in
the presence of the Commissionary of the Holy Office and his secretary,
not before the whole Congregation of the Inquisition, is a different story.
Galileo did *not* present his arguments for Copernicanism but declared
that he had *not* defended the theory, but merely discussed it, in his book.

Antonio Priuli, Procurator

In scene two, the Procurator Antonio Priuli introduces Galileo as the in-
ventor of the telescope that he had come to give to the Doge. Priuli says
nothing of the scientific use of the instrument but praises its military relevance in sighting and identifying far-off ships, and as "a highly mar-
ketable tube, for you to manufacture and sell as and how you wish."[53] The
real Antonio Priuli (1548–1623) was a distinguished officer who played a
major political role in the Venetian Republic, and was elected Doge in
1618. While Galileo was in Padua, Priuli was head of the police and the justice department in 1599, and Galileo probably met him at this time or, at
the latest, in 1602 when Priuli was appointed one of the three governors
of the University of Padua.

In August 1609, Galileo managed to make a telescope that enlarged objects nine times, and he took it to Venice. On 21 August, Antonio Priuli
and several worthy patricians climbed with Galileo to the top of the Cam-
panile in the Piazza San Marco. They were greatly impressed by the fact
that they could see distinctly the neighboring towns of Treviso and Padua,
watch people going in and coming out of a church on the island of Murano,
and observe passengers embarking and disembarking from gondolas on the
Canal Grande.[54] On 24 August, Galileo wrote to the Doge to say that he

wanted to give him the new instrument whose usefulness he outlined.[55] He was told to show up at the Senate on the next day. When he arrived, the meeting had already started and he took a seat in the waiting room. Shortly thereafter, Antonio Priuli, who was in the chair that day, came out to inform him that a motion had been tabled to double his salary, and confirm his professorship for life. Priuli promised to have the motion voted immediately. According to Galileo, the Senate approved it unanimously,[56] but the minutes show that this was not the case: 98 were in favor, 11 against and 30 abstained.[57] The large number of abstentions may have resulted from the fact that some senators had heard that similar instruments were already on sale in the market place. They were generally inferior to Galileo's but they were cheap. One such instrument had been seen in Padua two months earlier,[58] and Giovanni Battista Della Porta soon reminded his friends that he had described the instrument in a publication in 1593.[59]

In his letter to the Doge of 24 August, Galileo spoke of his telescope as "a remarkable and useful discovery," and "a new kind of spyglass derived from the innermost principles of optics." He handed it over to the Doge, he said, "to decide, as he saw fit, to make or not to make some more."[60] There can be no doubt that Galileo improved the magnification of the telescope but he never discovered the law of refraction that would have enabled him to explain how the instrument worked.

Antonio Priuli, who called for the vote that raised Galileo's income and gave him life tenure, believed that Galileo had designed a radically new instrument about which he understood the principles. Equally important is the fact that he assumed, along with his fellow senators, that Venice was being given the patent. When this turned out to be a puff of smoke, Priuli felt slighted, and he was still smarting years later.[61]

Brecht's Inheritance

We are not the first to find that Brecht abused Galileo's memory. In 1966, Eric Bentley wrote an introduction to the American version of Brecht's play in which he states that "Brecht was all wrong about the seventeenth century in general and about Galileo Galilei in particular."[62] A few years later, Paul Johnson painted a severe portrait of Brecht as the creator of the modern, sophisticated propaganda play, whose aim was to denounce capitalism and middle-class institutions.[63]

Brecht was not interested in people as individuals, and this is why he could not create characters, only types. His Galileo is too interested in himself to be a hero. He recants in the face of the Inquisition, but the terrible thing is the way he destroys his inquisitive daughter's spirit. In order to have the nagging specter of a reactionary Church in Galileo's own home, Brecht conceives Virginia as a spy. It is often said that a playwright cannot be accused of violating historical accuracy in order to provide an insight into human nature and enrich our knowledge over ourselves and the society we live in. But it would be naive to ignore that because Brecht's *Galileo* is considered factual by the majority of people who see the play, it becomes a powerful vehicle of falsehoods about Galileo, the Church and seventeenth-century society. We can only learn from history if we are honest about our past.

NOTES

1. John Willett and Ralph Manheim, "Introduction," in Bertolt Brecht, *Life of Galileo*, translated from the German by John Willett, edited by John Willett and Ralph Manheim (London: Methuen, 1980), p. vii.
2. *Ibid.*, p. ix.
3. Bertolt Brecht, "Texts by Brecht," *ibid.*, pp. 119–120.
4. *Ibid.*, p. 120.
5. *Ibid.*, p. 132.
6. *Ibid.*
7. *Ibid.*, pp. 132–133.
8. *Ibid.*, p. 118.
9. *Ibid.*, p. 158.
10. Quoted in John Willett and Ralph Manheim, "Introduction," *ibid.*, p. x.
11. Bertolt Brecht, "Texts by Brecht," *ibid.*, p. 160.
12. Bertolt Brecht, *Life of Galileo, ibid.*, p. 24.
13. *Ibid.*, pp. 27–28.
14. *Ibid.*, p. 32.
15. *Ibid.*, p. 15.
16. *Ibid.*, pp. 79–80.
17. Dava Sobel, *Galileo's Daughter* (London, Fourth Estate, 1999).
18. Maria Celeste Galilei to Galileo Galilei, 22 March 1629, *Le Opere di Galileo*, edizione nazionale, Antonio Favaro, ed., 1890–1909, reprint (Florence: Barbèra, 1968), vol. XIV, p. 26.
19. Geri Bocchineri to Galileo Galilei, 13 July 1633, *ibid.*, vol. XV, p. 177.
20. Maria Celeste Galilei to Galileo Galilei, 13 July 1633, *ibid.*, vol. XV, p. 179.
21. Maria Celeste Galilei to Galileo Galilei, 3 October 1633, *ibid.*, vol. XV, pp. 292–293.

22. Maria Celeste Galilei to Galileo Galilei, 22 October 1633, *ibid.*, vol. XV, p. 308.
23. Letter of Geri Bocchineri to Galileo Galilei, 7 April 1634, *ibid.*, vol. XVI, pp. 73–74.
24. Bertolt Brecht, *Life of Galileo, ibid.*, p. 63.
25. *Ibid.*, p. 69.
26. *Ibid.*, p. 96.
27. Bertolt Brecht, "Texts by Brecht," *ibid.*, p. 153.
28. Bertolt Brecht, *Life of Galileo, ibid.*, p. 40.
29. *Ibid.*, p. 43.
30. *Ibid.*, p. 34.
31. *Ibid.*, p. 90.
32. *Ibid.*, p. 50.
33. *Ibid.*
34. *Ibid.*, p. 52.
35. *Ibid.*, p. 54.
36. *Ibid.*, p. 60.
37. *Ibid.*, p. 61.
38. Bertolt Brecht, "Texts by Brecht," *ibid.*, p. 119.
39. Bertolt Brecht, *Life of Galileo, ibid.*, p. 93.
40. *Ibid.*, p. 94.
41. Bertolt Brecht, "Texts by Brecht," *ibid.*, p. 125.
42. *Ibid.*, p. 137.
43. *Ibid.*, pp. 148–149.
44. Bertolt Brecht, *Life of Galileo, ibid.*, p. 20.
45. *Ibid.*, p. 22.
46. *Ibid.*, p. 33.
47. Bertolt Brecht, "Texts by Brecht," *ibid.*, p. 144.
48. Bertolt Brecht, *Life of Galileo, ibid.*, p. 27.
49. *Ibid.*, pp. 65–66.
50. *Ibid.*, p. 69.
51. *Ibid.*, p. 81.
52. *Ibid.*, pp. 96–97.
53. *Ibid.*, p. 20.
54. "From the chronicle of Antonio Priuli," *Opere di Galileo*, vol. XIX, p. 587.
55. Galileo Galilei to Leonardo Donato, 24 August 1609, *ibid.*, vol. X, pp. 250–251.
56. We have Galileo's version of what happened in the letter he wrote four days later to Benedetto Landucci, his brother-in-law (Galileo Galilei to Benedetto Landucci, 29 August 1609: *ibid.*, vol. X, pp. 253–254).
57. Deliberation of the Senate, *ibid.*, vol. XIX, p. 116.
58. Lorenzo Pignoria to Paolo Gualdo, 1 August 1609, *ibid.*, vol. X, p. 250.
59. Giovanni Battista Della Porta to Federico Cesi, 28 August 1609, *ibid.*, vol. X, p. 252. Della Porta refers to his book, *De refractione optices parte* (Naples, 1593) where the telescope is mentioned in Chapter VIII.
60. Galileo Galilei to Leonardo Donato, 24 August 1609, *Opere di Galileo*, vol. X, pp. 250–251.

61. "He does not even want to hear the name of Galileo," writes Bernardo Pisenti to Ingolfo de' Conti, 3 May 1613, *ibid*., vol. XI, p. 503.
62. Eric Bentley, "Introduction," in Bertolt Brecht, *Galileo*, edited, with an Introduction, by Eric Bentley (New York: Grove Press, 1966), p. 9.
63. Paul Johnson, *Intellectuals* (London: Weidenfeld and Nicolson, 1988), Chapter 7 ("Bertolt Brecht: Heart of Ice"), pp. 173–196.

CHAPTER FOUR

Foul Play?

It is often said that Galileo was not treated fairly, and in this chapter we examine five such accusations: (1) Galileo's judges knew that he was right; (2) Galileo was granted permission to write his *Dialogue on the Two Chief World Systems* but charges were nonetheless laid against him; (3) a spurious injunction was used as evidence at the trial; (4) Galileo was offered a mild sentence if he admitted his guilt, but the agreement was violated and he was condemned to life imprisonment, not a light sentence even if he was allowed to dwell in his own house; and (5) he was tortured.

First Charge: The Judges Knew that Galileo Was Right

John William Draper claimed in *A History of the Conflict between Religion and Science*, published in 1874, that Galileo's judges acted in bad faith.[1] The accusation is baseless. Galileo's telescopic discoveries had altered contemporary knowledge of astronomy in a decisive way but they did not prove that our observatory, the Earth, is in motion. Galileo saw mountains and craters on the Moon, spots on the Sun, satellites around Jupiter, and the phases of Venus, but none of this refuted the age-old hypothesis that the Earth is at rest. The phases of Venus were a strong argument for saying that it revolved around the Sun, rather than the Earth, and this discovery dealt a blow to the Aristotelian and the Ptolemaic models. But the Danish astronomer Tycho Brahe had devised a new persuasive system in which the planets revolved around the Sun, which continued, however, to circle the Earth. Galileo rejected this new model and argued that the ebb and flow of the tides was the outcome of the combined effects of the diurnal rotation and the annual revolution of the Earth. The idea was ingenious, but it did not work. Cardinal Robert Bellarmine was perfectly reasonable when he said that he could not embrace Copernicanism "until he was shown a proof."[2] Urban VIII took an even stronger line and claimed that astronomers would never be able to know how the heavens go because they cannot carry out an empirical study of things that lie outside their reach.

How seriously people took Galileo in his own day is not always easy to determine because scientists did not enjoy the credibility that we are willing to give to them today. We see the Sun rise and set, but we know that it is the Earth that is really moving. Even if we are individually unable to prove this, we accept it because we know that it can be shown by qualified members of the scientific community. We have become accustomed to believe that scientific explanations possess a greater objectivity than sense impressions. For instance, we feel that a wooden table is solid, but we know that it is really made of small atoms surrounded by a considerably larger amount of empty space. The ease with which we withdraw from perceptual reality was only slowly acquired, and Galileo's contemporaries did not suspect that he would one day be hailed as the pioneer of the Scientific Revolution. In was only in 1638, five years after his trial, that he published his *Two New Sciences*, the great work that contains his two famous laws: (1) freely falling bodies have the same acceleration regardless of their weight, and (2) projectiles follow a parabolic path.

Second Charge: Galileo Was Allowed to Print His Book and then Charged for Doing So

When questions were raised about the compatibility of the Copernican theory with the Bible, Galileo thought that the best way of answering his critics was to go to Rome. He was confident that he could win over the leading members of the Roman College and the Curia, and he put forward his views in fashionable salons. Antonio Querengo, a man around town, wrote to his patron, Cardinal Alessandro d'Este, on 20 January 1616, and gave details about Galileo's campaign. Six are particularly interesting: (1) the meetings were held "now in one house, now in another;" (2) the audience varied between fifteen and twenty persons; (3) the question period was lively; (4) Galileo offered witty rebuttals of "the greater part" of the arguments that were raised against Copernicus; (5) before answering objections, Galileo added new ones that seemed even stronger so that when he went on to demolish them he appeared even more impressive; (6) he did not win over all open-minded persons but he made his opponents look ridiculous.[3] This last point boded ill. Some people were beginning to feel that he was too clever by half, and others suggested that he probably had been summoned to Rome to explain how the motion of the Earth could be reconciled with the Bible.[4]

When Copernicus's book was banned less than two months later, even Querengo thought that it was a good joke on a man who enjoyed making other people look foolish. But if Querengo was willing to laugh, the Florentine ambassador, Piero Guicciardini, thought that Galileo's one-upmanship was no jesting matter. Rome was not a place for people with new ideas and Galileo was bound to get himself and others into trouble. "Galileo," he wrote, "gets all worked up about his ideas, and has a hard time controlling himself . . . He is passionately involved in this quarrel as if it were a personal matter. He does not see or sense what can follow. He is deceiving himself and will get himself and those who follow him into trouble."[5] The Florentine ambassador was anxious to see Galileo leave as soon as possible, but he outstayed his welcome and only left Rome on 4 June.

In spite of the Ambassador's misgivings, Galileo did not resume his campaign in favor of Copernicanism until his friend Cardinal Maffeo Barberini was elected to the See of Peter. In the Spring of 1624, Galileo went to Rome to congratulate the new Pope Urban VIII and had the rare privilege of seeing him six times in the brief span of six weeks. It has generally been assumed that Galileo talked matters over with Urban VIII and that he was given permission to write about the motion of the Earth on two conditions. The first was that he present it as a conjecture, and the second that he stress that God, who is omnipotent, can make the world in an infinite number of ways that are beyond our ken. The latter was one of the Pope's favorite arguments. At first blush, it seems likely that Galileo would have worked out such a deal with the Pope, especially since they met on six occasions, but the evidence to the contrary is twofold: the first is circumstantial, the second rests on the testimonial of Cardinal Zollern. We shall examine both in turn.

The circumstantial evidence is that the Pope was an inveterate talker and that it was very difficult to say anything in his presence. Even high-ranking ambassadors, who had a weekly audience with the Pope, complained that if they could not put in a word at the beginning of the meeting they stood no chance of opening their mouth during the rest of the time. Galileo probably did not fare better than the ambassadors, and had no chance of making a clear appeal to the Pope. The second piece of evidence is even more cogent. Galileo was acquainted with the German Cardinal Frederic Eutel von Zollern (the name was later changed to Hohenzollern), a member of the Curia who had just been appointed to the bishopric of Olmütz in Bohemia. He was about to call on the Pope, as was the custom, to take formal leave before departing for his diocese. Galileo had two lengthy conversations with the Cardinal, and he reported to Cesi that he had convinced him to raise the matter with the Pope.[6] This is confirmed by what Galileo's friend, Giovanni Faber, wrote to Cesi on 24 May: "Galileo, who came to see me at my home yesterday, plans to leave Rome in six days. I hope that Cardinal Zollern will help him and put in a word about the Copernican system when he sees the Pope."[7] The Cardinal did see the Pope on 7 June and reminded him that Protestants had no quarrel with Copernicus, to which Urban VIII replied that the motion of the Earth had been censured as rash, not as heretical, and that there was no danger that it would be condemned as such, although he personally believed that it could not be proved.[8] Now if Galileo had personally heard Urban VIII say this on one of the six occasions when he saw him, he surely would have mentioned it to Cesi, whereas all he told him was that the Dominican Niccolò Riccardi and the scholar Gaspar Schopp held that the motion of the Earth "is not a matter of Faith, and that Scripture is irrelevant in this case."[9]

Third Charge: A Forged Injunction Was Used at the Trial

Since the full publication of all surviving documents concerning Galileo's trial, none have given rise to as much controversy as those relating to the order that was given to Galileo to refrain from advocating Copernicanism. The relevant documents are dated 25 February, 26 February, and 3 March 1616, and we shall examine them in turn. But let us first recall that in the winter of 1615–1616, Galileo held forth in Rome about the Earth's motion. He succeeded in demolishing the arguments of his opponents, but he did not win many converts to his own views. It was inevitable, however, that if the Earth moved, certain statements in the Bible would have to be reinterpreted, and since freedom to interpret biblical statements was a particular issue between Protestants and Catholics at the time, Galileo's position was a delicate one.

On 19 February 1616, the Holy Office asked an Advisory Committee of eleven theologians to examine two propositions about the matter. When they met on 24 February, they unanimously agreed that the first proposition, which stated that the Sun is stationary at the center of the world, was "foolish and absurd in philosophy, and formally heretical since it explicitly contradicts in many places the sense of Holy Scripture according to the literal meanings of the words, and according to the common interpretation and understanding of the Holy Fathers and the doctors of theology."[10] The second proposition, to the effect that the Earth has an annual and a diurnal motion, received "the same censure in philosophy" and was judged "at least erroneous in faith" in theology. Now consultants were only asked for their opinion; the Holy Father and the Cardinals of the Holy Office were the ones who took decisions. On the next day, 25 February, they met and the minutes record that after the Committee's assessment "of the propositions of the mathematicians" had been read out, the Pope ordered Cardinal Bellarmine "to call Galileo before himself and warn him to abandon these opinions. Should he refuse to obey, the Father Commissary, in the presence of a notary and witnesses, is to give him an injunction to abstain completely from teaching or defending this doctrine and opinion or from discussing it; and further, should he not acquiesce, he is to be imprisoned."[11]

This document, the first of the three to be considered, makes it clear that the Pope personally instructed Cardinal Bellarmine to tell Galileo to abandon the heliocentric theory, and that he envisaged three possible scenarios: (a) Galileo acquiesces and no further steps are taken; (b) Galileo refuses to obey, and he is formally enjoined by the Commissary, before a notary and witnesses, to refrain not only from *teaching or defending* the theory but even from *discussing* it; (c) Galileo does not submit and is incarcerated. The authenticity of this first document is not questioned. The second document, dated 26 February, is the one that raises problems. It states that Galileo was summoned by Cardinal Bellarmine who, in the presence of Commissary Michelangelo Segizzi, warned him that the Copernican opinion was erroneous and that he should abandon it. Now comes the disputed passage, which reads,

> Immediately thereafter, in my presence, etc., and in the presence of witnesses, etc., the Cardinal being also still present, the above-mentioned Father Commissary, in the name of His Holiness the Pope and the whole Congregation of the Holy Office, ordered and enjoined the

said Galileo, who was himself still present, to abandon completely the above-mentioned opinion that the Sun stands still at the centre of the world and that the Earth moves, and henceforth not to hold, teach, or defend it in any way whatever, either orally or in writing. Otherwise the Holy Office would start proceedings against him. The same Galileo acquiesced in this and promised to obey. And so, etc. Done in Rome at the place mentioned above, in the presence, as witnesses, of the Reverend Badino Nores of Nicosia in the Kingdom of Cyprus and Agostino Mongardo from the Abbey of Rose in the diocese of Montepulciano, both belonging to the household of the said Cardinal.[12]

We shall presently return to this document, but let us first look at the third, dated 3 March 1616, which mentions that on that day, at a meeting of the Inquisition, presided over by Pope Paul V and attended by six cardinals and the Commissary, Cardinal Bellarmine reported "that the mathematician Galileo Galilei had acquiesced when warned of the order of the Holy Congregation to abandon the opinion that the Sun stands still at the centre of the spheres and that the Earth is in motion."[13] At the same session, the Pope approved a Decree of the Congregation of the Index banning Copernicus's *On the Revolutions of the Heavenly Spheres*, Diego de Zuñiga's *Commentary on Job*, and Paolo Antonio Foscarini's *Letter on the Pythagorean and Copernican Opinion of the Earth's Motion*. This Decree was duly published two days later.

We now return to the second document, bearing the date of 26 February, the day Cardinal Bellarmine notified Galileo that he had to abandon the view that the Earth moves. What is incongruous about this document is that although Galileo was willing to comply with the order that he was given, matters did not end there, but the second scenario envisaged by the Pope was enacted forthwith. The Commissary, Father Segizzi, is said to have served him a formal injunction in the presence of the Cardinal, two members of his household, and the author of the memorandum who is not further identified. The document is neither notarized nor signed and, hence, had no legal status. This led Giorgio de Santillana to argue in his influential book, *The Crime of Galileo*, that the document was a forgery. But by whom? De Santillana suggested that Segizzi, annoyed with the ease with which Galileo had been left off the hook, went back to his office and told his assistant to arrange a more helpful minute of the proceedings. "And," he may have added, "make it stiff, just in case. What they don't know doesn't hurt them; when trouble arises, it is we who have to take it on."[14]

This hypothesis of a fraud did not originate with Santillana but with the German historian Emil Wohlwill,[15] who conjectured that the second part of the minute in which Segizzi's intervention is mentioned was written by an unscrupulous official at the time of Galileo's trial in order to indict him. But an examination of the document shows that it was entirely written by the same hand that was responsible for the other documents dated 1616. Furthermore, an X-ray analysis made in 1927 revealed that the document had not been tampered with after it had been written.[16]

De Santillana's own conjecture seems to be undermined by the publication in 1984 of a document that Sergio M. Pagano found in the Archive of the Inquisition. It repeats word for word what we find in the first document of 25 February, with the following addendum: "Cardinal Bellarmine warned Galileo about the above-mentioned opinion, etc., after which the Father Commissary issued the injunction as above, etc."[17] The use of *etc.* in this kind of minute is not unusual, and is shorthand for words that can easily be filled in. Here the first *etc.* stands for "that the Sun stands still at the centre of the world and that the Earth moves with diurnal motion," and the second *etc.* for "to abstain completely from teaching or defending this doctrine and opinion or from discussing it." We remain in the dark about the identity of the official who wrote this note, but this document apparently confirms that the Commissary served Galileo with an injunction, although scholars still have to decide whether it was written in 1616 or is a copy made at some later date.

We know too little about Father Segizzi's character to be able to guess why he proceeded as he did. But we know that Cardinal Bellarmine was an able theologian who held that as long as astronomers took the idea of the Earth's motion only hypothetically, there was no overt contradiction of the Bible. We also have evidence that he was a kind man and that he intended to spare Galileo. Two events that followed shortly thereafter corroborate this. On 6 March 1616, the day after the publication of the Decree banning Copernicus's book, Galileo was able to set forth in a letter the precise corrections that were to be made to the book of Copernicus, although these were not officially divulged until 1620.[18] It is difficult to account for this, unless Bellarmine himself, or an official acting on his behalf, wanted to make things easier for Galileo by providing him with all the information they had. The second event occurred less than a week later, on 11 March, when Galileo was granted an audience by Paul V with whom he strolled up and down for three quarters of an hour. The Pope reassured him against any lingering suspicion in his mind, and added that as long as he (Paul V) lived, Galileo would have no cause for alarm.[19] This remark is so unusual as to suggest that the Pope, who had been briefed by Bellarmine, was aware of the wagging of tongues in Rome. Galileo's friend, Antonio Querengo, joked about it in a letter to Cardinal d'Este: "Galileo's disputations have dissolved into alchemical smoke for the Holy Office has declared that to maintain this opinion is to dissent manifestly from the infallible dogmas of the Church. So here we are at last, safely back on a solid Earth, and we no longer have to fly with it as so many ants crawling on a balloon."[20]

Other people did not let matters pass off so lightly and spread rumors that Galileo had been forced to abjure and do penance. This gossip reached the ears of friends in Pisa and Venice from whom Galileo received condolences.[21] The way out of this unpleasantness was to call on Cardinal Bellarmine and explain the situation. Galileo took this step and received, in return, the following handwritten testimonial, dated 26 May 1616:

> We, Robert Cardinal Bellarmine, having heard that it is calumniously reported that Signor Galileo Galilei has abjured in our hands, and has also been punished with salutary penances, and being requested to state the truth of the matter, declare that the said Galileo has not abjured either in our hands, or in the hands of any other person here in Rome, or anywhere else so far as we know, any opinion or doctrine held by him; neither has any salutary penance been imposed upon him. He was only notified of the declaration made by the Holy Father and published by the Sacred Congregation of the Index, wherein it is set forth that the doctrine attributed to Copernicus (that the earth moves around the sun, and that the sun is stationary at the centre of the world, and does not move from east to west) is contrary to Holy Scripture, and therefore cannot be defended or held. In witness whereof we have written and signed this with our own hand, on this 26th day of May 1616. The same as above, Robert Cardinal Bellarmine.[22]

We now return to the controversial injunction of 26 February. It has been the object of a variety of reconstructions, some completely fanciful. We mention three that have some likelihood. First, Bellarmine acted so kindly and courteously toward Galileo that Segizzi felt that he had to intervene. This would explain why, immediately after the Cardinal's admonition, he delivered a more severe injunction. Second, Galileo expressed surprise when he was admonished by Bellarmine and showed some

ILLUSTRATION 7   Pope Paul V by Gian Lorenzo Bernini.

reluctance in accepting it, and Segizzi, following the Pope's injunction, went ahead with the injunction. Third, Bellarmine, annoyed at Segizzi's overbearing attitude, declined to sign the minute.

To our mind, the admonition by the Cardinal was all that was intended, and the further interference of the Commissary was due to overzealousness on his part. Let us imagine the case of a culprit brought up for sentence on his first offence before a judge and a fussy clerk. Expecting (as we know Galileo did) something mild, he is startled at being admonished to abandon his opinions and gives expression to this surprise by word or look. He seems not to comprehend. "What," he then blurts out, "must I abandon them altogether? Can I not even dis—." "No, no," cuts in the clerk, "You are commanded to abstain altogether from teaching or defending, and even from discussing them in any way whatsoever, and if you do not acquiesce you will be imprisoned." The culprit, crestfallen, says no more, bows and retires, noting only the Cardinal's admonition, and disregarding the Commissary's remark altogether, or regarding it as no part of the decision but merely a repetition in stronger words of the Cardinal's simple admonition.[23]

The absence of the signatures of the notary and the witnesses at the bottom of the injunction should not cause surprise. They were usually omitted in the draft minutes, which were called *imbreviatura* (shortened version) or *"matrix, seu originale instrumenti"* (original draft of the instrument). The *imbreviatura* is distinct from the "authentic instrument," which had to be witnessed and notarized. As Francesco Beretta explains, "most of the documents to be found in a judicial file—the interrogations of the witnesses and of the accused person, the decisions of the Tribunal concerning the conduct of the trial, copied in the trial files, and the prescriptions given to the accused—are written out in the form of *imbreviatura*. In all these instances, the authenticity of the document is guaranteed by its having been written by the notary."[24]

The *imbreviatura* was duly inserted into the series of *Decreta* of the Holy Office. But why the absence of an "authentic instrument"? It should have been inserted, not in the *Decreta* with the draft minute, but in the *Libri extensorum*, the register of the documents written in a public form and signed. Unfortunately, the series of "authentic documents" was almost completely lost as a result of the transport of the Archives of the Holy Office to Paris under Napoleon.[25] The absence of the authentic document of Segizzi's injunction (if, indeed, the document was ever compiled) in the acts of Galileo's trial is not a mystery, but the unfortunate result of war and looting.

When Galileo returned to Florence, he had Bellarmine's testimonial in his briefcase but he showed it to no one. He hoped that with a bit of luck the unfriendly gossip would soon die out and that he would never have to use his secret weapon. When he was summoned to the Holy Office in 1633, he produced a copy of Bellarmine's certificate at his first hearing on 12 April 1633. This came as a surprise to the examining magistrate, Commissary Vincenzo Maculano, but it did not help Galileo. It confirmed, rather, that Cardinal Bellarmine had personally notified him that the motion of the Earth was contrary to Holy Scripture and, therefore, could not be defended or held. By this time Bellarmine and Segizzi were both dead, but Carlo Sinceri, who had been Segizzi's assistant,[26] was not only alive and well but continued to exercise the position of Procurator-Fiscal that he held under Segizzi.[27] Furthermore, he was the only person who attended the four formal hearings that were held during the trial (12 April, 30 April, 10 May, and 21 June) when the new Commissary, Vincenzo Maculano, interrogated Galileo in the absence of any other witness. Sinceri wrote down the minutes of those meetings, and had the injunction seemed strange, he would have been the person to spot the irregularity.

Fourth Charge: The Extra-Judicial Deal Was Violated

If the injunction is not a forgery, we can still ask whether Galileo was manipulated during the trial. At his first hearing on 12 April 1633, Galileo denied that his *Dialogue on the Two Chief World Systems* was a defense of Copernicanism. When Commissary Maculano asked him whether he had mentioned the injunction when he applied for permission to print his book, Galileo replied that he did not, "because I have neither maintained nor defended the opinion that the Earth moves and that the Sun is stationary in my book. On the contrary, I have demonstrated the opposite, and shown that the arguments of Copernicus are weak and inconclusive."[28] With this answer, the first hearing of the trial came to an end. Silence on matters connected with the proceedings having been imposed on oath, Galileo was led to his apartment in the private quarters of the Procurator-Fiscal, where he received kind and considerate treatment. A servant was allowed to remain with him, Ambassador Niccolini was permitted to send him his meals, and no obstacle was opposed to his free correspondence with the Florentine Ambassador. Writing to the private secretary of the Grand Duke, Geri Bocchineri, on 16 April, Galileo says, "Contrary to custom, three large and comfortable rooms have been assigned to me, with permission to walk about in the spacious corridors. My health is good, for which, next to God, I have to thank the great care of the Ambassador and his wife, who have a watchful eye for all comforts—far more than I require."[29]

We have seen that Galileo formally denied under oath that he had defended Copernicanism in his book, a foolish move since, in fact, he had offered an extended vindication of the Copernican theory. Three counselors of the Holy Office, who had been asked to read the *Dialogue* to determine whether Galileo argued in favor of the motion of the Earth, handed in their reports on 17 April, five days after the first hearing. The first counselor, Agostino Oreggio, who was to become a cardinal that year, declared that Galileo's *Dialogue* defended the doctrine that the Earth moves and that the Sun is stationary. The second, the Jesuit Melchior Inchofer, stated that Galileo not only taught and defended that doctrine, but also almost certainly held it. The third, Zaccaria Pasqualigo, added that Galileo had infringed the injunction of 1616 not to teach or defend the prohibited doctrine.

Ten days after the first hearing, Galileo fell ill. From the letter that he wrote to Geri Bocchineri on 23 April, we know that Commissary Maculano and Procurator-Fiscal Sinceri were anxious to expedite matters:

> I am writing in bed to which I have been confined for sixteen hours with severe pains in one of my thighs, which according to my experience will last as much longer. A little while ago I had a visit from the Commissary and the Fiscal who conduct the enquiry. They have promised and intimated it as their settled intention to terminate the case as soon as I am able to get up again, encouraging me repeatedly to keep up my spirits. I place more confidence in these promises than in the hopes held out to me before, which as experience has shown were founded rather upon surmises than real knowledge. I have always hoped that my innocence and uprightness would be acknowledged and I now hope it more than ever.[30]

The second examination, originally fixed for 28 April but held on 30 April, took a different course from the first. While at the close of the first hearing Galileo not only denied having defended the Copernican doctrine, but asserted that he had done just the opposite, at this second hearing he made a declaration that, roundabout though it is, contained a confession that he had defended those doctrines. How this change of heart came about is explained in a letter from Maculano to the Pope's nephew Cardinal Francesco Barberini, who was at Castelgandolfo with his uncle at the time. After telling him that the day before, on 27 April 1633, he had reported to the Cardinals of the Holy Office what had been done in the case of Galileo, he adds that he requested "to treat extra-judicially with Galileo in order to render him sensible of his error, and bring him to a confession of the same."[31] Some cardinals were skeptical but Maculano had his way and was allowed to call on Galileo after lunch on the same day. After a long discussion, he convinced Galileo "to confess his error judicially," but Galileo requested a little time in order to consider the form in which he might most fittingly make his confession. Maculano concluded his letter by expressing the hope "that in this way the affair can be settled without difficulty. The Court will maintain its reputation, and it will be possible to deal leniently with the culprit."[32]

Maculano planned to return to Galileo's apartment on the same day to obtain Galileo's confession, which, once made, would allow him to return to the residence of the Tuscan ambassador, under house arrest, as Cardinal Francesco Barberini had suggested. The second hearing did not take place on that day as Maculano had intended, perhaps on account of Galileo's indisposition, but two days later on 30 April. Procurator-Fiscal Sinceri was present as on the first time. The usual oath to speak the truth was administered, and Galileo was requested to state what he had to say. Galileo then made a long and melancholy confession in which he declared that being at leisure to reread his book, and

> to note carefully whether, contrary to my most sincere intention, there had by any inadvertence fallen from my pen anything from which a reader or the authorities might infer not only some taint of disobedience on my part, but also other particulars which might induce the belief that I had contravened the orders of Holy Church. And being by the kind permission of the authorities at liberty to send about my servant, I succeeded in procuring a copy of my book, and having procured it I applied myself with the utmost diligence to its perusal and to a most minute consideration thereof. And, owing to my not having seen it for so long, it presented itself to me as if it were a new writing and by another author. I freely confess that in several places it seemed to me set forth in such a form that a reader ignorant of my real purpose might have had reason to suppose that the arguments adduced on the false side, and which it was my intention to refute, were so expressed as to be calculated rather to compel

conviction by their cogency than to be easy of refutation. Two arguments there are in particular—the one taken from the Sunspots, the
other from the ebb and flow of the tide—which in truth come to the
ear of the reader with far greater show of force and power than ought
to have been imparted to them by one who regarded them as inconclusive and who intended to refute them; as, indeed, I truly and sin-
cerely held and do hold them to be inconclusive and admitting of
refutation. And as excuse to myself for having fallen into an error so
foreign to my intention, not contenting myself merely with saying that
when a man repeats the arguments of the opposite side with the object of refuting them, he should, especially if writing in the form of dialogue, state them in their strictest form, and should not cloak them
to the disadvantage of his opponent. Not contenting myself with saying this, I now see I was misled by that natural complacency that
every man feels with regard to his own subtleties and in showing
himself more skilful than the majority of men in devising, even in
favor of false propositions, ingenious and plausible arguments. However, although with Cicero *avidior sim gloriae quam satis est* [I have
been more eager for glory than it is advisable], if I had now to set forth
the same arguments, without doubt I should so weaken them that
they should not be able to make an apparent show of force of which
they are really and essentially devoid. My error then has been—and
I confess it—one of vainglorious ambition and of pure ignorance and
inadvertence.[33]

After making this humiliating declaration, Galileo was allowed to
withdraw, and no questions were put to him. But he had no sooner left
the room than he returned to suggest that the *Dialogue on the Two Chief
Systems* be reprinted with the addition of one or two "days" in which he
would confute the arguments in favor of Copernicanism "in the strongest
way that God would suggest."[34] To this unexpected proposal, Maculano
and Sinceri made no reply. Galileo was then permitted to return to the
Tuscan Embassy, on oath not to leave it, not to hold intercourse with any
but the inmates of the house, to present himself before the Holy Office
when summoned, and to maintain the strictest silence on the subject of
the trial.

On 10 May, Galileo was summoned for the third time before Commissary Maculano, who informed him that he had eight days in which to
prepare a defense if he wished to do so. But Galileo at once handed in a
paper, from which we may conclude that it was written to order, and
under the same extra-judicial pressure as made him prepare his confession

of 30 April. The greater part of this document is taken up with an explanation of why he had not mentioned the prohibition of 1616 when applying for the *imprimatur* in 1630. Coming then to the last paragraph he declared:

> Lastly, it remains for me to pray you to take into consideration my pitiable state of bodily indisposition, to which at the age of seventy years, I have been reduced by ten months of constant mental anxiety, and the fatigue of a long and toilsome journey at the most inclement season, together with the loss of the greater part of the years of which, from my previous condition of health, I had the prospect. I am encouraged to ask this indulgence by the clemency and goodness of the most eminent lords, my judges, and hope that they will be pleased to remit what may appear good to their entire justice, and to consider my sufferings as adequate punishment.[35]

We cannot read this touching appeal without feeling pity for the old man who was compelled to sue cravenly for mercy, but Galileo was not crushed. He was sixty-nine at the time, and when he declared that he was seventy he was not suffering from partial loss of memory but using the fact that he had entered his seventieth year to good advantage. The rules of the Inquisition excluded the use of torture for people over seventy. After his declaration had been received, and the same obligations imposed on him on oath as after the second hearing, he was allowed to return to the Embassy. The nearer the time approached when his illusions were to be dispelled, the more sanguine was the news he sent to his friends. A favor granted just at the last, on the urgent solicitation of Niccolini, and unheard of in the annals of the Inquisition, might have encouraged these confident hopes. He was permitted to take the air in the gardens of the Villa Medici on the Pincio, to which, however, he was always conveyed in a closed carriage, as he must not be seen in the streets! Niccolini did not share in the hopes of his guest. After an audience with the Pope and Cardinal Barberini, he wrote to Cioli on 22 May: "I very much fear that the book will be prohibited, unless it is averted by Galileo's being charged (as I suggested) to write an apology. Some salutary penance will also be imposed, as they maintain that he has transgressed the command given to him by Cardinal Bellarmine in 1616. I have not yet told Galileo all this, because I want to prepare him for it by degrees, in order not to distress him."[36]

A lull now took place in the proceedings. For four weeks no one, not even Ambassador Niccolini, could learn anything. Galileo's fate was settled on 16 June at a meeting of the Holy Office at which the Pope presided. It was decided to try Galileo as to his intention, under threat of torture, and afterwards to call upon him to recant before a plenary assembly of the Holy Office. He was then to be condemned to imprisonment at their pleasure, and ordered in future not to discuss in writing or speaking the opinion that the Earth moves, under pain of further punishment. Further, Galileo's *Dialogue* was to be prohibited, and in order to make this known everywhere, copies of the sentence were to be sent to all Papal envoys and to all Inquisitors into heretical crimes, and especially to the Inquisitor in Florence, who was to read it publicly to all professors of mathematics summoned for the purpose.

Two days after these proceedings had been determined on, the Pope received Niccolini, who had come to beg for a speedy termination of the trial. Urban replied that it had already been terminated, and that the next week Galileo would be summoned to hear his sentence. The Ambassador implored the Pope to mollify any severity that he and the judges might, perhaps, have thought necessary. He mentioned the great complaisance already shown by the Grand Duke, who was only waiting the end of the business to express his gratitude in person. The Pope replied that the Grand Duke need not take this trouble, that he had readily showed every possible leniency to Galileo on account of his affection for his Highness. As to Galileo's opinions they could do no less than prohibit them as erroneous and contrary to Holy Scripture, which came from God's own mouth, and as to his person, he would according to usage be imprisoned for a time because he had transgressed the mandate issued to him in 1616. "However," added Urban, "after the publication of the sentence we will meet again and consult together so that he may suffer as little distress as possible." In his report of this audience to the Secretary of State, Niccolini added that he had simply informed Galileo of the approaching end of the trial and the prohibition of his book, but had said nothing about the personal punishment, in order not to trouble him too much at once. The Pope had also enjoined this course, "because in the course of the proceedings things might perhaps take a better turn."[37]

The drama now rapidly proceeded to a climax. On the evening of 20 June 1633, Galileo was warned to appear before the Inquisition on the following morning, when, as we know from the program outlined on 16 June, he was to be questioned under threat of torture about his intention, that is, his real convictions. On the morning of the 21st, Galileo appeared for the last time before Maculano and Sinceri. After he had taken the usual

ILLUSTRATION 8   Grand Duke Cosimo II byAdrian Haelweg,
17th century.

oath, and had answered in the negative the query whether he had any
statement to make, the examiner asked three separate questions, slightly
varied but all to the effect whether he held that the Sun is the center of
the world, and that the Earth is in motion. Galileo replied that he had not
held the opinion of Copernicus since he received the command that he
must abandon it. He then signed his deposition, and was taken to his suite
of rooms in the building of the Holy Office and detained until 24 June.[38]
He was never *thrown into the dungeons of the Inquisition,* as so many historians are fond of repeating. Neither is there, as we shall presently see,
the slightest foundation for another vulgar error—that he was actually put
to the torture.

101

Fifth Charge: Galileo Was Tortured

Like cats, myths have several lives and reappear in unlikely places at unexpected times. The myth that Galileo was tortured was revived by Italo Mereu in *The History of Intolerance in Europe* published in Italian in 1979, and reprinted several times since.[39] Mereu's claim that Galileo was tortured rests on the mention of "a rigorous examination"[40] in the sentence. We believe that Mereu has misunderstood the meaning of this expression, but let us first ask when Galileo could possibly have been tortured. Galileo was driven to the Holy Office in the Vatican on Tuesday, 12 April 1633, and remained there until Saturday, 30 April. He was interrogated upon arrival and on the day he returned to the Palazzo Firenze, the official residence of the Florentine ambassador. In the minutes of these two meetings, torture is not referred to at any time, and Galileo was not placed in a cell but provided with a three-room suite. There can be no question of torture during this period.

Galileo was summoned back to the Holy Office on 10 May to submit the defense that he had already written. He returned to the Florentine embassy on the same day, "half dead," as the Ambassador wrote.[41] Galileo was tired and stressed but he had not been tortured. We are left with one last possibility. Near the end of the trial, at a meeting of the Holy Office on 16 June, Pope Urban VIII decided that Galileo was to be summoned for a final time to determine what were his intentions in writing his book, "even with the threat of torture."[42] On 21 June, Galileo duly appeared before Maculano and Sinceri for the fourth and last time. He was asked whether it was true that he held or had held that the Earth moved when he wrote his book, and told, "that unless he decided to tell the truth, the law would be applied and appropriate steps taken against him (*devenietur contra ipsum ad remedia iuris et facti opportuna*)." The minutes then go on as follows:

> Reply: "I do not hold this opinion of Copernicus, and I have not held it since the command was given me that I must abandon it. For the rest, I am here in your hands; do as you please."
>
> And he was told to tell the truth; otherwise recourse would be had to torture (*devenietur ad torturam*).
>
> Reply: "I am here to obey. I have not held this opinion after the decision was pronounced, as I have stated."
>
> And as nothing further could be done in execution of the decree [of 16 June], his signature was obtained to his deposition, and he was sent back to his place.[43]

The threat of torture was not understood by Galileo or his judges as an actual menace. Galileo was only asked to sign his deposition, an act of compliance that must have been painful enough. On the next day, Wednesday 22 June, he was conducted to the Dominican convent of Santa Maria sopra Minerva, where in the presence of seven Cardinals of the Congregation of the Holy Office his sentence was read out to him. It contained a summary of his trial and stressed that he had failed to mention the injunction of 1616 when he requested permission to publish his book. It then went on: "Since it seemed to us that you had not disclosed the whole truth with regard to your intention [namely that he wanted to argue in favor of Copernicanism] we have considered it necessary to proceed to a rigorous examination, in which you answered like a good Catholic, without any prejudice to what was deduced, as said above, about your intention and to which you confessed." [44]

Next came the formal sentence:

> We pronounce, judge, and declare, that you, the said Galileo, by reason of these things which have been deduced in the course of this trial, and which, as above, you have confessed, have rendered yourself vehemently suspected by this Holy Office of heresy, that is of having believed and held the doctrine, which is false and contrary to Holy and Divine Scriptures that the sun is the centre of the world, and that it does not move from east to west, and that the earth does move, and is not the centre of the world; also, that an opinion can be held and defended as probable, after it has been declared and decreed contrary to the Holy Scripture, and, consequently, that you have incurred all the censures and penalties enjoined and promulgated in the sacred canons and other general and particular constitutions against delinquents of this description. From which we are willing that you be absolved, provided that with a sincere heart and an unfeigned faith, in our presence, you abjure, curse, and detest, the said errors and heresies, and every other error and heresy, contrary to the Catholic and Apostolic Church of Rome.[45]

Mereu fastened on the words "rigorous examination" as though they implied torture, but the expression was a formula that covered a sequence of five eventual stages: (1) threatening that extreme measures would be resorted to; (2) taking the accused into the torture chamber, renewing the threat, and showing him the instruments of torture; (3) undressing and binding; (4) laying him on the rack; (5) actual torture (*territio realis*). The actual proceedings of Galileo's trial clearly show that it was not necessary

103

to go beyond the first stage. Galileo saved his judges from this crowning infamy.

Mereu went to the extreme of saying that Galileo was actually tortured because he believed that most documents in the archives of the trial were of dubious authenticity. Writing in 1979, he rightly called upon the Vatican to open her archives, as many others urged at the time. In 1998 the archives were finally opened to the public, and the documents have since been studied in great detail by scholars from different or no religious inclination. Francesco Beretta, who has traced their history in great detail, concludes that the documents are genuine.[46] Mereu assumed that the only absolutely reliable documents were the ones that contain Galileo's sentence and Galileo's abjuration. The irony is that we do not have the originals of these two documents, which are only known from copies.

Another error that early biographers were fond of repeating, but of which a moment's reflection would have shown the absurdity, was that Galileo on rising from his knees after reciting the abjuration muttered *Eppur si muove* (it moves, nevertheless). Some writers, doubtless to render the story more plausible, provide a friend to whom the words are whispered. But consider for a moment the situation: an old man of seventy years, suffering in body, and distressed in mind by a lengthy trial, alone and without support in the midst of that stern assembly of Inquisitors. Is it likely that at such a moment he would have muttered or uttered these words? He must have known that the slightest indication by words or gesture of such a state of mind would have ruined all chance of clemency. Galileo did not choose to be a martyr.

NOTES

1. See Chapter 1, footnote 15.
2. Robert Bellarmine to Paolo Antonio Foscarini, 12 April 1616, in *Le Opere di Galileo*, edizione nazionale, Antonio Favaro, ed., 1890–1909, reprint (Florence: Barbèra, 1968), vol. XII, p. 172.
3. Antonio Querengo to Alessandro d'Este, 20 January 1616, *ibid.*, vol. XII, pp. 226–227.
4. Antonio Querengo to Alessandro d'Este, 1 January 1616, *ibid.*, vol. XII, p. 220.
5. Piero Guicciardini to Cosimo II, 4 March 1616, *ibid.*, vol. XII, p. 242.
6. Galileo Galilei to Federico Cesi, 15 May 1624, *ibid.*, vol. XIII, p. 179.
7. Giovanni Faber to Federico Cesi, 24 May 1624, *ibid.*, vol. XIII, p. 181.
8. Galileo Galileo to Federico Cesi, 8 June 1624, *ibid.* XIII, p. 182.
9. *Ibid.*, p. 183.

10. *Ibid.*, vol. XIX, p. 321. In Maurice A. Finocchiaro, *The Galileo Affair. A Documentary History* (Berkeley: University of California Press, 1989), p. 146.
11. *Opere di Galileo*, vol. XIX, p. 321, *The Galileo Affair*, p. 147.
12. *Opere di Galileo*, vol. XIX, pp. 321–322, *The Galileo Affair*, pp. 147–148.
13. *Opere di Galileo*, vol. XIX, p. 278, *The Galileo Affair*, p. 148.
14. Giorgio de Santillana, *The Crime of Galileo* (London: Heinemann, 1961), p. 266.
15. Emil Wohlwill, *Der Inquisitionsprozess des Galileo Galilei* (Berlin: Oppenheim, 1870), pp. 5–15.
16. See: Annibale Fantoli, "The Disputed Injunction and Its Role in Galileo's Trial," in *The Church and Galileo*, ed. Ernan McMullin (Notre Dame, Indiana: University of Notre Dame Press, 2005), p. 120.
17. Sergio M. Pagano, *I Documenti del Processo di Galileo Galilei* (Vatican: Pontifical Academy of Sciences, 1984), p. 223.
18. Galileo Galilei to Curzio Picchena, 6 March 1616, *Opere di Galileo*, vol. XII, p. 244.
19. Galileo Galilei to Curzio Picchena, 12 March 1616, *ibid.*, vol. XII, p. 248.
20. Antonio Querengo to Alessandro d'Este, 5 March 1616, *ibid.*, vol. XII, p. 243.
21. Benedetto Castelli to Galileo Galilei, from Pisa, 20 April 1616, *ibid.*, vol. XII, p. 254; Giovanfrancesco Sagredo to Galileo Galilei, from Venice, 23 April 1616, *ibid.*, vol. XII, p. 257.
22. *Ibid.*, vol. XIX, p. 348, *The Galileo Affair*, p. 153.
23. See J. J. Fahie, *Galileo His Life and Work* (London: John Murray, 1903), pp. 168–170.
24. Francesco Beretta, *Galilée devant le Tribunal de l'Inquisition. Une relecture des sources* (Fribourg: Université de Fribourg, 1998), p. 170.
25. See Francesco Beretta, "L'archivio della Congregazione del Sant'Ufficio: Bilancio provvisorio della storia e natura dei fondi d'antico regime," in *L'Inquisizione romana: Metodologia delle fonti e storia istituzionale*, Andrea Del Col and Giovanna Paolin, eds. (Trieste: Università di Trieste, 2000), p. 124.
26. *Opere di Galileo*, vol. XIX, p. 277.
27. For instance, he was present at the meeting of the Holy Office on 25 November 1615 when it was decided to examine Galileo's *Letters on the Sunspots*, *Opere di Galileo*, vol. XIX, pp. 277–278.
28. *Opere di Galileo*, vol. XIX, p. 341, *The Galileo Affair*, pp. 261–262.
29. Galileo Galilei to Geri Bocchineri, 16 April 1633, *Opere di Galileo*, vol. XV, p. 88.
30. Galileo Galilei to Geri Bocchineri, 2 April 1633, *ibid.*, vol. XV, p. 101.
31. Vincenzo Maculano to Francesco Barberini, 28 April 1633, *ibid.*, vol. XV, p. 106.
32. *Ibid.*, vol. XV, p. 107.
33. *Ibid.*, vol. XIX, pp. 342–343, *The Galileo Affair*, pp. 277–278.
34. *Opere di Galileo*, p. 344, *The Galileo Affair*, pp. 278–279.
35. *Opere di Galileo*, p. 347, *The Galileo Affair*, p. 281.
36. Francesco Niccolini to Andrea Cioli, 22 May 1633, *Opere di Galileo*, vol. XV, p. 132.

37. Francesco Niccolini to Andrea Cioli, 19 June 1633, *Opere di Galileo*, vol. XV, p. 160.
38. *Opere di Galileo*, vol. XIX, p. 362.
39. Italo Mereu, *Storia dell'intolleranza in Europa*, 6th ed. (Milan: Bompiani, 2000).
40. *Opere di Galileo*, vol. XIX, p. 405, *The Galileo Affair*, p. 290.
41. Francesco Niccolini to Andrea Cioli, 15 May 1633, *Opere di Galileo*, vol. XV, p. 123.
42. *Opere di Galileo*, vol. XIX, p. 360. English translation in Maurice A. Finocchiaro, *Retrying Galileo* (Berkeley: University of California Press, 2005), p. 247.
43. *Opere di Galileo*, vol. XIX, p. 362, *The Galileo Affair*, p. 287.
44. *Opere di Galileo*, vol. XIX, p. 405, *The Galileo Affair*, p. 290. The original Italian has "rigoroso essame," which we have translated literally as "rigorous examination."
45. *Opere di Galileo*, vol. XIX, pp. 405–406, *The Galileo Affair*, p. 291.
46. Francesco Beretta, "The Documents of Galileo's Trial. Recent Hypotheses and Historical Criticism," in *The Church and Galileo*, ed. Ernan McMullin (Notre Dame, Indiana: University of Notre Dame Press, 2005), pp. 191–212.

CHAPTER FIVE

The Courtier Who Promised More than He Could Deliver

Simple-minded explanations, such as the one that presents the Galileo Affair as the natural outcome of the conflict between science and religion, may be attractive but they fail to account for the facts. We may be dealing with a case of "mutual mistake," as Walter Brandmüller suggests in his book, *Galileo and the Church or the Right to Err*, that appeared in German,[1] and in an enlarged Italian version that was published by the Vatican Press in 1992.[2] Brandmüller claims in the preface that he made a contribution to the work of the Pontifical Commission created by Pope John Paul II to study the Galileo Affair. No wonder, therefore, that Brandmüller's ideas are sometimes quoted as representing the official position of the Church.

Brandmüller's approach is appealing for those who are keen on defending the Church. "We are thus led to the paradoxical result," he writes, "that Galileo erred in the field of science and the Curia in the field of theology, and that the Curia was right in the field of science and Galileo in the interpretation of the Bible."[3] This sounds plausible: Galileo thought that his theory of the tides was a decisive proof of Copernicanism, and in this he was wrong; he claimed that Copernicanism and Scripture were compatible, and in that he was right. Church officials considered that Copernicanism had not been proved, which was true; they believed that it was contrary to Scripture, and here they were mistaken. In order to assess Brandmüller's interesting proposal, let us examine his four claims in turn: (1) Galileo was wrong in science, (2) but right in theology; (3) the Roman Officials were wrong in theology, (4) but right about science.

Was Galileo Wrong in Science?

Galileo wanted to call his book *A Treatise on the Tides*, in order to highlight what he considered the most important and original of his arguments in favor of the motion of the Earth. Had he been allowed to keep the title he proposed, most people today would want to say that although the Earth really moves around the Sun, Galileo completely failed in his attempt to prove it, since he offered the tides as a rigorous scientific demonstration. Writing to his friend Prince Cesi, Galileo declared, "If the Earth is at rest, the tides cannot occur, but if it moves with the motions that I have described, they necessarily follow with all that is actually observed."[4] We know now that the tides are not caused by the motion of the Earth but by the gravitational pulls that are exerted by the Moon and the Sun. The idea of attraction was discussed in Galileo's day but it was not scientifically confirmed until Newton published his *Principia* in 1687, almost half a century after Galileo's death. When he wrote his *Dialogue*, Galileo was understandably distrustful of the idea of *attraction*. It seemed to him an *occult quality*, namely a non-scientific concept. Paradoxically, it was Pope Urban VIII who prevented him from using the title, *A Treatise on the Tides*, because this gave the impression that there was a physical fact that could only be explained if the Earth were in motion. In order to comply, Galileo changed the title to *A Dialogue on the Two Chief World Systems, the Ptolemaic and the Copernican*, under which the book is known to the present day.

Although Galileo's theory of the tides was wrong, Brandmüller does not do justice to Galileo as a scientist when he criticizes him for this mistake. Galileo was looking for a mechanical cause of the ebb and flow of the oceans and he thought that the combination of the Earth's diurnal rotation and its annual revolution would give rise to a to and fro, or tidal motion. In his enthusiasm, he neglected to ascertain the exact period of the tides, and he neglected to take seriously Kepler's discovery that the orbit of the Earth is not circular but elliptical. Let us recall that Galileo had also other reasons for endorsing Copernicanism. His telescopic discoveries of the phases of Venus and the satellites of Jupiter suggested that these two planets go around the Sun, not the Earth, and he showed that Aristotelian physics and traditional astronomy were seriously flawed. A pioneering scientist, Galileo promised more than he could deliver, but he delivered much more than any of his contemporaries did.

Was Galileo Right in Theology?

On 10 November 1979, speaking to the Pontifical Academy of Sciences, Pope John Paul II recognized that Galileo was right when he argued that Copernicanism was not contrary to the Bible:

> He, who is rightly called the founder of modern physics, declared explicitly that the two truths, of faith and of science, can never contradict each other, "Sacred Scripture and nature proceeding equally from the divine Word, the former dictated as it were, by the Holy Spirit, the latter as a very faithful executor of God's orders," as he wrote in his letter to Father Benedetto Castelli on 21 December 1613. The Second Vatican Council does not express itself otherwise: it even takes up again similar expressions when it teaches: "Methodical research in all brands of knowledge, provided it is carried out in a truly scientific manner and does not override moral laws, can never conflict with the faith, because the things of the world and the things of faith derive from the same God" (*Gaudium et Spes*, 36). Galileo feels in his scientific research the presence of the Creator, who stimulates him, inspires and helps his intuitions.[5]

The Pope equated what Galileo wrote to Castelli with what the Second Vatican Council declared. Galileo would have been delighted, and in his own day the *Letter to Castelli* had not been dealt with harshly by the Church. When Niccolò Lorini, a Dominican who was dissatisfied with Galileo, sent a copy of the *Letter* to the Holy Office, it was reviewed by an anonymous consultant who reported that he found nothing to question beyond three passages that sounded bad because they were poorly formulated. "As for the rest," he added, "although words are not always properly used, it does not depart from the highroad of Catholic expression."[6] It was on account of these terminological infelicities that Galileo revised his *Letter to Castelli* and wrote the expanded version known as *The Letter to the Grand Duchess Christina of Lorraine*. It is a brilliant essay and much ahead of what was commonly written in those days. It is not without its difficulties, however, and to these we must now turn. Quoting the *bon mot* of Cardinal Cesare Baronio, "The intention of the Holy Spirit is to teach us how to go to heaven, not how the heavens go,"[7] Galileo argues that the Bible was not written to provide scientific knowledge but religious teaching. When it refers to natural events, it uses everyday language that is intelligible to everyone, be he or she educated or not. So far so good, but Galileo does not draw the line here. He is so convinced that he is right about Copernicanism that he launches into a different argument that would have the Bible say something about natural knowledge:

> In the learned books of worldly authors are contained some propositions about nature that are truly demonstrated and others that are simply taught. In regard to the former, the task of wise theologians is to show that they are not contrary to Holy Scripture; as for the latter (which are taught but not conclusively demonstrated), if they contain anything contrary to Holy Writ, then they must be considered indubitably false, and must be demonstrated such by every possible means.[8]

Were the "wise theologians" to act upon the methodological precept that Galileo has just formulated, they would have to consider the motion of the Earth as "indubitably false." The problem is that Galileo is still relying on the Aristotelian "necessary demonstration" that is outlined in the *Posterior Analytics*. Galileo never developed a reliable way of discussing hypothetical reasoning or taking stock of a well-supported theory that falls short of actual demonstration. This explains why he overstates the cogency of his argument on the one hand and, on the other, uses scriptural texts to confirm his own hypothesis. At the end of the *Letter to the Grand Duchess Christina* he mentions that the miracle of the Sun's standing still in Joshuah is more easily understood if the Earth stopped than if the Sun and all the heavenly bodies came to a grinding halt.

Galileo's strategy is perhaps surprising, but it does not amount to an inconsistency. He is using an argument *ad hominem*, namely he assumes, without conceding, a premise relied upon by an opponent in order to show that the contradictory of what the opponent seeks to establish will follow. He writes, "Let us then assume and concede to the opponent that the words of the sacred text should be taken precisely in their literal meanings."[9] In no way does this commit him to the premise. What Galileo wants to show is that scientific knowledge can be used to clarify scriptural text, in this case the passage in Joshuah 10,13 where we read, "The Sun stopped in the middle of the sky." The Copernican system can help us understand what this really ("literally") means, but Galileo is not saying that we should initially turn to the literal ("everyday") reading of the text to support the Copernican position. Galileo is right in arguing that Copernicanism does not contradict the Bible. His rhetorical strategy, which implied that Scripture should automatically prevail over a serious but as yet unproved theory, is less fortunate.

Was the Church Wrong in Theology?

It seems evident nowadays that the Roman authorities made a mistake when they condemned Copernicanism. We were all brought up in the knowledge that the Earth goes around the Sun, but no one learned about this in school in Galileo's day, and it is by no means straightforward. One thing is certain: a *physical proof* that the Earth moves around the Sun and rotates on its axis was only found after Galileo's condemnation.

Cardinal Bellarmine had been clear in 1616: if the motion of the Earth were proved, the scriptural texts that appear to deny this would have to be reinterpreted. Personally, Bellarmine very much doubted that such a proof would ever be forthcoming. Pope Urban VIII held the same view, and he advised Galileo to use Copernicanism as a convenient mathematical tool without assuming that it was true. If one admits, as Galileo did, that the literal meaning of Scripture should prevail against mere conjectures in the natural sciences, then Bellarmine and Pope Urban VIII may be said to have been right. It is only with the advantage of hindsight that we can say that they were wrong. But Bellarmine and Pope Urban VIII cannot be completely excused if we consider two other aspects of the problem. The first is that Galileo, helped by friends who were priests and theologians, was able to find in Saint Augustine, Saint Jerome, and other eminent early writers known as the "Church Fathers," a number of considerations that opened the door to interpreting the Bible in a way that allowed the Earth and not the Sun to be in motion. The Council of Trent had declared that Scripture should be interpreted in conformity with the consensus reached by the Church Fathers, but had wisely added "in matters of faith and morality." Cardinal Bellarmine was aware of the problem and anticipated an argument that Copernicans might make: "Nor may it be replied that this is not a matter of faith, since if it is not so with regard to the subject matter, it is with regard to the speaker. Thus that man would be just as much a heretic who denied that Abraham had two sons and Jacob twelve, as one who denied the virgin birth of Christ, for both are declared by the Holy Ghost through the mouths of the prophets and apostles."[10] The issue was therefore more complex than is sometimes believed.

A second aspect of the question is the threat that Copernicanism posed for those who unconsciously identified the geocentric worldview with Christian cosmology. This is something that Brandmüller vigorously denies: "there was not, as often has been said, any confusion or distress in the authorities of the Church facing the collapse of the world view accepted until that moment. They were only interested in the inerrancy of the Scriptures that they mistakenly thought was compromised by the Copernican system."[11] That there was more at stake cannot be so lightly dismissed. Cardinal Bellarmine and Pope Paul V (the former Cardinal Camillo Borghese) had both been members of the Holy Office when Giordano Bruno was condemned to the stake in 1600. Although Bruno was not an astronomer, he had used Copernicanism as a platform from which to launch his new cosmology, in which stars are suns surrounded by inhabited planets, and the universe a necessary manifestation of the infinity of God and, hence, boundless. The outcome was a radical form of pantheism that overturned the basic tenets of Christianity. Bruno was executed in Rome in 1600 and it is unlikely that only sixteen years later Pope Paul V and Cardinal Bellarmine would have forgotten the overtones of Bruno's Copernicanism. On 27 February 1615, Galileo's friend Giovanni Ciampoli sounded Cardinal Maffeo Barberini, the future Pope Urban VIII, on the issue. The Cardinal said that he would like "greater caution in not going beyond the arguments used by Ptolemy and Copernicus," and "in not overstepping the limits of physics and mathematics." The future Pope also warned about the danger of misguided extensions of Copernicanism. As Ciampoli explained to Galileo,

> Your opinion regarding the play of light and shadow in the bright and dark spots of the moon creates some analogy between the lunar globe and the earth; somebody expands on this, and says that you place human inhabitants on the moon; the next fellow starts to dispute how these can be descended from Adam, or how they can have come off Noah's ark, and many other extravagances you never dreamed of.[12]

We have come to see our planet Earth as one among a vast number that circle their own Sun, and speculation on life on other planets has become common. Such was not the case in the seventeenth century. When Benedetto Castelli, Galileo's closest collaborator, mentioned the motion of the Earth in a conversation with Cardinal Francesco Barberini, Pope Urban VIII's nephew, he was told that if the Earth really moved, "it would have to be considered a planet, something that seems too much at variance with theology." To which Castelli replied that Galileo intended to prove that the Earth was not a planet, and the Cardinal rejoined that indeed he should.[13]

Was the Church Right about Science?

In Galileo's time, Copernicanism was a conjecture that awaited confirmation. If Galileo had been less dogmatic, he could have avoided a clash with the Church. "Therefore," concludes Brandmüller, "we face the grotesque fact that the Church, so often accused of error in this affair, was right precisely in the ambit that was not her own, namely that of the natural science, when she required Galileo that he treat the Copernican system only as a hypothesis."[14] Brandmüller overstates his case. The churchmen who held, in agreement with current methodology, that astronomical models were merely hypothetical constructions were entitled to *advise* Galileo to discuss Copernicanism as a conjecture. But could they *demand* this of him? When they laid upon Galileo the duty to speak hypothetically or to hold his peace, they were talking as *theologians*, not as scientists. When Pope Urban VIII declared that God's ways are inscrutable and that He could have designed the world after a fashion that escapes us entirely, he was basing his argument on God's omnipotence. The implication, only thinly disguised, was that to query this was tantamount to a denial of His omnipotence. At the time, it was not realized that a new science was emerging and no one guessed that it would prove extremely powerful. The position of Bellarmine and Pope Urban VIII was reasonable, but it was a reasonableness of a limited kind. The Cardinal and the Pope were men of their time, not heralds of the future. We know, in retrospect, that the road to modern science lay along the path that Galileo was following, not along the conventional highway that they were busy signposting.

Are Theories Underdetermined?

It may come as a surprise to some of our readers that the argument of Pope Urban VIII from the omnipotence of God resonates with contemporary accounts in the philosophy of science, and can be considered a theological version of the thesis concerning the *underdetermination* of theories. As Larry Laudan explains,

> The term underdetermination refers to a broad family of arguments about the relations between theory and evidence. All share the conclusion that evidence is more or less impotent to guide choice between rival theories or hypotheses. In one or other of its guises, underdetermination has probably been the most potent and most persuasive idea driving twentieth-century forms of skepticism and epistemological relativism.[15]

Underdetermination has a long pre-history. In Antiquity and the Middle Ages, the realization that we can account for the same data using different theories led to an "instrumentalist" notion of scientific explanation. On this view, an astronomical system aims at "saving the appearances," namely at providing mathematical instruments to compute the position and apparent size or speed of celestial bodies. A good astronomical theory can be used to predict eclipses but should not be taken as a true account of how the planets actually move. In order to know the *real* nature of the world, another kind of science was required, a demonstrative science, like Aristotelian philosophy purported to be, where the *real* causes of observed facts were investigated. This dichotomous approach to cosmology had important institutional consequences. The professor of astronomy was expected to teach how to "save the appearances," not what caused them. It was the job of the professor of natural philosophy to look behind or beyond the phenomena. Galileo taught mathematics not philosophy at Padua, and he had to deal with professors of philosophy who had no clue that mathematics could teach them something about the real world. This division of tasks also had financial implications. A professor of philosophy could be paid four to six times the salary of his colleague who taught mathematics. Hence Galileo's insistence that he be made not only *mathematician* but also *philosopher* to the Grand Duke when summoned back to Florence in 1610.

Bellarmine and Pope Urban VIII had no doubt that the traditional division of methods was sound. They had logic on their side, something that Brandmüller is eager to stress:

> Already in 1908 Pierre Duhem, when he expressed his point of view on the Galileo Affair, made the astounding statement that "logic was on the side of Osiander, Bellarmine, and Urban VIII, and not on the

side of Kepler and Galileo. The former understood the true meaning of the experimental method, the later misunderstood it."[16]

A startling assertion, to say the least!

Andreas Osiander, who is mentioned by Duhem, was a Lutheran theologian who wrote, without Copernicus's knowledge, a preface to his book in which the heliocentric theory is considered a way to "save the appearances," not a realist proposal. Osiander did not sign his preface and for decades readers assumed that it was by Copernicus even if heliocentrism is presented in the body of the book as a description of how the planets *really* move. Bellarmine and Pope Urban VIII cannot be blamed for taking the preface at face value. They were theologians not astronomers and, hence, unable to grasp the difference between the preface and the content of the book itself. Kepler and Galileo, who were in a position to judge, realized that Copernicus spoke like a realist not an instrumentalist. They were realists who believed that we can know the true system of the universe, and their realism played an important role in the establishment of the new science.

The position that Duhem takes in his book, *To Save the Phenomena*,[17] is nuanced. He does not deny that an external reality exists but that the goal of science is to discover regularities in the world and to express these regularities as "laws," which should not be regarded as identifying "the way things actually are." Scientific "laws" are simply convenient shorthands. A theory is not judged true or false according to how well it gives an explanation of reality. Instead, we judge a theory according to how well it accounts for the observations—for how the world appears. Good science leads to laws that are remarkably compelling and accurate, and it is understandable that scientists are tempted to believe that the laws represent the underlying reality, but this is incorrect.

Duhem's view of science was shared by his contemporaries, Henri Poincaré and Ernst Mach, and is frequently referred to as *conventionalism*. In a more modern guise, it has been given currency by Willard Van Orman Quine, one of the most influential philosophers of the twentieth-century, and is sometimes called the "Duhem-Quine thesis." The new twist is the emphasis on the impossibility of using evidence to bear against a particular hypothesis and none other. For instance, a physical experiment may be said to virtually depend on the whole of physics. The design of the apparatus and the interpretation of its output may involve not only the hypothesis supposedly to be tested, but also current theories about electronics, optics, thermodynamics, and so on. If the experiment does not give the expected result, the hypothesis to be tested might be blamed, but from a logical point of view any of these other physical theories might be faulted instead. In other words, no principled way exists to localize the bearing of evidence.

The Right to Make Mistakes

Brandmüller highlights what he takes to be Galileo's errors in an attempt to restore a better balance between Galileo's science (as it was in his own day and not as it later became at the hands of Newton) and Catholic theology (as it was generally understood in the seventeenth century before the rise of historical criticism). He claims that both sides made serious mistakes because neither of them could predict the future development of science. Galileo undoubtedly overestimated the strength of his argument from the tides, but we cannot categorically say that he considered it absolutely certain. It was his best argument, and he presented it in its most favorable light, which is not the same as offering it as indubitable. Galileo was a formidable debater who loved to show off, but he also had the good sense to realize that verbal fireworks do not amount to rigorous proof. In spite of what Brandmüller intimates, Galileo had a better feeling for science than either Bellarmine or Pope Urban VIII. The Jesuits, of which Bellarmine was a member, were interested in the scientific status of Copernicanism but they generally shied away from taking what might be construed as a controversial stance about the motion of the Earth. After all, they were first and foremost priests, and their scientific endeavors, however distinguished, were ancillary. Religion was their vocation; science their avocation.

This is even more the case of the eleven consultants who were asked by the Holy Office to assess the orthodoxy of the heliocentric theory, as Brandmüller recognizes: "The fact that the experts of the Holy Office provided a purely philosophico-theological evaluation shows that they did not consider the scientific aspect of the problem, and therefore that they did not deal with the scientific reasons in favor or against Copernicus."[18] The same can be said of what occurred at the trial in 1633. Galileo was faulted for disobeying the injunction given to him in 1616, not for having been wrong about the method of science. The idea that a "mutual mistake" occurred provides us with the opportunity of looking at the Galileo Affair afresh, but it is a view that is open to serious qualifications.

Galileo Courtier

The single-minded dedication to science and the overwhelming demonstrative force that earlier writers ascribed to Galileo has been called into question from yet another direction. Mario Biagioli, in *Galileo Courtier*, has argued that Galileo was essentially a social climber, or a *courtier* in the language of his day.[19] He made his first trip to Rome in order to secure the patronage of Christopher Clavius, the Jesuit professor of mathematics and astronomy at the Roman College, who agreed to write a letter of recommendation for him when he applied for a university post. In 1610, Galileo called "Medicean stars" the four satellites of Jupiter that he had discovered in order to win favor with the ruling family of Florence. He was fulsome in the praise of his would-be patron:

> The Maker of the Stars has Himself given me clear reasons to assign to these new planets Your Highness' famous name in preference to all others. For just as these stars, like children worthy of their sire, never leave Jupiter's side by much, so—and indeed who does not know this?—clemency, kindness of heart, gentleness of manner, splendor of royal blood, nobility in public affairs, and excellency of authority and rule have all fixed their home and habitation in Your Highness.[20]

This form of flattery is no longer practiced in democratic societies, but funding and jobs are as topical as ever. In order to obtain financial support, researchers write grant proposals, visit foundations, and contact the "right" people. Biagioli provides us with a lively and revealing description of how patronage worked in the seventeenth century. As he points out, the very first of Galileo's extant letters contains an explicit reference to one of his "patrons." Writing to Clavius, Galileo mentions that his letter will be delivered by Cosimo Concini, whom he calls "my most beloved patron (*mio amorevolissimo padrone*)" in whose favor he hopes to be confirmed thanks to Clavius's esteem, "which will weigh very much."[21] In his reply, Clavius says that he did not see Concini when he brought the letter but that he will gladly do what Galileo requested as soon as he sees him.[22] Galileo thanked him and renewed his request that he be "kept in the good graces of Signore Cosimo Concini."[23] Galileo's choice of a patron was judicious. Concini became Tuscan ambassador to the Emperor in Prague and, subsequently, ambassador to Spain.

Galileo was not born a courtier, but he became one at the age of forty-six when he was appointed Mathematician and Philosopher of the Grand

Duke of Tuscany. Biagioli believes that Galileo's troubles were typical of a princely court, and "resembled what is known as *the fall of the favorite.*"[24] The snag is that the relevant court is not the Tuscan one but the Papal Court at Rome. Galileo met Cardinal Maffeo Barberini for the first time when he went to Rome in March 1611. Six months later the Cardinal, as a guest of the Grand Duke in Florence, attended a staged discussion between Galileo and Flaminio Papazzone, a professor at the University of Pisa. The topic was the reason why some bodies float while others sink in water. During the question period, Barberini sided with Galileo, while another guest of the Grand Duke, Cardinal Ferdinando Gonzaga, upheld the position of his opponent. A few years later Barberini, who was a poet in his hours of leisure, praised Galileo's telescopic discoveries in a Latin ode and sent him a copy.[25] When the Cardinal's nephew, Francesco Barberini,

ILLUSTRATION 9   Cardinal Francesco Barberini by Guillame Vallet, 1679.

attended the University of Pisa some time thereafter, Galileo helped him get his doctorate. The Cardinal was more than pleased and sent him a warm letter of thanks, to which he added a postscript in his own handwriting: "I am much in your debt for your continuing goodwill towards myself and the members of my family, and I look forward to the opportunity of reciprocating. I assure you that you will find me more than ready to be of service in consideration of your great merit and the gratitude that I owe you."[26]

Less than two months later, Maffeo Barberini had been elected Pope Urban VIII and, on 2 October 1623, Francesco, then only twenty-seven, was created Cardinal and became his right hand man. When Galileo went to Rome in 1624, he was received by Urban VIII six times in a few weeks, a clear sign of the esteem in which he was held. With the Pope as friend and admirer, Galileo thought that he could now resume his campaign for Copernicanism as long as he did not declare that he personally subscribed to the arguments presented. The device that he chose was a written dialogue in which the pros and cons of heliocentrism could be put forward by different interlocutors. The winner would not be named, but the intelligent reader would have no trouble identifying him. Galileo's *Dialogue on the Two Chief World Systems* appeared in 1632, and his plan could have worked, had he not made the case for Copernicanism so strong that it was clear where he stood. He also made the mistake of putting in the mouth of Simplicio, a silly pedant who raised objections against the motion of the Earth, the argument that Pope Urban VIII was very fond of, and which consisted in stressing that God could have made the world in a number of unfathomable ways. When the Pope was told that Simplicio was his standard bearer, he was so irritated that he asked that the matter be investigated.

Whatever we think of the sociology of patronage in the seventeenth century, there can be no doubt that several other factors greatly influenced the outcome of Galileo's trial. At least eight were particularly unfavorable to Galileo. First, the death in 1630 of prince Federico Cesi, the Head of the Lincean Academy, whom Galileo had expected not only to pay for the publication of his *Dialogue* but to see it through the shoals of censorship. Cesi was a great diplomat and would have known how to avoid any possible hitch. Second, the dismissal of Giovanni Ciampoli, the friend who took upon himself to say to the Censor that Pope Urban VIII was willing to have the *Dialogue* published when he had never actually heard the Pope say anything of the kind. Third, the outbreak of the plague that rendered difficult the passage of any goods, including books to and from Rome. This created problems for the transmission of the manuscript of Galileo's book, which should have been completely revised in Rome. Fourth, Raffaello Visconti, the Roman consultant who had praised Galileo's manuscript, was suspected of collaborating with Orazio Morandi, the Abbot of San Prassede in Rome, who was accused of writing a horoscope in which he predicted the imminent death of the Pope. To add to this evil, Galileo was known to have dined with Visconti and Morandi when he came to Rome in 1630 to obtain the license to print his book. Fifth, the Holy See became embroiled in the Thirty Years War (1618–1648), and Pope Urban VIII was accused by some Catholics of siding with the Protestant King of Sweden. The matter came to a head in a Consistory on 8 March 1632 (two weeks after the publication of Galileo's book) when the Spanish Cardinal Gaspare Borgia attacked the Pope and charged him with dishonoring the Church. The supporters of Urban VIII were outraged and the cardinals almost came to fisticuffs. The Swiss Guard had to be called in to restore order. Now Giovanni Ciampoli, whom we mentioned above as Galileo's sanguine friend, seems to have cast his lot with the Pope's adversaries. Sixth, the hostility of university professors in Pisa, where Galileo never gave a course in spite of being a paid faculty member. Seventh, the resentment of some Jesuits whom Galileo had treated harshly when they disagreed with him on physical and astronomical questions. Eighth, the generally conservative outlook of Vatican officials, who neither rocked the boat of St. Peter nor enjoyed seeing others trying to do so.

Biagioli, who is cognizant of these factors, sees them from the vantage point of patronage, and he sums up as follows at the end of his book:

> This volume has presented a study of the interaction between the culture of political absolutism and Galileo's new natural philosophy. Once we see it in this context, Galileo's trial appears as a sign of the structural limits of the type of socioprofessional legitimation offered by court society and political absolutism. Galileo's trial was as much a clash between Aristotelian natural philosophy, Thomistic theology, and modern cosmology as it was a (structurally predictable) clash between the dynamics and tensions of a baroque court society and culture.[27]

The "Dynamics of Patronage"

Science does not exist in a cultural vacuum, and Biagioli's sociological approach is a useful reminder of this fact. But unless we believe in determinism (fatalism in high gear) we must also bear in mind that politics is only part of a larger picture. What Biagioli characterizes as the "dynamics of patronage" is a process that involves: (1) the fall of the favorite, (2) its justification on the grounds of betrayal, and (3) its absolute and inexorable character. Evidence for this kind of behavior of court is provided by Matteo Pellegrini, a contemporary of Galileo, who published in 1624, the year Cardinal Maffeo Barberini was elected Pope, a book dedicated to Antonio Barberini, the brother of Urban VIII.[28] It is essentially a handbook for winning favor at court and it cautions against the instability and mutability of princely benevolence. Courtiers who rise up can suddenly crash down if the ruler transfers his affection or chooses to use him as a scapegoat when an error is committed. "In short," writes Biagioli, "the fall of the favorite was no accident but rather a routine process of seasonal rejuvenation" of the court and of "cleansing" of the prince's power image. It was almost a ritualized sacrifice that worked both for the prince and aspiring courtiers."[29] Moreover,

> to be effective, the fall of the favorite had to be quick and inexorable. It was only by being absolute that it would be perceived as a sign of the prince's absolute power in determining the fate of its courtiers. Also, the prince could not under any circumstance admit that he had previously misevaluated the now-disgraced courtier. By doing so, he would present himself as fallible and consequently as not absolutely in control, that is, as not absolutely powerful.[30]

This is an interesting piece of information about the workings of a Baroque court, but its relevance to the Galileo Affair is never established, something that Biagioli admits: "Obviously I am not claiming that Galileo was Urban's favorite. There were no official favorites in Rome and, although Galileo was well connected at the papal court *and visited it every few years*, he was not a local courtier."[31] In his eagerness to strengthen this case, Biagioli has Galileo visit Rome *every few years*. This is a slip of the pen or a gross exaggeration since Galileo only went three times to Rome under the pontificate of Urban VIII (and not more than six times in all his life), always in connection with his scientific work. The first time, in 1624, to explore the possibility of writing about Copernicanism. The second time, to show the manuscript of his book and obtain permission to publish it. The third time, much against his will, to face trial.

Since Galileo cannot be said to have been the Pope's political favorite, Biagioli shifts his ground and declares that "he certainly was his intellectual one."[32] This is a startling claim, to say the least. Urban VIII admired

Galileo and spoke highly of his telescopic discoveries but it never entered his mind to confer upon him a post at the Vatican as, say, a consultant on scientific matters. Indeed, Urban VIII thought he knew more than Galileo about the philosophy of science, if not about actual scientific practice. He held that scientific realism (the theory that scientific theories are true and not mere conjectures) was naive and, hence, that the task of astronomers was not to find the true orbits of the planets but only to devise computational methods to predict where the planets would be observed at some future time. When Galileo made a strong case for realism in his *Dialogue*, Urban VIII felt he had been let down by a person whom he thought he had convinced that astronomical models could only be hypothetical.

Pope Urban VIII may have felt "betrayed" by Galileo, but this does little for Biagioli's thesis since Urban VIII was not looking for an excuse to downgrade a courtier. If the *Dialogue* had not been a pro-Copernican book, there would have been no trial. A purely mathematical or instrumentalist discussion of the motion of the Earth would have caused no problem. What shocked and angered the Pope was that Galileo went beyond the limits imposed on scientific speculation. We are not dealing here with an inexorable "fall of the favorite." In 1616, Maffeo Barberini, then still Cardinal, had intervened at a meeting of the Congregation of the Index to remove the word "heretical" from the decree banning Copernicus's *On the Revolutions of the Heavenly Spheres*. Because he was not a member of the Holy Office, Barberini was not apprised at the time that Galileo had been warned by Cardinal Bellarmine not to teach Copernicanism. When he found out about this injunction after the publication of Galileo's *Dialogue*, he was understandably annoyed that Galileo should not have mentioned this to him in 1624 or to the Roman censor when he applied for the license to print his book in 1630. We can sympathize with Galileo's reluctance to refer to the set-back of 1616, but the Pope's reaction was human, perhaps too human.

Biagioli has made an important contribution to our knowledge of seventeenth-century politics but he has underestimated the passionate quest for truth that animated Galileo. Biagioli's sociological commitment is as single-minded as that of the positivists whom he criticizes in his book:

> If it is a bit naïve to consider scientific credibility as related only to peers' recognition, even in modern science, such a view is seriously misleading when used to interpret the construction of scientific credit

ILLUSTRATION 10 Palazzo Barberini.

and legitimation in early modern science. I think it would be useful to suspend for a moment the 'natural' belief that Galileo, Kepler, and Clavius earned their titles simply because of the quality of their scientific work, and to consider, instead, that they also gained scientific credibility because of the titles and patrons they had.[33]

There is no doubt that sociological factors play a role in science, but Biagioli ascribes too much to the "dynamics of honor, power, challenges and duels" in order to "contextualize the repeated invitations of Galileo's patrons (from Cosimo II to Cesi and Urban VIII) to present his arguments as hypotheses, to write dialogues rather than treatises, to argue *ex suppositione*."[34] The fact that Urban VIII tried to impress upon Galileo that he should speak hypothetically has been taken by Biagioli as evidence that Cosimo II and Prince Cesi harbored the same feelings. But Cosimo II does not seem to have ever asked Galileo to consider the motion of the Earth as a mere hypothesis, and Prince Cesi shared Galileo's astronomical ideas although he urged, as was his wont, caution from all his colleagues. We cannot assess the Galileo Affair without some insight into the society in which he lived, but we shall miss much of what was at stake if we forget that Galileo considered science to be a quest for truth, and Copernicanism an instance of the correct application of scientific reasoning. What we have to do is not suspend our "natural" belief in the scientific quality of the work of Galileo, but the "unnatural" disbelief that would have us neglect his contribution to knowledge.

NOTES

1. Walter Brandmüller, *Galilei und die Kirche oder Das Recht auf Irrtum* (Regensburg: Verlag Friedrich Pustet, 1982).
2. Walter Brandmüller, *Galilei e la Chiesa ossia il diritto ad errare* (Città del Vaticano: Libreria Editrice Vaticana, 1992). The work is translated into Spanish: *Galileo y la Iglesia* (Madrid: Rialp, 1987). Brandmüller also published a documentary study in Italian, entitled *Copernicus, Galileo and the Church*, the outcome of extensive research in the Archives of the Holy Office. Walter Brandmüller and Johannes Greipl, *Copernico, Galilei e la Chiesa: fine della controversia (1820), gli atti del Sant'Uffizio* (Firenze: Olschki, 1992).
3. Brandmüller, *Galilei e la Chiesa*, p. 196.
4. Galileo to Federico Cesi, 23 September 1624, in *Le Opere di Galileo*, Antonio Favaro, ed., 1890–1909, reprint (Florence: Barbèra, 1968), vol. XIII, p. 209.

5. John Paul II, Address of 10 November 1979, in *Papal Addresses to the Pontifical Academy of Sciences 1917–2002* (Vatican City: The Pontifical Academy of Sciences, 2003), p. 242. *Gaudium et Spes* is the name of an official document of the Council Vatican II.
6. *Opere di Galileo*, vol. XIX, p. 305; Maurice A. Finocchiaro, *The Galileo Affair. A Documentary History* (Berkeley: University of California Press, 1989), pp. 135–136.
7. *Opere di Galileo*, vol. V, p. 319; English translation, *Letter to the Grand Duchess Christina* in Stillman Drake, ed., *Discoveries and Opinions of Galileo* (New York: Doubleday, 1957), p. 186.
8. Galileo Galilei, *Letter to the Grand Duchess Christina*, in *Opere di Galileo*, vol. V, p. 327; Finocchiaro, *The Galileo Affair*, pp. 101–102. See also Ernan McMullin, "Galileo's Theological Venture," in ed. Ernan McMullin, *The Church and Galileo* (Notre Dame, Indiana: University of Notre Dame Press, 2005), pp. 88–116.
9. Galileo Galilei, *Letter to the Grand Duchess Christina*, in *Opere di Galileo*, vol. V, p. 285; Finocchiaro, *The Galileo Affair*, p. 52.
10. Robert Bellarmine to Paolo Antonio Foscarini, 12 April 1615: *Opere di Galileo*, vol. XII, p. 172; Finocchiaro, *The Galileo Affair*, p. 68.
11. Brandmüller, *Galilei e la Chiesa*, p. 74.
12. Giovanni Ciampoli to Galileo, 28 December 1615: *Opere di Galileo*, vol. XII, p. 146.
13. Benedetto Castelli to Galileo Galilei, 9 February 1630: *ibid.*, vol. XIV, p. 78.
14. Brandmüller, *Galilei e la Chiesa*, p. 194.
15. Larry Laudan, "Underdetermination," in *Routledge Encyclopedia of Philosophy*, ed. E. Craig, vol. 9 (London: Routledge, 1998), p. 527.
16. Brandmüller, *Galilei e la Chiesa*, p. 194.
17. Pierre Duhem, *To Save the Phenomena: an Essay on the Idea of Physical Theory from Plato to Galileo*, translated by Philip P. Wiener (New York: Atheneum, 1962). The French edition appeared in 1908.
18. Brandmüller, *Galilei e la Chiesa*, p. 73.
19. Mario Biagioli, *Galileo Courtier. The Practice of Science in the Culture of Absolutism* (Chicago: The University of Chicago Press, 1993).
20. Galileo Galilei, *Sidereus Nuncius*, in *Opere di Galileo*, vol. III, p. 57.
21. Galileo Galilei to Christopher Clavius, 8 January 1588: *ibid.*, vol. X, p. 22.
22. Christopher Clavius to Galileo, 16 January 1588: *ibid.*, p. 24.
23. Galileo Galilei to Christopher Clavius, 25 February 1588: *ibid.*, pp. 27–28.
24. Biagioli, *Galileo Courtier*, p. 313.
25. Maffeo Barberini to Galileo Galilei, 28 August 1620: *Opere di Galileo*, vol. XIII, pp. 48–49.
26. Maffeo Barberini to Galileo, 24 June 1623: *ibid.*, vol. XIII, p. 119.
27. Biagioli, *Galileo Courtier*, p. 352. Biagioli acknowledges the influence of Richard S. Westfall's pioneering essay, "Patronage and the Publication of the *Dialogue*, Essays on the Trial of Galileo" (Vatican City: Vatican Observatory, 1989), pp. 58–83.

28. Matteo Pellegrini, *Che al savio è convenevole il corteggiare* [*It Behooves the Wise to Be a Courtier*] (Bologna: Tebaldini, 1624); reissued a year later as *Il Savio in Corte* [*The Wise Man at Court*] (Bologna: Mascheroni, 1625).
29. Biagioli, *Galileo Courtier*, p. 327.
30. *Ibid.*, p. 328.
31. *Ibid.*, p. 331. Emphasis ours.
32. *Ibid.*, p. 333.
33. *Ibid.*, p. 59.
34. *Ibid.*, p. 82. For an extended discussion of Biagioli's views, see Michael H. Shank, "Galileo's Day in Court" (Essay Review of Mario Biagioli, *Galileo, Courtier: The Practice of Science in the Age of Absolutism*, *Journal for the History of Astronomy* 25 (1994) 236–243, and "How Shall We Practice History? The Case of Mario Biagioli's *Galileo, Courtier*," *Early Science and Medicine* (1996), pp. 106–150.

CHAPTER SIX

Galileo Another Bruno?

G iordano Bruno (1548–1600), an admirer of Copernicus, ended his life on the stake in Rome in 1600. Galileo, who wrote in defense of Copernicanism some years later, was condemned in 1633. Was there a connection? Alexandre Koyré, a leading historian of science, has suggested that there is, and that Bruno's trial is "the occult but real cause of the condemnation of both Copernicus and Galileo."[1] This claim has to be considered, but let us first recall who was Giordano Bruno.

A Daring Friar

Giordano Bruno was born in Nola, twenty miles from Naples, in 1548. He entered the Dominican Order in Naples and was ordained a priest in 1572. After completing the prescribed course in theology in 1575, he entered into discussions about the divinity of Christ and, as a result, a trial for heresy was prepared against him by the Provincial Father of the Order. Bruno escaped to Rome in February 1576 where a second process was started, and in April 1576 he fled again. He left the Dominican Order, and after wandering in northern Italy, he went in 1578 to Geneva where he earned his living by proofreading. Bruno formally embraced Calvinism, but when he wrote a broadsheet against a Calvinist professor he discovered that the Reformed Church was no less severe than the Catholic. He was arrested, excommunicated, rehabilitated after retraction, and finally allowed to leave the city. He moved to France, first to Toulouse—where he unsuccessfully sought to be absolved by the Catholic Church, but was nevertheless appointed to a lectureship in philosophy—and then in 1581 to Paris. The French king, Henry III, appointed him to a temporary professorship, and in 1582 Bruno published three mnemonic works and a vernacular comedy, *Il Candelaio* (*The Candlemaker*), a vivid representation of contemporary Neapolitan society. In the spring of 1583 Bruno went to London, and in the summer lectured in Oxford. In 1584 he quarreled with some Oxonian doctor and began writing a series of dialogues among which was *La Cena de le ceneri* (*The Ash Wednesday Supper*) that we describe below.

In 1585 Bruno returned to Paris but he found the atmosphere uncongenial and soon left for Germany where he wandered from one university to another, lecturing and publishing a variety of works, including the *Articuli centum et sexaginta* (*One Hundred and Sixty Articles*) in which he expounded his theory of the peaceful coexistence of all religions based upon mutual understanding and the freedom of reciprocal discussion. At Helmstedt, however, he was excommunicated by the local Lutheran church in January 1589 and had to resume his travels. In August 1591, he returned to Italy at the invitation of the Venetian patrician Giovanni Mocenigo. Bruno was still looking for an academic platform from which to expound his theories, and he had probably heard that the chair of mathematics at the University of Padua was vacant. He went almost immediately to Padua, then the official state university of the Republic of Venice, and started a private course of lectures for students of the German College. At the beginning of the winter when it appeared that he was not going to receive the chair (it was offered to Galileo in 1592), he returned to Venice, as the guest of Mocenigo, who wanted private lessons on the art of memory. Disappointed with his new teacher and shocked by his theological positions, Mocenigo denounced him to the Venetian Inquisition in May 1592. Bruno was arrested and tried. He defended himself by admitting minor theological errors, and emphasizing the philosophical rather than the theological side of his basic tenets. The Roman Inquisition demanded his extradition, and on 27 January 1593 Bruno entered the jail of the Holy Office. During the seven-year period of the trial, Bruno at first developed his previous defensive line, disclaiming any particular interest in theological matters and reaffirming the philosophical character of his speculation. This distinction did not satisfy the inquisitors, who demanded an unconditional retraction of his theories. Bruno then made a desperate attempt to demonstrate that his views were not incompatible with the Christian conception of God and creation. The inquisitors rejected his arguments and pressed him for a formal retraction. Bruno finally declared that he had nothing to retract and that he did not even know what he was expected to retract. At this point, Pope Clement VIII ordered that he should be sentenced as an impenitent and pertinacious heretic. On 17 February 1600 he was burnt on the Campo dei Fiori in Rome.

Bruno's Copernicanism

Bruno was not a scientist, and he was not interested in astronomy as such but in Copernicanism as a launching pad for his cosmological ideas. He poorly understood some of the basic features of the heliocentric system, for instance he held that the Earth, the Moon, and the planets were—like animals of the same species—approximately the same in size and had roughly the same period of revolution around the Sun. His arrangement of the planets differed entirely from that of Copernicus, and he rejected most emphatically the mathematical astronomy on which Copernicus rested his case. As Ernan McMullin writes, "to call Bruno a Copernican requires one to empty the label of all content save the assertion that the earth and planets move around the sun."[2] Bruno did not rely on observational evidence or geometrical reasoning but on Renaissance Neoplatonism and Hermeticism. He believed that the universe is alive and actively striving towards ends consciously entertained. In *The Ash Wednesday Supper*, Bruno claims that the Earth and the planets have a soul. "Do you think that this soul is sensitive?" asks one of the interlocutors. To which Bruno replies, "Not only sensitive, but also intellective, and not only intellective as our souls, but perhaps even more so."[3]

Bruno had a flash of insight when he saw that the Sun, not the Earth, must be taken as the center of our local system of celestial motions. He pointed people's attention in the right direction, but he used the wrong sort of discourse in the mistaken belief that he could see further in virtue of his superior powers of discernment. He declared that he held the mobility of the Earth "on other, more solid grounds of his own. On this basis, not by authority but through keen perception and reason, he [Bruno] holds it just as certain as anything else of which he can have certainty."[4]

Frances Yates has argued in her influential book, *Giordano Bruno and the Hermetic Tradition*, that Bruno is best understood against the background of Renaissance Hermeticism.[5] This movement looked back to a collection of texts that were believed to have been written by Hermes Trismegistus in remote Antiquity, but actually dated from the second century after the birth of Christ. They were alleged to contain an arcane wisdom arrived at through a combination of magic and mystical inspiration. Bruno saw this "ancient philosophy" as announcing the cosmological doctrines he had taken upon himself to proclaim: the presence of a living principle in all things, and the participation of the Sun, the Earth and the stars in divinity itself. He developed a natural philosophy that could have become a rival of the Aristotelian one had it not been superseded by the new science of Galileo and Newton.

Galileo and Bruno

Bruno was no Galileo, but this does not preclude the possibility that his fate had important consequences for Galileo. Several ideas associated with Bruno may have sprung to mind when Galileo independently advocated the motion of the Earth. The main ones are: (1) the Sun is but one of many stars; (2) there exist many inhabited planets; (3) the universe is infinite; and (4) celestial bodies are alive and godlike. As far as the first point is concerned, the claim that the Sun is a star at the center of several revolving bodies, including the Earth, was startling but hardly heretical. Nonetheless, if the Church had never defined geocentrism as part of the Creed, it was the astronomical model that was taken for granted from the time of its Founder. The second issue concerning life on other planets raised more immediately theological questions about such issues as original sin, since extraterrestrial rational beings could not be descended from Adam, about the Incarnation of the Son of God on our planet, or again about the notion that Adam (and not some alien creature) was created in the image of God. The third point, Bruno's cherished belief in the infinity of the universe, hinged on what was meant by "infinity," a topic that Galileo avoided when discussing the size of the universe. Finally, the pantheism implied in the "divine" nature of everything, including cosmic bodies, was something that was foreign to Galileo's outlook.

But let us take a closer look at Bruno's extended discussion of Copernicanism, which is found in a series of five dialogues purported to have been held on Ash Wednesday 1584, hence the title *The Ash Wednesday Supper* that was given to the book. The characters are four in number: Teofilo (God-loving) is Bruno's mouthpiece; Smith stands for the educated layman willing to listen and to learn; Prudenzio is an academic pedant who invariably slips into Latin tags that are as worn-out as his ideas; and Frulla, who enlivens the conversation with biting remarks. When Bruno published his book in 1584, four decades after the appearance of Copernicus's *On the Revolutions of the Heavenly Spheres*, not more than a handful of persons had endorsed his system, and Bruno was the most vocal and the most prominent in Italy. Anyone embracing Copernicanism would find himself willy-nilly walking in his shadow.

Galileo's *Dialogue* is a far cry from Bruno's *Supper* but here are similarities: (1) whereas the common scientific language was Latin, both Bruno and Galileo chose to write in Italian; (2) both elected to present their ideas in the form of a dialogue in which their spokesman is clearly the winner: Teofilo in Bruno's *Supper*, and Salviati in Galileo's *Dialogue*; (3) Bruno made a fool of the pedant Prudenzio, and Galileo deals in the same way with Simplicio, the simpleton who rehearses Aristotelian arguments; (4) Smith represents the sensible and open-minded layman in the *Supper*, and Sagredo plays the same role in Galileo's *Dialogue*. A further similarity lies in the fact that Bruno never appears personally in the *Supper* but is praised by Teofilo as the *Nolan* (from his native town of Nola), and that Galileo, who is also absent from his *Dialogue*, has his spokesman, Salviati, refer to him as the *Lyncean* (belonging to the Academy of the Lynxes), always approvingly of course.

As far as specific arguments are concerned, Bruno anticipated Galileo's refutation of the commonsensical but fallacious objection that, if the Earth rotates on its axis, a stone dropped from a tower would not fall at its foot but some distance to the east because the tower would have moved westward while the stone was falling straight down. Bruno and later Galileo showed that this is wrong because the stone shares the motion of the revolving earth whether it is at rest on top of the tower or grazing its side as it falls. The point is brought home with a thought-experiment. Imagine that you climb the mast of a moving ship and drop a stone. It will clearly fall at the foot of the mast, not some distance sternward. The argument can be extended to clouds and birds to explain why they are not swept away by the whirling of the Earth.[6] Equally interesting, and of even greater interest in the case of Galileo's trial, is Bruno's understanding of Scripture as a source of moral insight accessible to all because it uses plain language. The Bible does not consider, says Bruno, "those truths that would not have helped the common people in turning away from evil and following what is good," for God chose "to speak to the common people according to their way of understanding, so that they might know what is of vital importance."[7] This view was echoed in Galileo's *Letter to the Granduchess Christina* of 1615, and is now taken for granted by everyone in the Catholic Church. But Bruno and Galileo after him were going against a growing trend toward biblical fundamentalism and Scholastic rigidity motivated to a large extent by the determination to show Protestant Reformers that Catholics also took the Bible seriously.

Bruno's Trial

Bruno was not put on trial mainly for his cosmological ideas but for his theological views. We have a full record of the proceedings in Venice between May 1592 and January 1593. After this date, he was handed over to the Roman Inquisition, and the documentation concerning the Roman trial is scanty. The reason in this case, as in several others, is the fate of the Vatican Archives under Napoleon, who had them transported to Paris by the French army. After his defeat at Waterloo and the restoration of the monarchy, the Vatican asked that the Archives be returned. The new French government acquiesced but on condition that the transport be paid for by the Catholic Church. The Pope sent Father Marino Marini and Count Giulio Ginnasi to Paris, but the amount of material was so vast and their resources so limited that they found they could not cover the expense of sending all the documents back to the Vatican. They selected the more obviously important ones, including the complete file on Galileo, and sold the rest to paper manufacturers.

The Holy Office was mainly interested in records that dealt with doctrinal or jurisdictional matters. The fate of the vast collection of trial documents was left at the discretion of their two envoys, who had no choice but to part with some four thousand volumes of criminal records, the collections of sentences and abjurations, and almost all the registers of correspondence.[8] This explains why the records of Bruno's trial are missing.

In 1942, the Director of the Vatican Secret Archives, Angelo Mercati, had a stroke of luck. He came across a summary of the trial that was presented to the tribunal on 16 March 1598.[9] It consists of 261 paragraphs, each containing an accusation against Bruno or an answer by him. They are grouped under 34 headings, and we list them below to give the reader an idea of the variety of issues that were discussed at the trial:

1. Bruno's views against the Catholic Faith and its ministers (paragraphs 1–23);
2. the Trinity, the divinity, and the Incarnation (24–40);
3. Jesus Christ (41–56);
4. whether Jesus Christ committed sin (57–64);
5. transubstantiation and Holy Mass (65–71);
6. hell (72–81);
7. that many worlds exist (82–97);
8. the adoration of the Magi (98–100);
9. the eternity of the world (101–109);
10. Cain and Abel (110–117);
11. Moses (117–123);
12. the prophets (124–129);
13. the decisions of the Church (130–132);
14. the doctors of the Church (133–135);
15. the invocation of saints (136–144);
16. the relics of saints (145–149);
17. sacred images (150–154);
18. the virginity of the Virgin Mary (155–156);
19. the sacrament of penance (157);
20. the breviary (158–167);
21. blasphemy (168–177);
22. the soul of men and animals (178–189);
23. divination (190–197);
24. that sins must not be punished (198–200);
25. carnal sins (201–205);
26. the Supreme Pontiff (206–207);
27. Bruno's stay in England and in other places with heretics (208–212);
28. eating meat on forbidden days (213–214);
29. reading forbidden books (215);
30. other trials before the Holy Office (216–217);
31. what Bruno intends to do if allowed to return to his [Dominican] Order (218–225);
32. other issues (226–241);
33. arguments against the witnesses (242–251);
34. Bruno's answers to the censure made against propositions taken from his books (252–261).

Out of the 34 headings, only two refer to cosmology: number 7, "that many worlds exist," and number 9, "the eternity of the world." Under these headings we find 25 paragraphs out of a total of 261. Under number 7, we find the accusations formulated by Giovanni Mocenigo, the Venetian nobleman who denounced Bruno to the Inquisition. Mocenigo declared that he had heard Bruno say that there are infinite worlds, that God is continually and endlessly producing things because he wants everything possible, that the world is eternal, that all stars are worlds, that God needs the world as the world needs Him, that God would be nothing without the world, and that this is why he continually creates new worlds. Under heading 9, we again find Mocenigo's claim that Bruno advocated that the world is eternal, and the testimonial of four persons who heard him say that God did not create the world. To which Bruno replied that the world depends on God for its existence.

On their own, these accusations carried little juridical weight because Bruno's conversations with Mocenigo were not confirmed by witnesses. They reveal, however, that Bruno's ideas about God and his relations to the world could seriously clash with Christian doctrine. That Bruno repeatedly stated that many worlds exist and that the stars are worlds is known from the testimony of others beside Mocenigo. There is also evidence that Bruno inclined to believe that there are rational beings elsewhere than on Earth and that he maintained that this is not contrary to the Catholic Faith.

From a doctrinal point of view, the paragraphs under headings 7 and 9 were not sufficient proof that Bruno was a heretic, given his disclaimer that he intended anything at variance with Catholic doctrine. Bruno was an impetuous man, given to overstatements, but he was also skillful at shifting his ground and leaving his judges in a quandary about where he really stood. From time to time he added to their perplexity by sending them written defenses against the accusations that had been raised against him. This seems to have unsettled some of his judges who did not feel they had the dialectical skill to follow him. Someone who was more than able to do this was Robert Bellarmine, a Jesuit theologian, soon to become a cardinal, who worked in the Holy Office. Now Bruno had manifested on several occasions his willingness to recant, and Bellarmine suggested that he be questioned about a number of objectionable propositions that he had published or made during his interrogation. Bellarmine and the Commissary of the Holy Office prepared a list of eight such proposals, which were approved on 14 January 1599 at a meeting of the Holy Office presided over

by Pope Clement VIII. Unfortunately, we do not have these eight propositions and we are left to speculate about their content. We know, however,
that the trial was not limited to what they contained, since the minutes of
the meeting of the Holy Office contain the follow sentence, "See also other
heretical propositions in the trial and in the books."[10] The attitude of
Bruno's judges seems to have hardened after they were informed around
September of that year that Bruno had published in London in 1584 a
work in Latin entitled *The Expulsion of the Triumphant Beast*. The book
contains an indictment of Christianity and a thinly disguised mockery of
Jesus, and must have convinced the Holy Office that Bruno was a confirmed heretic.

The Long Shadow of Bruno

Two members of the Congregation of the Holy Office who judged Bruno
were to play a decisive role in the injunction that Galileo received in 1616
not to teach Copernicanism. The first was Robert Bellarmine whom we
have already mentioned. He served as a consultant and, after his appointment as a Cardinal in March 1599, as one of the seven members of
the Congregation of the Holy Office who condemned Bruno on 20 January 1600. The second person was Cardinal Camillo Borghese, who took
part in the deliberations of the Holy Office concerning Bruno from September 1596 onwards, and became Pope Paul V. The two men could not
have forgotten Bruno when Copernicanism became a hot issue in 1616.
Galileo was not suspected of any form of deviance, beyond his rash support of a theory that contradicted passages in the Bible that described the
Sun, and not the Earth, as moving. The connection between Bruno and
Galileo is their common advocacy of Copernicanism, and it must have
been in people's mind only sixteen short years after Bruno's horrific death.
It seems clear, however, that neither Bellarmine nor Pope Paul V considered the motion of the Earth as heretical although they felt uncomfortable
about its apparent clash with the Bible.

A Delayed Reaction?

The publication of Copernicus's *On the Revolutions of the Heavenly Spheres*
in 1543 did not send shock waves throughout Christendom. The author
was a canon of the Catholic Church and the editor, Andreas Osiander, was

ILLUSTRATION 11   Portrait of Galileo by Ottavio Leoni,
painted in 1624.

a Protestant pastor and theologian. More importantly, the book opened
with a Foreword, *To the Reader about the Hypotheses of this Work*, that
declared that the heliocentric theory was not meant to be taken as a factual description of how the planets move but as a mathematical model to
work out their positions. The reason given is that astronomy, by its very
nature, does not aim at knowing the causes of celestial motions, but only
at "saving the appearances." Hence there is no principled way to determine which set of hypotheses are the true ones.

ILLUSTRATION 12   Villa Borghese.

The Foreword was actually penned by Osiander (as we discussed in Chapter Five) but, as it was unsigned, it was assumed to have been written by Copernicus himself. This may be the reason why the book was not condemned for over seventy years after its publication. The opponents were disarmed by the representation of the theory as a mere means of computation, although some astronomers, such as Michael Maestlin, Kepler's teacher in Tübingen, knew that Copernicus meant to be taken in earnest. Osiander's authorship was made known for the first time in print on the back of the title page of Kepler's book on Mars issued in 1609. What is notable is that Bruno realized as early as 1581 that the Foreword was at variance with the rest of the book, and was the work of "I know not what ignorant and conceited jackass."[11]

Bruno had expressed a sufficient number of startling ideas to provide stakes for a score of heretics, and his advocacy of the Earth's motion could hardly have determined his fate. But it might be argued that the Church only awakened to the full theological implications of the motion of the Earth after they saw how Bruno handled it. As Thomas S. Kuhn writes,

> Bruno was not executed for Copernicanism, but for a series of theological heresies centering on his view of the Trinity, heresies for which Catholics had been executed before. He is not, as he has often been called, a martyr of science. But Bruno had found Copernicus' proposal congenial to his Neoplatonic and Democritean vision of an infinite universe containing infinity of worlds generated by a fecund deity. He had propounded Copernicanism in England and on the Continent and had given it a significance not to be found in the *De Revolutionibus*. Certainly the Church feared Bruno's Copernicanism, and that fear may also have stimulated their reaction.[12]

The theological implications of Copernicanism were bound to be considered as soon as Galileo set foot in Rome to advertise his telescopic discoveries in 1611. On 19 April 1611, Cardinal Bellarmine, a prominent member of the Holy Office, asked the professors of astronomy at the Roman College to give him in writing their opinion of Galileo's celestial discoveries.[13] Shortly afterwards, Piero Dini, one of Galileo's best friends in Rome, received a letter from Perugia informing him that Galileo's discoveries were hotly debated and that a number of issues were raised, "beginning with the creation of Adam, and so on, as your Lordship knows better."[14] Dini passed on the letter to Galileo, who made it clear in his reply that he had no intention of entering into theological waters, "Regarding the numerous arguments taken from Adam onwards, as they are not specified but are supposed well known by your Lordship, and in a sense addressed to you, I shall leave their examination to you."[15] The reference to "arguments taken from Adam onwards," may conceivably anticipate an objection that was explicitly formulated some four years later when Giovanni Ciampoli, at Galileo's request, asked Cardinal Maffeo Barberini (the future Pope Urban VIII) about the advisability of openly promoting Copernicanism. The Cardinal felt scientists should stay within their field, "because theologians claim that the interpretation of the Scriptures is their business." To which Ciampoli commented that he had personal experience of what the Pope meant because he had heard people infer from the physical resemblance that Galileo established between the Moon and the Earth that he believed that the Moon was inhabited. "And someone else goes even further," he added, "and asks how they can have descended from Adam, or have come out Noah's ark, and many other wild ideas that you never dreamed of."[16]

A couple of weeks later, Benedetto Castelli wrote to Galileo in Florence that he had been summoned by Francesco Bonciani, the Archbishop of Pisa, who urged him to abandon Copernicanism, "for otherwise it would cause my ruin because these ideas, in addition to being silly, are rash, dangerous, and a cause of scandal because they go straight against Holy Scripture."[17] Castelli protested that he was anxious to do as bidden but that he would like to know Bonciani 's reasons. The Archbishop, no astronomer, finally came up with the following argument: "all creatures were made to serve man, from which it follows, as a necessary consequence, that the Earth cannot move like a planet."[18]

After Galileo was admonished by Cardinal Bellarmine not to teach Copernicanism on 26 February 1616, he immediately took steps to allay any suspicion that he might have entertained the possibility that there are living beings on the Moon. On 28 February, he wrote a letter to Giacomo Muti, a nephew of Cardinal Tiberio Muti in whose apartment he had spoken about mountains on the Moon a few days earlier. Alessandro Capoano, one of the persons present, had recalled as something obvious that nature produced mountains on Earth for the benefit of the flora and the fauna, which, in turn, existed for the benefit of man. Now, Capoano continued, if there were mountains on the Moon, we would have to draw the same consequences. But this is wrong. Hence, there can be no mountains on the Moon. To which Galileo wanted his reply recorded. It ran as follows: there can be no life on the Moon because there is no water there and the soil is different from ours. But even if the lunar soil were similar to the kind we find on Earth, life on the Moon would still be impossible because a solar day is 24 hours on Earth but about one month on the Moon. This means that it is scorched by the Sun for 15 days and subject to sub-zero temperature for the next 15 days.[19]

Between 1616 and the election of Pope Urban VIII in 1623, Galileo was discretion itself about the motion of the Earth. But after meeting the new Pope in Rome in 1624, he resumed work on his *Dialogue on the Two Chief World Systems*. It was practically completed by Christmas 1629, and he informed his friend and patron, Prince Federico Cesi, whom he assumed would pay for the publication, that he would be happy to go to Rome to correct the galleys. He also wrote to Benedetto Castelli, who was teaching in Rome, to ask him to contact the Dominican Niccolò Riccardi, a Florentine and an old friend, who had become Master of Sacred Palace and, as such, was entitled to grant permission to publish books in Rome. Castelli replied on 9 February 1630 that he had called on Riccardi who told him that Galileo could count on him. In the same letter, however, Castelli also mentioned a less satisfactory meeting with Cardinal Francesco Barberini, the nephew and right hand man of the Pope, who said to Castelli that if the Earth moved, "it would have to be considered a planet, something that seemed quite contrary to what we know from theology." Castelli replied that Galileo could show that the Earth is not a planet. Not completely convinced, Cardinal Barberini rejoined, "Well, let him do that. The rest seems acceptable."[20] Galileo may have had little in common with Bruno, but no Copernican could eschew the theological implications of setting the Earth in motion.

The Pope's Assessment

That Urban VIII thought that Copernicanism posed genuine theological problems can be seen from the stormy interview that the Florentine Ambassador, Francesco Niccolini, had with him on 5 September 1632, shortly after Galileo's *Dialogue* had exploded like a bombshell in Rome. "As we were talking about those tiresome matters of the Holy Office," he wrote to the Secretary of State of the Grand Duke, "His Holiness flew into a rage and all of a sudden declared that our Galileo had ventured where he should not have and dealt with the most serious and dangerous matters that can be raised in these times."[21] When the Ambassador interposed that Galileo had not published his book without permission, the Pope once again flew off the handle and said in an injured voice that Galileo and his friend Ciampoli had tricked him. He also added, "that in such matters, that can seriously damage religion in a way that far exceeds any done before, His Lordship [the Grand Duke of Tuscany] should help to punish Galileo, as becomes a Christian prince." The Pope even instructed Ambassador Niccolini to write to the Grand Duke that Galileo's opinion was "wicked in the extreme."[22]

The Pope did not say this merely because he was out of sorts on that day. A few days later, Riccardi confirmed in a private conversation with the Ambassador that the Pope thought that Copernicanism was dangerous, "because we are not dealing here," he said, "with mathematics but with Sacred Scripture, religion and the Faith."[23] A week later, on 18 September, Niccolini reported a conversation that he had with the Pope that very morning. The Pope said that Galileo was a friend but that these opinions were condemned 16 years ago and that he had got himself into a real mess. The Pope added,

> Galileo's work is really pernicious and the matter is more serious than His Highness [the Grand Duke] thinks. He then began to tell about these matters and these opinions, but with the express order, under penalty of censure, that I should not mention this to anyone, included His Highness. When I asked to speak only to His Highness, he replied that he was telling me this in confidence as a friend, not as a minister.[24]

What made the Pope so nervous? Pietro Redondi has suggested that Galileo had been accused of something completely different, namely the incompatibility between his atomism and the doctrine of the Eucharist. The opposition between Copernicanism and Scripture could hardly motivate the stringent secrecy that the Pope demanded, but we are left without any clear understanding of what troubled the Pope so much, unless it was a case of wounded pride combined with theological misgiving about the possibility of an entirely new cosmology. Referring to the events of 1616 when, while still a Cardinal, he had intervened to remove the word "heretic" from the condemnation of Copernicanism, the Pope exclaimed, "May God forgive Galileo for having made the mistake of getting himself into a mess from which I had freed him."[25]

Ambassador Niccolini had several audiences with the Pope after Galileo arrived in Rome for his trial. On 26 February 1633, Urban VIII repeated that Galileo, by arguing in favor of Copernicanism, had contravened the injunction given to him by Cardinal Bellarmine in 1616.[26] The Ambassador next called on the Pope's nephew, Cardinal Francesco Barberini, who said that he respected and admired Galileo but that the matter, which was very sensitive, might give rise to who knows what "fantastic tenets" (*qualche dogma fantastico*).[27] What these were is not stated, but the Cardinal could have been thinking of Bruno's ideas about the plurality of worlds and life on other planets. Ambassador Niccolini had two other audiences with the Pope on 13 March 1633 and 9 April 1633. Urban VIII once again complained that Galileo had entered into religious matters.[28] There is little doubt that Urban VIII was incensed at having been hoodwinked by a man whom he had considered his friend, but he was also concerned about a revolution in theology that might prove more subversive than merely making the Earth move around the Sun.

NOTES

1. Alexandre Koyré, *Galileo Studies*, translated by John Mepham (Atlantic Highlands, NJ: Humanities Press, 1978), p. 136.
2. Ernan McMullin, "Bruno and Copernicus," *Isis*, 78 (1987), p. 64.
3. Giordano Bruno, *The Ash Wednesday Supper*, edited and translated by Edward A. Gosselin and Lawrence S. Lerner (Hamden, Connecticut: Archon Book, 1977), p. 156.
4. *Ibid.*, p. 139. Bruno writes of himself in the third person in *The Ash Wednesday Supper*.
5. Frances A. Yates, *Giordano Bruno and the Hermetic Tradition* (London: Routledge, 1964).
6. Giordano Bruno, *The Ash Wednesday Supper*, pp. 162–165; Galileo Galilei, *Dialogue Concerning the Two Chief World Systems*, translated by Stillman Drake, 2nd revised edition (Berkeley: University of California Press, 1967), pp. 126, 141–145, 154–155, and 180.
7. Giordano Bruno, *The Ash Wednesday Supper*, p. 177. We have revised the translation.
8. See Francesco Beretta: "The Documents of Galileo's Trial: Recent Hypotheses and Historical Criticism," in *The Church and Galileo*, Ernan McMullin, ed. (Notre Dame, Indiana: University of Notre Dame Press, 2005), pp. 195–196.
9. Angelo Mercati, *Il sommario del processo di Giordano Bruno con appendice di documenti sull'eresia e l'inquisizione a Modena nel secolo XVI* (Vatican: Biblioteca Apostolica Vaticana, 1942). The document is also reproduced in

Luigi Firpo, *Il processo di Giordano Bruno* (Napoli: Edizioni scientifiche italiane, 1949), pp. 247–304.

10. Firpo, *Il processo di Giordano Bruno*, pp. 312–313.
11. Bruno, *The Ash Wednesday Supper*, p. 137.
12. Thomas S. Kuhn, *The Copernican Revolution* (New York: Vintage Books, 1959), p. 199.
13. Robert Bellarmine to the Mathematicians of the Roman College, 19 April 1611, *Opere di Galileo*, ed. Antonio Favaro, 1890–1909, reprint (Florence: Barbèra, 1968), vol. XI, pp. 87–88.
14. Cosimo Sassetti to Piero Dini, 14 May 1611, *ibid.*, vol. XI, p. 103.
15. Galileo Galilei to Piero Dini, 21 May 1611, *ibid.*, vol. XI, p. 116.
16. Letter of Giovanni Ciampoli to Galileo Galilei, 28 February 1615, *ibid.*, vol. XII, p. 146.
17. Letter of Benedetto Castelli to Galileo Galilei, 12 March 1615, *ibid.*, vol. XII, p. 154.
18. *Ibid.*
19. Letter of Galileo Galilei to Giacomo Muti, 28 February 1616, *ibid.*, vol. XII, pp. 240–241.
20. Letter of Benedetto Castelli to Galileo Galilei, 9 February 1630, *ibid.*, vol. XIV, p. 78.
21. Letter of Francesco Niccolini to Andrea Cioli, 5 September 1632, *Opere di Galileo*, XIV, p. 383.
22. *Ibid.*, p. 384.
23. Letter of Francesco Niccolini to Andrea Cioli, 11 September 1632, *ibid.*, p. 388.
24. Francesco Niccolini to Andrea Cioli, 18 September 1632, *Opere*, XIV, p. 392.
25. Letter of Francesco Niccolini to Andrea Cioli, 13 November 1632, *ibid.*, p. 428.
26. Letter of Francesco Niccolini to Andrea Cioli, 27 February 1633, *ibid.*, XV, p. 56.
27. *Ibid.*
28. Letters of Francesco Niccolini to Andrea Cioli of 13 March and 9 April 1633, *Opere di Galileo*, XV, pp. 68, 85.

CHAPTER SEVEN

Galileo Son of the Church

The relations of Galileo with the Church are often considered as essentially antagonistic. He was indeed tried and sentenced, but it is also the case that he was a genuine believer and that he sought to prevent the Church from condemning Copernicanism because he thought such a mistake would damage its spiritual authority. As he wrote to a French correspondent after his trial,

> I have two sources of continuous comfort. First, that in my writings there cannot be found the faintest shadow of irreverence towards the Holy Church; and second, the testimony of my own conscience, which only I and God in Heaven thoroughly know. And He knows that in the cause for which I suffer, though many might have spoken with more learning, none, not even the ancient Fathers, has spoken with more piety or with greater zeal for the Church than I have.[1]

Galileo was prone to hyperbole, and he may have overstated the case for his piety or zeal, but there can be little doubt that he earnestly believed that a condemnation of the motion of the Earth would hurt the Church. In this chapter, we shall consider two books that bear this in mind and offer an account of his life that brings us closer to the real, historical Galileo. The first is Dava Sobel's *Galileo's Daughter: A Historical Memoir of Science, Faith and Love*,[2] which is based on letters that Galileo's eldest daughter wrote to him from her convent in Arcetri, a suburb of Florence. She had been christened Virginia, after Galileo's sister, but she took the name of Sister Maria Celeste when she became a nun. The second book is Annibale Fantoli's *Galileo for Copernicanism and for the Church*,[3] an objective study of Galileo's commitment to both science and religion. We shall examine these books in turn, beginning with Dava Sobel's more personal and often moving account of a single parent and a singular daughter.

The Professor and his Daughters

Galileo never married but he had a long-standing relationship with Marina Gamba, a Venetian woman who belonged to the common folk, and with whom he had three children: Virginia was born in 1600, Livia in 1601, and Vincenzo in 1606. The three children were baptized in the Catholic Church, but the name of Galileo is not mentioned in the parish register. It is a sign of the times that Galileo installed his common-law wife in an apartment rather than in the house that he had rented and where he let out rooms to young noblemen who had come to study in Padua. Marina Gamba was probably unable to read or write, as was generally the case in those days, and she never appeared in polite society with Galileo. There was no question of his marrying her and, in 1610, when he left for Florence to take up his prestigious appointment as Mathematician and Philosopher of the Grand Duke of Tuscany, Marina was not expected to follow. The two girls went along, but Vincenzo, who was only four years old, stayed with his mother.

Galileo, who prided himself on belonging to the Tuscan nobility, had no hope of finding husbands of rank for his two daughters born out of wedlock. Like many others in his position, he thought of placing them in a nunnery. Virginia, barely thirteen, and Livia, hardly twelve, were entered into the Convent of San Matteo in Arcetri. Here they were to spend the rest of their life in poverty and reclusion, but honored and respected by contemporary society. Virginia adopted the name of Sister Maria Celeste when she took her vows at the canonical age of sixteen, and a year later Livia became Sister Arcangela. Livia never adapted to life in a convent and suffered from depression, but Sister Maria Celeste, as we shall now call her, became a deeply religious person, who spent most of her day in prayer but still found time for a number of other activities. She served at the convent's apothecary, tended the sick in the infirmary, composed business letters for the Abbess, directed the choir, and even wrote plays in which she performed. She also attended to the personal needs of her father, from mending his shirts to preparing the sweets that he was particularly fond of. Confined to her convent, Sister Maria Celeste communicated with her father in writing. The first of 124 surviving letters from the once voluminous correspondence was written on 10 May 1623, and the last, to welcome Galileo back to Florence after his trial, on 10 December 1633. Sister Maria Celeste was already gravely ill at this time, and she passed away four months later at the age of thirty-three.

ILLUSTRATION 13   Sister Maria Celeste, Galileo's daughter, around 1630.

Suor Maria Celeste and Pope Urban VIII

Galileo was elated when he heard that Cardinal Maffeo Barberini had been elected Pope on 6 August 1623. He had received a number of friendly letters from the Cardinal shortly before, and he had proudly passed them on to Sister Maria Celeste. On 10 August 1623 she returned them, overjoyed that someone who esteemed her father so much was now the Sovereign Pontiff. She requested that she be allowed to see her father's letter to the new Pope, and added charming thanks for his gift of fresh fruit,

> I can only imagine, Sire, what a magnificent letter you must have written to His Holiness to congratulate him on the occasion of his reaching this exalted rank and, because I am more than a little bit curious, I yearn to see a copy of that letter, if it would please you to show it, and I thank you so much for the ones you have already sent, as well as for the melons that we enjoyed most gratefully.[4]

Galileo replied that protocol prevented him from writing directly to the Pope. Instead, after a suitable interval of six weeks, he proffered his congratulations through the proper channel of Urban's nephew, Francesco, soon to be made a Cardinal. On 13 August, Maria Celeste apologized for her slight knowledge of the world, and mentioned how happy she was to receive Galileo's daily letters. Unfortunately, none of these have survived. At the time, Galileo lived in Bellosguardo, a hill outside Florence that commanded a magnificent view of the city, and a forty-minute walk across fields, or a shorter journey on donkey, brought him to the Convent of San Matteo. In 1623, Maria Celeste, who was then twenty-three years old, could have done it in even less time but she was barred from setting foot outside the convent, even when her father was sick. This happened in the summer of 1623, when Galileo had to move back to Florence to live with Benedetto Landucci, his recently widowed brother-in-law. It is here that Sister Maria Celeste sent the steward of the convent to see Galileo and hear from himself what state his health was in. She says, in an affectionate little note, of which the steward was the bearer, that she never regretted being a nun except when her father was ill.[5] Four days later, we find her writing again and sending, as an excuse for the steward's going so often to see her father, a present of marzipan baked in a mould in the shape of a fish.[6] Shortly thereafter she sent him "four plums, hoping that if they are not as good as I could have wished you shall take the will for the deed."[7]

When Galileo decided to go to Rome towards the end of 1623, he asked Sister Maria Celeste whether he could do anything for the nuns while in Rome. Although the Convent was really poor, she did not ask for money or alms but for something she considered much more important, that is, she wanted her father

> to implore His Holiness that we be given as our confessor a member of a religious order, or friar as they are called, under the understanding that he be changed every three years, as is the custom for other nuns. The reason is not to subtract ourselves from obedience to the local bishop, but to receive the Holy Sacraments from such a person. This is so serious that I can hardly convey its crucial importance. Nonetheless, I list some of the reasons in the enclosed paper.[8]

The background to this request is that the sisters of San Matteo, as was the custom with cloistered nuns, relied on a chaplain to celebrate mass and administer the sacraments. The priests who had been assigned to them by the local bishop were ill-prepared to provide spiritual guidance, and behaved in an unscrupulous way. The note that Maria Celeste enclosed makes this clear, and also gives us an insight into the deep religious life that she led:

> The first and principal reason for my making this request is that I see and know what scanty knowledge and experience these priests have of the rules and requirements of us nuns; and that in consequence they give us great occasion, or I might say permission, to lead a life with small attention to our rule. And who can doubt that, while we live without the fear of God, we must expect to be in perpetual misery regarding temporal matters? Thus we ought to begin by removing the cause of offence that I have already stated. The second reason is, that, owing to the poverty of the convent, we cannot satisfy the claims of the confessor, by paying them the salary owing at the expiration of the three years of office. I know that three of the former confessors have large sums still owing them, and they make this a pretence for coming here frequently to dine, and getting friendly with one or other of the nuns. And, what is worse, they make a common talk of us, and complain of us wherever they go, so that we are become the laughing stock of the whole Casentino [the region to the West of Florence] from whence these confessors, who are more apt at chasing hares than at guiding souls, originate. If I once began telling you all the absurdities committed by our present confessor, I should never have done; they are so numerous and so incredible.[9]

Galileo was successful and the nuns were provided with a Father Confessor who understood their rule and gave them sound advice.

Papal Audiences and the Issue of Copernicanism

Dava Sobel's description of the relationship between Galileo and his daughter Maria Celeste is a major contribution to our understanding of a great man and a truly remarkable woman. On the relations between Galileo and Urban VIII, Sobel relies on traditional accounts and is led to offer an interpretation of Galileo's dealings with the Pope that calls for qualification. This does not detract from the main theme of her book, but since it is relevant to our assessment of the Galileo Affair, it is worth considering. Sobel recalls that Galileo was received six times by Urban VIII between 24 April 1623, the day after he arrived in Rome, and 7 June, 9 days before he returned to Florence. Here is how she describes their encounters:

> The old friends strolled through the Vatican Gardens for an hour at a time, treating all the topics Galileo had hoped to discuss with His Holiness. Although no one recorded the content of Galileo's springtime sessions with Urban in 1624, there can be little doubt they assessed the fallout from the momentous decree that had dominated their last days together. . . . Urban, now more than halfway through the first year of his pontificate, was proud to say he had never supported that decree, and that it would not have seen the light had he been pope in those days. As a cardinal, he had successfully intervened, along with his colleague Cardinal Bonifazio Caetani, to keep "heresy" out of the edict's final wording. Thus, although the consulters to the Holy Office had called the immobility of the Sun "formally heretical" in their February 1616 report, the 5 March edict merely stated that the doctrine was "false" and "contrary to Holy Scripture." . . . The eight years since the edict had not swayed Urban from his position on Copernicus. He still saw no harm in using the Copernican system as a tool for astronomical calculations and predictions. The Sun-centered universe remained merely an unproven idea—*without*, Urban felt certain, any prospect of proof in the future. Therefore, if Galileo wished to apply his science and his eloquence to a consideration of Copernican doctrine, he could proceed with the Pope's blessing, so long as he labeled the system a hypothesis.[10]

Sobel captures the Pope's state of mind and his deep-seated conviction that the Copernican theory, published almost a century earlier, was as far as ever from proof. Where we believe that Sobel goes beyond the evidence is in assuming that Galileo raised the issue of Copernicanism with Urban VIII. It might seem natural that he should have done so. He had been silenced in 1616, when Copernicus's *On the Revolutions of the Heavenly Spheres* had been placed on the Index of Proscribed Books, but the new Pope was an open-minded and enlightened person and, praise the stars, a friend. Less than two months before his election to the papacy, the future Urban VIII had written to Galileo thanking him most warmly for helping his nephew, Francesco, obtain his doctorate in law at the University of Pisa. "I am much in your debt," he declared, "for your continuing goodwill towards myself and the members of my family, and I look forward to the opportunity of reciprocating. I assure you that you will find me more than ready to be of service in consideration of your great merit and the gratitude that I owe you." And he signed himself—with noteworthy warmth—"your most affectionate brother."[11] Furthermore, as soon as he was elected, the Pope promoted two of Galileo's closest friends to high positions in the Vatican. One was Virginio Cesarini, a gifted poet who had turned to science after hearing an inspirational lecture by Galileo in 1616. The other was Giovanni Ciampoli, a senior official, who read aloud to Urban VIII during meals, and had made a point of choosing select passages from a recent book from Galileo, much to the Pope's satisfaction.[12] Under these favorable circumstances, what could be more natural than that Galileo should ask if he could resume work on the motion of the Earth? Unfortunately, what we assume to be the normal course of events is often thwarted by a number of factors, not all of them perspicuous. In this particular instance, the evidence suggests that Galileo never got around to discussing Copernicanism with Urban VIII. He was never alone with him, and the Pope had the notorious reputation of doing most of the talking during audiences. We have all met inveterate talkers, and we can sympathize with Galileo.

All we know about his first meeting with Urban VIII (in company of the Pope's elder brother, Antonio) is what Galileo wrote to the Secretary of State of Tuscany three days later, "To my utmost pleasure, His Holiness kept me for an hour during which various topics were raised." In the same letter, we learn that Galileo also called on the Pope's nephew, Cardinal Francesco Barberini, and the Grand Duke's brother, Cardinal Carlo de Medici, but he does not mention what they discussed, and Galileo ends his letter on a despondent note: "The rest of the time I spend on various visits which, in the end, make me realize that I am old, and that to be a courtier one has to be young with the physical strength and the hope of preferment that make it possible to endure this kind of labor."[13] Galileo wrote in the same vein to his friend Prince Cesi, who replied that he was sorry that Galileo had to submit to the "infinitely tedious task" of playing the courtier, and urging him to be cautious and proceed without haste.[14] More easily said than done, for Galileo was not a diplomat by temperament or training. He found it exasperating to have to pussyfoot in order to publish what he considered a perfectly unobjectionable scientific theory. He was now over sixty and his rheumatism had not improved with age. He would follow Cesi's advice, he rejoined, if he could extend the remaining days of his life into as many years. There is a touch of cynicism but also genuine earnestness in this comment. The Vatican wheels were wont to grind very slowly, and he had to find someone who knew the Curia but could still speak his mind.

Galileo pinned his hopes on Cardinal Frederic Zollern (later Hohenzollern) who had just been appointed bishop of Olmütz in Bohemia, and was about to call on the Pope to take official leave from Rome. Galileo met him a couple of times, and convinced him to raise the issue of Copernicanism with Urban VIII. Zollern was as good as his word. He spoke to the Pope and mentioned that since the theory was accepted by all the Protestants, the Catholic Church would be wise to weigh the matter carefully. To which Urban VIII replied that the Church had condemned Copernicanism as temerarious but not as heretical, and that it had no intention of doing so. The Pope added, however, that he had no fear that it might one day be demonstrated.[15] There was no reference to Galileo, and no mention of revising the decree of 1616 that banned Copernicanism. Nonetheless, Galileo rushed in where angels would fear to tread and decided that he could now write his *Dialogue on the Two Chief World Systems*. He argued in favor of the motion of the Earth, protesting from time to time that the issue was not settled, and leaving it to the "intelligent reader" to determine where he really stood. He was running a huge risk and when the book appeared in 1632 he soon found that he had overplayed his hand. Urban VIII felt tricked, and instead of being a friend became a bitter foe.

Good Copernican and Good Catholic

The second book that achieves a considerable measure of objectivity about Galileo is Annibale Fantoli's *Galileo for Copernicanism and for the*

Church. Fantoli stresses that Galileo never saw a rift between his science and the Faith in which he had been brought up. While a professor at the University of Padua between 1592 and 1610, Galileo discussed the motion of the Earth with his colleagues, very few of whom, if any, were convinced by his arguments. None of them were sufficiently well versed in astronomy to read Copernicus, let alone assess his intricate geometrical demonstrations. Like most people trained in the humanities, they experienced awe for mathematics and no small amount of skepticism about its use in everyday life. They admired Galileo but did not consider him an oracle of the nascent science.

In his private life, Galileo was not a regular churchgoer, but some of his very best friends were ordained priests, and he had his three children baptized. It would never have occurred to him to describe himself as a dissenter or as harboring doubts about the Creed. As he grew older, he seems to have become more conventional in his religious practice. To put it bluntly, he was not a devout but a run-of-the-mill Catholic.

Galileo's status changed when he left his professorship at Padua to take up a prominent position as Mathematician and Philosopher of the Grand Duke at the Court in Florence. He was now in the limelight, and whatever stance he took could be interpreted as having the seal of approval of his employer. In Padua, the motion of the Earth had been a mere scientific conjecture; in Florence, it could at any moment become an affair of State. In Padua, questions were raised by colleagues and students in the tolerant atmosphere of Academe; in Florence, Galileo had to answer the queries of the mother of the Grand Duke, the Grand Duchess Christina, who was curious about science and greatly concerned about religion. To meet her demands, Galileo wrote a magisterial letter, known as the *Letter to the Grand Duchess Christina*, in which he set out what subsequently became the official Catholic position about science and Faith. To defend his scientific position, Galileo had to enter the minefield of exegesis, where theologians believed they were the only qualified experts. If Galileo had heavy scientific artillery, his opponents had the armor plate of tradition. They also had the ear of important people in Rome for whom novelty was not a good word.

Galileo went to the Eternal City in 1615 to wage his campaign, but he was routed and the result was that Copernicus's *On the Revolutions of the Heavenly Spheres* was condemned. Galileo escaped any official blame, but he was privately informed by Cardinal Bellarmine that, henceforth, he could neither teach nor defend Copernicanism. Cardinal Maffeo Barberini, the future Urban VIII, was in Rome at the time and he made it clear that he did not consider the theory heretical. He was not informed, however, that the Congregation of the Holy Office had instructed Bellarmine to warn Galileo not to write about the motion of the Earth. He only discovered of this after the publication of Galileo's *Dialogue on the Two Chief World Systems* in 1632. Galileo had been under no obligation to tell Urban VIII about the injunction he had received, but the Pope felt betrayed and duped by a friend.

At the time, the Pope was facing opposition from the Spaniards, who accused him of betraying the Catholic Church by supporting France (allied with the Swedish Protestants) in the Thirty Years War (1618–1648). In response, the Pope tried to bolster his position by showing that he was a strong defender of orthodoxy, including the traditional interpretation of the Bible. He also took care to purge his entourage of Spanish sympathizers such as Giovanni Ciampoli, who had got, by hook or by crook, permission to have Galileo's book printed. Ciampoli's behavior particularly incensed Urban VIII, and he suspected Galileo of having the same treacherous cast of mind.

Galileo made a number of unfortunate moves. In his determination to be "the head of the class," he had sniggered at the quality of the astronomical research of two very good Jesuit scientists, the German Christoph Scheiner and the Italian Orazio Grassi. This cost him the support of an influential and competent group of persons in Rome. Fantoli handles these matters in a judicious and dispassionate way in his book but there are two issues that seem to us controversial and that deserve closer scrutiny. The first is Galileo's relations with the Jesuits, which we will discuss here. The second is the Pontifical Commission created by Pope John Paul II to deal with the Galileo Affair, which we will consider in Chapter Nine.

Galileo and the Jesuits

The Society of Jesus (whose members were called Jesuits) was founded by Ignatius Loyola in the first half of the sixteenth century. The Jesuits were young, well-educated and dynamic, and they soon became famous for the quality of their schools, where students were admitted free of charge. Their main center of higher learning was the Roman College founded in 1551. Galileo's relations with the Jesuits were excellent until he clashed with some of them over the nature of sunspots and comets after he left Padua in 1610.

ILLUSTRATION 14   Galileo's Villa "Il Gioiello" on the outskirts of Florence.

As a young man of twenty-three, Galileo had traveled to Rome in 1587 to make the acquaintance of Christoph Clavius, the greatest Jesuit professor of mathematics of his day. He showed him some of his work on the center of gravity of solids, and the Jesuit was so impressed that the two subsequently corresponded. Clavius's favorable opinion helped Galileo get his first university appointment in Pisa in 1589 as well as his transfer to Padua in 1592. While in Rome, Galileo may also have made the acquaintance of another Jesuit, Paolo Valla, who taught philosophy, and was Galileo's senior by only three years. It would seem that Galileo returned to Pisa in 1587 with a set of the lecture notes that Valla dictated (as was the custom) during his course at the Roman College. In Galileo's early notebooks, posthumously published as *Juvenilia*, we find passages that seem inspired by him.[16] If this is the case, Galileo must have been pleased when he moved to Padua to learn that Valla had been appointed professor of theology at the Jesuit College. When calling on him, Galileo probably met his colleague, Antonio Menù, who had also lectured at the Roman College before being transferred to the Jesuit College in Padua, a post he held until his recall to Rome in 1600.

Some of Galileo's colleagues at the University and most prominently Antonio Riccoboni, the professor of rhetoric, felt that the Jesuits were encroaching on their rights, and they lodged a formal complaint with the Venetian authorities. Galileo kept out of the row, but he was happy to become one of the signatories when an agreement was reached between the University and the Jesuit College in 1597. A few years later, in the wake of a quarrel over jurisdiction, the Papacy placed an interdict, i.e. forbade priests from administering sacraments in the Venetian Republic. The Doge ordered the clergy to disregard orders from the Vatican and virtually everyone complied except the Jesuits, who were forced to leave Venice and its territory in 1606. It was not wise to have dealings with them, and Galileo suspended correspondence with Clavius. As soon as he returned to Florence, however, he wrote to Clavius to express his regret at having had to interrupt their exchanges of letters, and to assure him that his admiration for him had never cooled.[17] When Galileo went to Rome in 1611, the first time since 1587, he rushed to see him on the very next day after his arrival. As he reported to Belisario Vinta, the Tuscan Secretary of State,

I spent a long time with father Clavius and two other Fathers, who were his students and are experts in his field. . . . I found that these

Fathers, once they realized that the new Medicean planets were real, had been making continuous observations for the last two months. We compared them with mine and they agreed very well.[18]

Cardinal Bellarmine, who was also a Jesuit, asked the professors of the Roman College about the credibility of Galileo's celestial discoveries and they replied that they had been able to confirm them. The Jesuits even organized a well-attended public lecture at which Galileo was fêted and lionized. On his next trip to Rome, Galileo was admonished by Cardinal Bellarmine (acting on the instructions of the Pope) to refrain from advocating Copernicanism. But the Cardinal gave Galileo a letter of testimonial in which he stated that he had at no time been under a cloud or reprimanded.

Things turned sour with the Jesuits when a question of priority raised its ugly head. The issue was the discovery of sunspots that both Galileo and the Jesuit Christopher Scheiner observed in 1611. Galileo offered a better interpretation of their nature but Scheiner was the first to mention them in print. Both men were too proud to be gracious about the incident, and Scheiner developed an intense dislike of his rival. Another Jesuit who had trouble with Galileo was Orazio Grassi, a professor of mathematics at the Roman College.

Galileo Goes to War

In the autumn of 1618, three comets appeared in rapid succession. The last was of unusual size and brilliance, remaining visible from November until January of the following year. It was greeted (like any celestial novelty, be it a quasar or an orbiting station) with considerable interest, and Galileo was urged by his friends to swell the mounting tide of books and pamphlets that were flooding the astronomical and astrological market. Unfortunately, Galileo was bedridden at the time and unable to make any observations. Yet he was free to speculate, and his admirers wanted not so much an accurate description of the size, position and motion of the comet as an authoritative pronouncement—an oracular verdict—on its nature. His literary friends, siding with the "moderns" against the "ancients" in the current debate on poetry, were only too willing to embrace Galileo's "modern view" whatever it might be. Out of the scores of pamphlets that appeared, Galileo selected a lecture delivered by Fr. Orazio Grassi and published anonymously in 1619. Grassi located the comet between the Sun and the Moon. His tone was serene and he said nothing that was deliberately offensive to Galileo, whose name was not even mentioned.

It is puzzling why Galileo should have singled out this perfectly honest and unassuming address for special attention and criticism. He was, of course, fond of polemics, and it is possible that his friend Giovanni Battista Rinuccini pricked his pride when he informed him that the Jesuits were publishing something on the comet and added, in the same breath, that some people considered that it discredited Copernicanism altogether.[19] Grassi had been understood as favoring the compromise system of Tycho Brahe that postulated that the Earth was at rest while the other planets went around the Sun, a half-way house that particularly annoyed Galileo. He welcomed the opportunity of briefing one of his disciples, Mario Guiducci, who delivered a series of three lectures that were published under his name as the *Discourse on the Comets*. The manuscript, examined by Antonio Favaro, the editor of the National Edition of Galileo's *Works*, is largely in Galileo's own handwriting, and the sections drafted (or perhaps merely copied) by Guiducci show signs of revision and correction by the master.

As Guiducci was a lawyer and enjoyed no scientific reputation, it was clear to Grassi that Galileo was the real author, and he prepared a rejoinder that appeared in print in the autumn of 1619. Galileo was incensed and prepared a point-by-point rebuttal that he dedicated to the new Pope, Urban VIII. *The Assayer* (*Il Saggiatore* in Italian) is a model of brilliant wit and devastating irony. Grassi was no match for Galileo's ridicule, but the price Galileo paid was the loss of a potential ally in his crusade for the renewal of astronomy.

There is another Jesuit who was involved in Galileo's downfall. When the Master of the Holy Palace, the Dominican Niccolò Riccardi, was instructed to set up a Committee of three persons to determine whether Galileo actually advocated the motion of the Earth in his *Dialogue*, he cast around for a Jesuit who might have some sympathy for his plight. No professor at the Roman College, where Scheiner was now in residence, could be relied upon but, fortunately, a Jesuit had recently arrived to exculpate himself with the Congregation of the Index that had seen fit to ban one of his books. Could a man who had been through the ordeal of justifying his own work not show understanding for Galileo? Riccardi was so proud of his discovery that he boasted to the Tuscan Ambassador that he had personally nominated a Jesuit whose qualifications were impeccable.[20] This was Melchior Inchofer, an Austrian by birth, who had joined the Society of Jesus in 1607 and had been sent after his ordination to Messina, where he taught a variety of subjects including mathematics. He became interested in a local tradition that ascribed to the Blessed Virgin Mary a letter to the inhabitants of the city, and he set out to prove its authenticity in a lengthy monograph that appeared in 1629. The Congregation of the Index to whom it was referred looked askance at Inchofer's method of establishing historicity, and his book was proscribed "*donec corrigatur*," i.e. until amended. Inchofer rushed to Rome, professed his submission to the Church, and declared that what he claimed for his conclusions was not absolute truth but only high probability. This was all that the Congregation required and he was allowed to publish a revised edition of his book in which the only major change is the substitution of *Conjectatio* (Conjecture) for *Veritas Vindicata* (Truth Vindicated) on the title-page. Riccardi can be excused for believing that a man who could show such diplomatic litheness without abandoning his own controversial views would find a solution to the delicate problem of authorizing Galileo's *Dialogue* without appearing to contravene the ban on Copernicanism. We may well imagine Riccardi's shock when he found that Inchofer, far from sympathizing with Galileo, seemed to welcome the opportunity of ingratiating himself with the Holy Office by heaping coals on Galileo's head.

Of the three reports on the *Dialogue* that were submitted, Inchofer's is the longest and the most detailed. It is biased and goes as far as to state: "Galileo's main purpose at the time was to attack Fr. Christoph Scheiner who had just published a book against the Copernicans."[21] We have already seen that years earlier, Galileo had entered into a controversy with Scheiner over the nature of the sunspots. In his *Dialogue*, Galileo does take to task a slim anti-Copernican treatise by Johann Locher, a pupil of Scheiner, but Scheiner had got his word in first in a voluminous treatise, the *Rosa Ursina*, which appeared in 1630, almost two years before Galileo's own work. This is the refutation of Copernicus that Inchofer had in mind. We know that Scheiner heard of the publication of Galileo's *Dialogue* when he ran into an acquaintance in a Roman bookshop in June 1632. When the man innocently praised the book, Scheiner turned pale, became extremely agitated, and said that he would give ten scudi in gold to be able to answer on the spot.[22] Word of Scheiner's outburst soon spread, and Riccardi confided to Filippo Magalotti: "The Jesuits will persecute him with the utmost bitterness."[23] After the trial, Fr. Christoph Grienberger, the professor of mathematics at the Roman College, was heard to say, "If Galileo had remained a friend of the Fathers of this College, he would be honored in the world and would not have incurred any of his misfortunes. He could have gone on writing freely on any subject, including the motion of the earth." Galileo passed on this information to Elia Diodati in Paris, adding, "So you can see that it is not this or that of my opinions that caused and continues to cause the war, but having fallen in disgrace with the Jesuits."[24]

The Jesuits of the Roman College were neither that bad nor that influential. The only person who was clearly hostile to Galileo among the Jesuit scientists was Christoph Scheiner. But when he wrote a book against Galileo's *Dialogue*, he was unable to get permission to publish it during his lifetime, and it only appeared in a posthumous edition in Prague in 1651. Scheiner had assumed that a work "in defense of traditional astronomy against Galileo," would meet "the wish of the Pope, the General of our Order, the Assistant Generals, and all those who walk in the right path."[25] This querulous stance did not win the approval of most Jesuits. Orazio Grassi, who had been the butt of Galileo's ridicule, displayed not only moderation but charity in defending Galileo. In a letter to a friend on 22 September 1633, he writes,

> Concerning the trials of Galileo, let me tell you very sincerely that I was deeply sorry to hear about them because I have always had more affection for him than he has deigned to have for me. When I was asked in Rome last year what I thought of his book on the motion of the Earth, I did my best to calm those who were angry with him and make them see the strength of his arguments. Some marveled that I could speak so strongly in his favor since they thought I had been offended by him and, hence, was hardly a friend. What happened is that he ruined himself because he was too fond of his cleverness and had no esteem for anyone else. So don't be surprised if everyone tries to pull him down.[26]

Galileo had antagonized the Jesuits and this is why Grassi was asked why "everyone tries to pull him down." We find no trace of Jesuit outright opposition, however, beyond the report that Melchior Inchofer submitted or the irritation that Scheiner displayed. Fantoli stresses the lack of evidence against the Jesuits, and downplays the attendability of letters suggesting that Jesuits may have acted against Galileo. It seems to us, however, that some form of Jesuit involvement in the Galileo Affair cannot be completely ruled out, and that the issue will remain open as long as our information about Scheiner is incomplete. As we shall see in the next chapter, an historian of science, Pietro Redondi, believes that he has evidence that the Jesuits actually denounced Galileo to the Congregation of the Index.

Galileo and Catholicism Today

Pope John Paul II was anxious to foster the dialogue between science and religion, and he felt that an honest conversation could not begin without recognizing Galileo's contribution. In an address to the Pontifical Academy of Sciences in 1979, he said, "Allow me, gentlemen, to submit to your attention some points that seem to me important to set the Galileo Affair in its true light. In this affair the agreements between religion and science were more numerous and, above all, more important than the misunderstanding that led to a bitter and painful conflict."[27]

The Pope mentioned three points of agreement. The first is Galileo's conviction that science and Faith can never be at odds. Referring to Galileo's *Letter to Benedetto Castelli* of 21 December 1613, the Pope declared that the Second Vatican Council did not express itself differently. The second point is Galileo's belief that God enlightens those who try to understand his creation. Humility and open-mindedness, the Pope stressed, are the necessary conditions for a fruitful exchange between scientists and religious believers. The third point of agreement is Galileo's recognition that there are different literary styles in the Bible, "The various agreements that I have mentioned," the Pope concluded, "do not in themselves solve all the problems of the Galileo Affair, but they contribute to the creation of a starting point favorable to their honorable solution, a state of mind conducive to the honest and loyal resolution of old oppositions."[28]

Contemporary Catholic theology may have caught up with Galilean exegesis, but the reader will still want to have an idea of what kind of Christian Galileo was. We cannot know his inmost thoughts, but he genuinely felt himself part of a Church. In the seventeenth century, the Mathematician and Philosopher of the Grand Duke of Tuscany had to be a Roman Catholic even if his adherence was purely formal, but Galileo's commitment went beyond lip service.

We know that he considered pilgrimages and vows important. Never an avid traveler, he nonetheless made the journey from Florence to Loreto (some two hundred miles) in 1618 in order to visit the so-called House of our Lady that was very popular in his day. Ten years later he planned to go back on a second pilgrimage but was deterred by poor health. When he was ill in 1637, he prayed for recovery and made a vow "to save some miserable young girl from grave risks by taking upon myself to pay all the costs of having her placed in a monastery, or married, or in general to make her circumstances secure."[29] This sounds admirable and would have been even more impressive if Galileo had fulfilled his vow in 1637 and not in 1640 when he chose as the recipient of his bounty his niece, the daughter of his deceased sister, Virginia.

He also believed that God had singled him out to make all the new astronomical discoveries, and that God had granted him, and him alone, the privilege of making the telescopic ones. On 30 January 1610, he wrote to the Tuscan Secretary of State, "I am infinitely grateful to God that it should have pleased him to grant me to be the only person to make the first observations of admirable things unknown from all ages."[30] In the *Sidereus Nuncius* that appeared in 1610, Galileo added that "the Maker of the Stars clearly told him to give the satellites of Jupiter the name of the Grand Duke."[31] Several years later, when commenting on a book by the Jesuit Orazio Grassi, Galileo went even further, "What can you do," he says to his rival, "if it was only given to me and to no one else to make all the celestial discoveries."[32] Galileo's belief in the singularity of his destiny is not particularly linked to the person of Christ, a name that we never find under his pen. Of course, the religious commitment of a human being is not an observable quality and the deeper side of Galileo's faith is not open to inspection.

NOTES

1. Letter of Galileo to Nicolò Fabri di Peiresc, 21 February 1635, in *Le Opere di Galileo*, edizione nazionale, ed. Antonio Favaro, 1890–1909 (reprint Florence: Barbèra, 1968), vol. XVI, p. 215.
2. Dava Sobel, *Galileo's Daughter. A Historical Memoir of Science, Faith, and Love* (London: Fourth Estate, 1999).
3. Annibale Fantoli, *Galileo for Copernicanism and the Church*, translated by George V. Coyne, 2nd enlarged edition (Vatican: Vatican Observatory, 1996).
4. Letter of Maria Celeste to Galileo, 10 August 1623, in Dava Sobel (ed. and translator), *To Father. The Letters of Sister Maria Celeste to Galileo 1623–1633* (London: Fourth Estate, 2001), p. 5. The original Italian is on facing pages, and we have occasionally amended Sobel's translation in the passages that we quote.
5. Letter of Maria Celeste to Galileo, 17 August 1623, *ibid.*, p. 9.

6. Letter of Maria Celeste to Galileo, 21 August 1623, *ibid.*, p. 11.
7. Letter of Maria Celeste to Galileo, 28 August 1623, *ibid.*, p. 13.
8. Letter of Maria Celeste to Galileo, 10 December 1623, *ibid.*, p. 29.
9. *Ibid.*, pp. 31–33.
10. Sobel, *Galileo's Daughter*, pp. 140–142.
11. Letter of Maffeo Barberini to Galileo Galilei, 24 June 1623, *Opere di Galileo*, vol. XIII, p. 119.
12. Letter of Giovanni Ciampoli to Galileo, 4 November 1623, *Opere di Galileo*, vol. XIII, p. 146. The book is Galileo's *Assayer* (*Il Saggiatore*) that appeared at the end of October 1623.
13. Letter of Galileo Galilei to Curzio Picchena, 27 April 1624, *ibid.*, p. 175.
14. Letter of Federico Cesi to Galileo, 30 April 1624, *ibid.*, p. 177.
15. Letter of Galileo to Federico Cesi, 8 June 1624, *ibid.*, p. 182.
16. See William A. Wallace, *Galileo and his Sources: The Heritage of the Collegio Romano in Galileo's Science* (Princeton: Princeton University Press, 1984).
17. Letter of Galileo to Christopher Clavius, 17 September 1610, *ibid.*, vol. X, p. 431.
18. Letter of Galileo to Belisario Vinta, 1 April 1611, *ibid.*, vol. XI, pp. 79–80. The two other Jesuits were Christopher Grienberger and Odo Van Maelcote.
19. Letter of Giovanni Battista Rinuccini to Galileo, 2 March 1619, *ibid.*, vol. XII, p. 443.
20. As reported by Ambassador Francesco Niccolini to Andrea Cioli, the Tuscan Secretary of State, 11 September 1632, *ibid.*, vol. XIV, p. 389.
21. *Ibid.*, vol. XIX, p. 351.
22. Letter of Benedetto Castelli to Galileo, 19 June 1632, *ibid.*, vol. XIV, p. 360.
23. Letter of Filippo Magalotti from Rome to Mario Guiducci in Florence, 7 August 1632, *ibid.*, vol. XIV, p. 370.
24. As related by Galileo in his letter to Elia Diodati, 25 July 1634, *ibid.*, vol. XVI, p. 117.
25. Letter of Christopher Scheiner to Athanasius Kircher, 16 July 1633, *ibid.*, vol. XV, p. 184.
26. Letter of Orazio Grassi to Girolamo Bardi, 22 September 1633, *ibid.*, p. 273.
27. John Paul II, "Address to the Pontifical Academy of Sciences on 10 November 1979" in *Papal Addresses to the Pontifical Academy of Sciences 1917–2002* (Vatican: Pontifical Academy of Sciences, 2003), p. 242.
28. *Ibid.*, p. 243.
29. See Giorgi Spini, "The Rationale of Galileo's Religiousness" in C. L. Golino, ed., *Galileo Reappraised* (Berkeley and Los Angeles: University of California Press, 1966), pp. 44–66, and Olaf Pedersen, "Galileo Religion" in eds. G. V. Coyne, M. Heller and J. Zycinski, The *Galileo Affair*: A Meeting of Faith and Science (Vatican: Vatican Observatory, 1985), pp. 75–100.
30. Letter to Belisario Vinta, 30 January 1610, *Opere*, vol. X, p. 280.
31. *Sidereus Nuncius, Opere*, vol. III, p. 56.
32. Marginal note in Galileo's copy of Grassi's *Ratio Ponderum*, *ibid.*, vol. VI, p. 383 n.1.

CHAPTER EIGHT

Galileo Heretic

We live in an age of reinterpretations, and Pietro Redondi, an Italian historian of science, has offered a novel and provocative one under the title *Galileo Heretic*. It created a furor in the Italian press, and was given a rave review by the novelist Italo Calvino.[1] We shall outline Redondi's thesis before proceeding, as our readers will expect, to a reinterpretation of his reinterpretation. We shall also provide more recent evidence about the case. But first a word about the usual account of the trial.

The Standard Account

In 1616, Copernicus's *On the Revolutions of the Heavenly Spheres* was placed on the *Index of Proscribed Books*, and Cardinal Bellarmine personally told Galileo that he could no longer teach or write in favor of the motion of the Earth. Having infringed this order, Galileo was tried and sentenced in 1633. The *Proceedings* of the trial were published over 150 years ago, and although we are still in the dark about some details, no one, before Redondi, doubted that Galileo was condemned for advocating, under the spurious guise of impartiality, that the heliocentric system of Copernicus was superior to the geocentric one of Ptolemy. What is not altogether clear is why Pope Urban VIII reacted so strongly to the publication of Galileo's *Dialogue*, or what role the Jesuits played in the sorry affair. In the case of Urban VIII, it would seem that he had good reason to be affronted by the concluding speech of the *Dialogue* where his own theological point that God can create the world in a variety of ways is placed in the mouth of Simplicio, the clown who is kicked in the pants by the other two interlocutors, Salviati and Sagredo.

As we have seen in Chapter Seven, there is no proof that the Jesuits played a major role in Galileo's condemnation, but Redondi contends that they did and that Galileo scholars (at least the top dogs in the profession) have been barking up the wrong tree. In a sense, it is a case of discovering that the Emperor has no clothes or, rather, that the man who is wearing the clothes is not the Emperor but someone else. How Redondi made his alleged discovery is worth recounting. During the academic year 1981–1982, he was doing research in Paris on the history of light and, more specifically, on seventeenth-century discussions about the "stone of Bologna," a natural sulphate of barium that glows in the dark. It was an early instance of photoluminescence (phosphorus was only discovered at the end of the seventeenth century), and the phenomenon was poorly understood. The stone gave off heat without light, and Galileo created a sensation in Rome when he showed it to friends and admirers in 1611.

Redondi was looking up references to this "stone of Bologna" in library catalogues when he came across a reference to Galileo in the title of a manuscript that was said to be in the Archives of the Holy Office in Rome. He immediately wrote to the Holy Office (now the Congregation for the Doctrine of the Faith) to ask whether he could see the document. The source he had consulted gave the call number, something that made matters easy for the Roman librarians. Nonetheless, he received a curt reply: the relevant section of the records of the Holy Office was not open for consultation. Redondi showed the letter to Pierre Costabel, an eminent French historian of science and a priest of the Oratory of St. Philip of Neri. Costabel felt that the matter was ridiculous—if the call number was known, there could be no difficulty in fetching the manuscript. Using his clerical influence, Fr. Costabel obtained permission for Redondi to make *one* visit to the Archives to examine that *one and only* document. The letter granting authorization made much of the favor that was thus bestowed upon the world of scholarship.

We mention this because it explains the frame of mind in which Redondi went to Rome. He could not help wondering what the librarians of the Holy Office might be attempting to conceal. Were they sitting on a pile of unpublished letters? Were they hiding documents from the famous trial? Was Urban VIII implicated? Had the Holy Office done something reprehensible in 1633? The seventeenth century may seem a long way off for most of us, but for officials of the Roman Curia it is just a few generations ago. Furthermore, the Vatican does not wash its dirty linen in public.

Redondi's vision of a conspiratorial Rome was not allayed by the long waiting periods that he experienced at the Holy Office and at the Archives of the Gregorian University where the Head Librarian, Fr. Monachino, literally left him to cool his heels for hours before allowing him to examine part of the material he requested. At first blush, the situation seems deplorable, but there is actually nothing sinister about it. The Archives of the Gregorian University are notoriously understaffed, and Fr. Monachino must have been eighty if not ninety years old at the time. Redondi, however, was disposed to think the worst, and he saw studious delay where there was really nothing more dreadful than a combination of overload and old age.

Finally, the fated manuscript of the Holy Office (called G3 because of the letter and the number that appear at the top of the first page) was placed in Redondi's hands on the morning of 11 June 1982. It turned out to be an anonymous denunciation of Galileo, not for holding that the Earth moves but for jeopardizing the Catholic doctrine of the Eucharist. The background to this accusation is the following. The Council of Trent (1545–1563) had stressed against Protestant Reformers that the mystery of the Eucharist (the belief that the consecrated bread and wine become the body and blood of Christ) was to be understood in terms of transubstantiation. On this view, what remains of the bread and wine are only "accidental" qualities, such as their color, taste and texture. Transubstantiation is couched in terms of the distinction between substance and accidents in the Thomistic philosophy, in whose system it makes sense, but it might be considered incompatible with a philosophy where atoms are considered objective whereas secondary properties such as color, odor and taste are deemed subjective.

The person who wrote the anonymous G3 had more than a superficial acquaintance with theology, and Redondi surmised that he was probably a member of the clergy. He began looking around in the hope of tracking down a similar indictment of Galileo. He came across a book on comets in which the author, the Jesuit Orazio Grassi, claimed that Galileo imperiled the dogma of transubstantiation by pronouncing the sensible qualities of heat, color, smell and taste subjective.

Redondi needed no more: he had his man! Grassi, he surmised, must have penned the unsigned delation. All that remained to be done was to write a five-hundred page book to show what this implied. The story rests on the assumption that Galileo was suspect in the eyes of the Jesuits on account of his close association with two organizations that, on Redondi's view, were the rivals of the Society of Jesus. One is the Academy of the Lynxes to which Galileo was elected in 1611, the other the Roman University of La Sapienza, where Galileo's closest assistant, Benedetto Castelli, had become professor in 1626. The evidence adduced by Redondi is largely circumstantial. But even if we grant that the Jesuits were not fond of Galileo, we are left with a number of queries: Why should the anonymous delation be considered the work of Grassi whom we know to have expressed regret at Galileo's troubles?[2] Why was the delation not brought forward at the time of Galileo's trial? And how could this have been a cover-up by the Holy Office?

To these questions Redondi offers the following answer. The Jesuits, he opines, could not make a fuss about the suggestion that planets revolved around the Sun since several of their members were openly sympathetic to the system of Tycho Brahe in which all the planets are satellites of the Sun which, in turn, carries them around the Earth. So mum was the word. But we still have to ask why the Holy Office failed to clamp down on Galileo's atomism if it was perceived as a threat to the dogma of transubstantiation? In reply, Redondi conjectures that Urban VIII, himself a Florentine like Galileo, did not wish to condemn the official Philosopher and Mathematician of the Grand Duke of Tuscany for heresy. The blow, metaphorically speaking, would have ricocheted off Galileo's chin onto the Grand Duke's nose. The best way out of this unpleasant scenario was to replace the real charge by something relatively innocuous. The Grand Duke's top philosopher would not be saddled with heresy but with Copernicanism, a minor form of deviationism. And so it was done. Needless to say, adds Redondi, no documents that might substantiate this devious maneuver were allowed to survive. The Inquisition that burnt its last live heretic (Giordano Bruno) in 1600 still knew how to consign papers to the flames. In Redondi's able hands, the very absence of evidence becomes evidence of a special, surrealistic kind! Like so much of the Baroque architecture with which Urban VIII graced Rome, the trial of Galileo was a grandiose *trompe l'œil*. For centuries, claims Redondi, scholars repeated what the Holy Office wanted them to believe, not what really happened.

What are we to make of this clever piece of detection? For the record, let us mention that no one who has studied the trial thinks that Redondi has got it right. To which Redondi replies, of course, that this is just what

ILLUSTRATION 15   Villa Medici in Rome.

is to be expected. Modern historians cannot bring themselves to admit that they have been hoodwinked by a bunch of sly seventeenth-century Jesuits and the Holy Office. But things have changed now that the author of *Galileo Heretic* penetrated their smokescreen.

Galileo scholars are known for their lively disagreements, and they are not so easily deceived. We are also of the opinion that Galileo was condemned for arguing that the Earth moves and not for believing in the atomic theory. Nonetheless, a document that was discovered by one of us (Mariano Artigas) throws new light on the issue, and we shall say a few words about it.

The new piece of evidence surfaced in the Archives of the Holy Office that was instituted by Pope Paul III in 1542 to defend the Catholic Church from heresy, which at the time meant the Protestant Reformation. The Holy Office worked closely with the Congregation of the Index of Forbidden Books that was created in 1571, and published an *Index* (or list of censured books) during the period between 1559 and 1917 when the Congregation was merged with the Holy Office. In 1965, the Congregation was radically transformed and modernized by Pope Paul VI, who renamed it the Congregation for the Doctrine of the Faith. The Archives were opened to the public in 1998, and on 9 December 1999, Mariano happened to be in the Vatican with a couple of free hours to spare. It occurred to him that it might be interesting to look up the document that Redondi had seen. He knew that the volumes that contain the *Records* (*Protocolli*) of the Congregation of the Index are numbered with capital letters A, B, C . . . AA (or A^2), BB (or B^2), and so on. The new document that was discovered by Artigas was bound in volume EE (or E^2), the same one in which Pietro Redondi had found a three-page document, identified by the code "G3" that appears at the top of the first page (nobody knows what "G3" stands for).

Roman Gossip and the Background to G3

Redondi makes much of the fact that Galileo, upon his return to Florence from Rome in June 1624, heard that his theory of sensible qualities was being criticized. He asked his friend Mario Guiducci, who was in Rome, to investigate, and on 21 June 1624, Guiducci reported as follows:

> I hear from all sides rumors of the war with which Grassi is threatening us to the point that I am tempted to believe that he has his reply

ready. On the other hand, I cannot see how he can attack us since Count Virginio Malvezzi is practically certain that he cannot gain a foothold against your position about the nature of heat, taste, smell, and so on. The Count says that you wrote about this in order to stir up a debate for which you must be armed to the teeth.[3]

Over the next months, Guiducci kept his ears open but the rumor died out. On 18 April 1625, however, he had a new bit of gossip to pass on. It was provided by Federico Cesi, the founder of the Academy of the Lynxes, and concerned "a pious person" who had asked the Holy Office to ban Galileo's *Assayer* because he argued for the motion of the Earth. The Pope's nephew, Cardinal Francesco Barberini, agreed to look into the matter and entrusted his theological adviser, Father Giovanni Guevara, with the task of examining the work. Guevara saw no reason to condemn the "doctrine concerning motion" that was found in the book, and the Holy Office let the matter drop. Now Galileo does not argue for the motion of the Earth in *The Assayer*, and this incident puzzled historians until Pietro Redondi discovered G3, which indeed sheds light on the problem.

The "doctrine concerning motion" in G3 does not refer to the motion of the Earth but to that of atoms, precisely what is at issue in *The Assayer*. The information that Guiducci had passed on to Galileo was not only second-hand, it was distorted. He, or his informant, had misunderstood "motion" as referring to the Earth when it was about atoms, and the way they cause heat. Here is how Galileo expresses himself in *The Assayer:*

As soon as I think of a material object or a corporeal substance, I immediately feel the need to conceive that it is bounded and has this or that shape, that it is big or small in relation to others, that it is in this or that place at a given time, that it moves or stays still, that it touches or does not touch another body, and that it is one, few, or many. I cannot separate it from these conditions by any stretch of my imagination. But my mind feels no compulsion to understand as necessary accompaniments that it should be white or red, bitter or sweet, noisy or silent, of sweet or of foul odor. Indeed, without the senses to guide us, reason or imagination alone would perhaps never arrive at such qualities. I think that tastes, odors, colors and the like are no more than mere names so far as pertains to the subject wherein they seem to reside, and that they only exist in the body that perceives them. Thus, if all living creatures were removed, all these qualities would also be removed and annihilated.[4]

171

ILLUSTRATION 16   Portrait of Galileo by Giusto Sustermans,
painted in 1640.

The author of G3 may, in good faith, have considered this passage as
incompatible with the permanence of real accidents in the Eucharist, but
the Holy Office saw no grounds to proceed against Galileo. Although the
Church used the concept of transubstantiation when speaking of the Eucharist, it did not give the word a technical meaning. The Church declared
that the bread and wine are transformed into the body and blood of Jesus

172

Christ while the appearances of wine and bread remain. It is noteworthy that in the definitions of the Council of Trent, the word "accident" is not used. Instead, the Council speaks of "species," i.e. appearance, namely "the species of bread" or "the species of wine" in the singular. The concept of substance was borrowed from Aristotelian philosophy, but the Council explicitly stated that it did not intend to enter into a philosophical discussion. The appearance of bread and wine after the consecration remain the same whatever scientific or philosophical explanation is offered for the reality of sensible qualities. Cardinal Francesco Barberini's adviser, Father Guevara, was quite correct in saying that Galileo's theory about the motion of atoms did not contradict the doctrine of the Church. If the accusation had concerned the motion of the Earth, Guevara would surely have pointed out that this matter was not raised in *The Assayer*.

The Unsigned New Document: EE 291

When Redondi had been handed the volume in 1982, he had not been allowed to look at more than one document. Seventeen years later the Archives had become fully accessible to scholars and Artigas was allowed to peruse the volume at leisure. After examining G3, which occupies sheets 292 (*recto* and *verso*), and 293 (*recto*), Artigas went through the volume in the hope of finding other documents in the same handwriting. He did not find any, but when he came to the document just before G3 he discovered that it was another anonymous and undated document that dealt with the same subject. It filled sheet 291 *recto* and half of sheet 291 *verso*, and will henceforth be referred to as EE 291.

Whereas Redondi's G3 is in Italian, EE 291 is in Latin. Galileo is not mentioned by name, but the text begins with the words, "I saw the discourse of the Lyncean," an unmistakable reference to Galileo, who was a member of the Lyncean Academy and was fond of putting *Linceo* on the frontispiece of his books, as he did in the case of *The Assayer*, the work that is considered in G3. The fact that EE 291 comes just before G3 confirms that the discussion of the alleged incompatibility of Galileo's interpretation of sensible qualities with the doctrine of the Eucharist is related to what he had written in *The Assayer*.

EE 291 is written with less care than is G3, and has a number of handwritten corrections. This would seem to indicate that the author of EE 291 worked for the Congregation of the Index and had been asked to write an internal report on whether to proceed with the accusation made in G3. The author of EE 291 is critical of Galileo's views on atomism, and concludes that the Holy Office could proceed with a formal inquiry.

The Author of EE 291

Artigas communicated his discovery to Shea, and both asked Rafael Martínez, a Roman professor, to help them determine the author and the date of composition.[5] Martínez undertook a systematic study of the volume in which EE 291 appears, and he came across two documents in the same handwriting. Both are signed by Melchior Inchofer, a Jesuit, who was born in Hungary around 1585, and died in Milan on 28 September 1648. He came to Rome to study at the Roman College in 1605 and entered the Society of Jesus in 1607. He spent the rest of his life mainly in Italy except for a brief period in Austria. Martínez also examined other manuscripts by Inchofer and the handwriting leaves no doubt about his authorship of EE 291.

In all likelihood, Inchofer was a member of the Preliminary Commission appointed by Urban VIII to examine Galileo's *Dialogue on the Two Chief World Systems* in the summer of 1632.[6] The next year he was asked, along with Agostino Oregio and Zaccaria Pasqualigo, to assess the work for the Holy Office and determine whether Galileo had disobeyed the injunction not to write on Copernicanism, which he had received in 1616. They concurred that Galileo had contravened the order, but Inchofer was particularly damning in his report and, in the very same year, he published a book entitled *Tractatus Syllepticus* against the motion of the Earth.[7]

The Date of EE 291

Inchofer was sent to Messina in Sicily to teach mathematics, philosophy and theology. He was also interested in local history and in 1629 he published a work in favor of the authenticity of a letter, supposedly written by the Virgin Mary to the people of Messina, which had been declared apocryphal by the Holy Office. Objections were raised, and Inchofer went to Rome to defend himself. He was so successful that he was allowed to publish a revised edition of his book and remain in Rome. He became a consultant of Niccolò Riccardi who, as Master of the Apostolic Palace, had close ties with the Holy Office and the Congregation of the Index.

Inchofer could not have started working in the Vatican before he had been cleared of the charges against him. This only occurred in December 1630, so he could not have begun to act as a consultant for Riccardi or the Congregation of the Index before that date. Hence, EE 291 cannot have been written prior to December 1630. We also know that it could not have been written later than 1642, because the criticism of the "Lyncean" that it contains is directed against a living person, and Galileo died that year. Furthermore, EE 291 recommends that the Holy Office examine the matter more closely, and this would make no sense if Galileo were already dead. But we can be even more precise. Since there is no reference to Galileo's condemnation on 22 June 1633, which the author would have mentioned had the document been written after the trial, it seems clear that the document was written before that date.

The Date and Authorship of G3

Having determined the date of EE 291, we must ask about the date and authorship of G3 in order to determine why Inchofer wrote EE 291. Redondi conjectured that it was written after the publication of Galileo's *Assayer* in 1623, before Father Grassi retorted in a book that was printed in 1626. It was around this time that Galileo heard the rumor that his theory of "motion" had been denounced. We cannot exclude, however, that G3 was written some years *after* the publication of *The Assayer*. There have been instances of delayed attacks in more recent times. For example, at the end of the nineteenth century, a book on evolution by a Dominican priest, Marie-Dalmace Leroy, was denounced to the Index several years after it was published. Nevertheless, it seems more reasonable to assume that G3 was written in 1624, shortly after *The Assayer* appeared. This date would agree with what we know about Galileo's concerns upon his return to Florence in June 1624, and the denunciation mentioned by Mario Guiducci in his letter to Galileo of April 18, 1626.[8] The only detail that does not seem to fit so well is Guiducci's reference to the motion of the Earth as the cause of the denunciation, but as we have seen, this was surely a mistake because there is no mention of the motion of the Earth in *The Assayer*. That the person who informed Cesi had difficulties in grasping that the real issue was the motion of atoms is quite understandable, and Cesi himself, or Guiducci for that matter, could have missed the point. The second time Guiducci refers to the denunciation in his letter he only speaks of "motion," not "the motion of the Earth." Once this matter is understood, the denunciation reported by Cesi and transmitted by Guiducci makes perfect sense: Galileo had indeed claimed in *The Assayer* that the motion of atoms are responsible for the sensations of heat, color, and odor that we experience.

But who wrote G3? It is difficult to identify the author because the neat copy of G3 in the Archives is almost certainly the work of a copyist. Redondi conjectured that the author was none other than Father Orazio Grassi, but this is now believed to be most unlikely.[9] Several persons in Rome disliked Galileo, on personal or doctrinal grounds, but none seem to qualify as the author of G3. One possibility is Francesco Ingoli (1578–1649) with whom Galileo had clashed in Rome in 1616. Ingoli carried out the revisions to Copernicus's *De Revolutionibus* that the Index had requested, and he had a share in the prohibition of Kepler's *Epitome Astronomiae Copernicanae*. Rafael Martínez examined several of his manuscript notes in the Archives of the Congregation for the Evangelization of the Peoples (formerly the *Propaganda Fidei*) and determined that he did not write G3. Martínez also examined writings of several copyists who worked at the *Propaganda Fidei* at the time, but their handwriting does not match that of G3.

Sergio Pagano has drawn attention to what might be another clue: the watermark of G3. It is an ecclesiastical coat of arms, probably that of Cardinal Tiberio Muti, the bishop of Viterbo between 1611 and 1636. Martínez found several variants of this watermark in documents in the diocesan archive of Viterbo. The Mutis were a noble Roman family and Galileo was acquainted with them. When he went to Rome in 1611, he carried a letter of recommendation to Tiberio Muti from Antonio de' Medici, and he saw Tiberio again in 1616. He was even closer to Carlo Muti, Tiberio's nephew, who became a member of the Lyncean Academy, and with whom he corresponded until Carlo's death in 1621.

Cardinal Tiberio Muti was a member of the Congregation of the Index, whose meetings he attended at least until 1633. It is most unlikely that Cardinal Muti was involved in drafting G3 because his handwriting is different, and the tone of the document is not what we would expect from a Cardinal who belonged to the Congregation of the Index. Several persons in the entourage of the Cardinal could have had access to paper with his watermark, but thus far we are in the dark about who these people may have been.

The New Documents and Galileo's Trial

When the Holy Office investigated the conditions under which Galileo's *Dialogue* had been published in 1632, G3 probably surfaced in the files. The author of G3 had experienced what he called "doctrinal scruples" after reading *The Assayer*, a statement that would have been welcomed by those who wanted to see Galileo taken down a peg or two. In August 1632, Rome halted the sale of the *Dialogue*, and the Pope appointed a Commission of Inquiry that probably numbered Inchofer among its members. The Commission met in August and September 1632, but we do not know its mandate or how it went about its task. But one thing is clear: the injunction given to Galileo in 1616 was discovered in the Archives of the Holy Office, and the Commission recommended that Galileo be called before the Holy Office. On 11 September 1632, the Tuscan ambassador in Rome, Francesco Niccolini, wrote to Florence to say that Father Riccardi, the Master of the Apostolic Palace, had mentioned that a trusted Jesuit confidant (probably Inchofer) had been appointed to the Commission, and that Riccardi had added that the injunction of 26 February 1616, intimating to Galileo to abandon Copernicanism, had been found in the Holy Office.

When this came to light, Urban VIII was surprised that his much-admired friend Galileo had told him nothing about the orders received from Cardinal Bellarmine. But this is what one should expect in normal circumstances. In 1616 the Holy Office was anxious to protect Galileo's reputation, and there was no reason why Galileo should have told anybody about the precept. Galileo had even obtained a certificate from Cardinal Bellarmine, a man who respected confidentiality. But secrecy was so strict at the Vatican that Bellarmine could not refer to the minutes of the Holy Office, or explain in detail the orders received from the Pope. Nonetheless, Galileo would have been wise to mention that he had received such orders when he brought the manuscript of his *Dialogue* to Rome in 1630 in order to have it approved for publication. The discovery of the records of 1616 turned against him, and it became the focus of the trial. Galileo's only defense was to claim that he did not argue for Copernicanism in the *Dialogue*. The three experts, who read the work, realized that he argued as persuasively as he could for the motion of the Earth, and they told the Pope. When G3 turned up, it came as a surprise, since it is not about Copernicanism. A report on its relevance was necessary, and Inchofer was the right person to prepare it since he knew some science and had probably been a member of the Preliminary Commission.

The violation of the 1616 injunction regarding Copernicanism was sufficient to have Galileo summoned before the Holy Office, and G3 and EE 291 were not needed. Yet after his arrival in Rome on February 1633, Galileo was not immediately summoned before the Holy Office. On 26 February, Ambassador Niccolini asked the Pope for a rapid trial, but Urban VIII told him that the case was still being investigated.[10] Since the Pope was the head of the Holy Office, it is clear that the matter was taken very seriously. It was only on April 12, two months after his arrival in Rome, that Galileo appeared before the Holy Office to make his deposition. There could be no doubt that Galileo had disobeyed the orders given to him in 1616. Philosophical niceties about sensible qualities seemed irrelevant, and G3 and EE 291 were probably returned to the Archives where they laid dormant until recently. Thomas Cerbu suggests that EE 291 was "a strictly personal memorandum, drafted in conjunction with the meetings of the special commission. . . . The two pieces [G3 and EE 291] may well have remained in his [Inchofer's] possession for several years after he drafted his opinion."[11] It seems difficult to admit, however, that a member of the Preliminary Commission, such as Inchofer, could have kept G3 for himself. And if this were the case, it would be hard to explain how G3 and EE 291 came to be deposited in the Archives some years later.

There are two lacunae in our knowledge of the discussions that took place prior to Galileo's trial. The first concerns what happened in the summer of 1632 prior to his being summoned to Rome, and, the second, what went on behind the scenes between his arrival in February 1633 and the beginning of the trial began on 12 April. The investigation focused on the contents of the *Dialogue*, and EE 291 could have influenced the examiners during those crucial months. Official documents do not mention who was the first to formally accuse Galileo or whether anyone approached the Pope personally. Neither do we know if only the *Dialogue* was examined or whether other writings by Galileo were taken into consideration. It is unlikely that Urban VIII would have read the *Dialogue* and initiated proceedings on his own. When the Holy Office or the Congregation of the Index proceeded against a book, the case was often set in motion by a denunciation in the form of a letter or a deposition. Who, then, denounced Galileo?

At the time, everyone was jumpy in Rome because the Papacy was implicated in the Thirty Years War. At a private consistory, the pro-Spanish Cardinal Borgia accused the Pope of favoring the Protestants on the grounds that his support of France served the interests of their ally, Sweden. In such a context, if Galileo's *Dialogue* was represented as going against Scripture, the Pope, not wanting to appear weak on doctrinal matters, would have felt obliged to act with great firmness.

It would help to know who wrote G3 and when it was sent to the Holy Office. Other documents may one day surface and enlighten us on the circumstances that led to Galileo's trial. We do not believe, however, that the facts about the Galileo Affair will be undermined. Galileo was condemned for failing to comply with a formal order not to teach that the Earth moves. The background issues were the authority of Scripture in scientific questions and, more specifically, the relevance of geocentrism to Christian doctrine. Many high-ranking members of the Church were aware of these problems and felt that there was no clash between science and religion. Galileo's condemnation is regrettable but it was not inevitable.

NOTES

1. Pietro Redondi, *Galileo Heretic*, translated by Raymond Rosenthal (Princeton: Princeton University Press, 1987). Original Italian 1983.
2. Letter of Orazio Grassi to Girolamo Bardi, 22 September 1633, *Opere di Galileo*, vol. XV, p. 273, quoted above, chapter seven, p. 160.
3. Mario Guiducci to Galileo Galilei, 21 June 1624, *Opere di Galileo*, vol. XIII, p. 186.
4. Galileo Galilei, *Il Saggiatore*, *Opere di Galileo*, vol. VI, pp. 347–348.
5. Artigas, Martínez, and Shea drafted an article in 2000 but it had not appeared when they heard in 2001 that two other scholars had also seen the document. One is Ugo Baldini, the other is Thomas Cerbu. Both subsequently published EE 291, and Cerbu agrees with us on the authorship of EE 291. See Thomas Cerbu, "Melchior Inchofer, *un homme fin & rusé*," in *Largo campo di filosofare: Eurosymposium Galileo 2001*, José Montesinos and Carlos Solís, eds. (La Orotava, Tenerife: Fundación Canaria Orotava de Historia de la Ciencia, 2001), pp. 587–611.
6. Francesco Niccolini to Andrea Cioli, 11 September 1632, *Opere di Galileo*, vol. XIV, p. 389.
7. William R. Shea, "Melchior Inchofer's *Tractatus Syllepticus*: A consultor of the Holy Office answers Galileo," in *Novità celesti e crisi del sapere*, Paolo Galluzzi, ed. (Florence: Barbèra, 1983), pp. 283–292; Francesco Beretta, "*Omnibus Christianae, Catholicaeque Philosophiae amantibus*: Le *Tractatus syllepticus* de Melchior Inchofer, censeur de Galilée," *Freiburger Zeitschrift für Philosophie und Theologie*, 48 (2001), pp. 301–325.
8. Mario Guiducci to Galileo Galilei, 18 April 1626, *Opere di Galileo*, vol. XIII, p. 265.

9. See Sergio Pagano, ed., *I documenti del processo di Galileo Galilei* (Vatican: Pontifical Academy of Sciences, 1984), pp. 43–48.

10. Francesco Niccolini to Andrea Cioli, 26 February 1633, *Opere di Galileo*, vol. XV, p. 56.

11. Cerbu, "Melchior Inchofer, un homme fin & rusé," p. 598.

CHAPTER NINE

The Man to Whom the Church Apologized

At a commemoration of the centenary of Albert Einstein's birth, on 10 November 1979, Pope John Paul II spoke about the relations between science and religion. Referring to Galileo, he declared that "he had to suffer a great deal—we cannot conceal the fact—at the hands of men and organisms of the Church."[1] The Pope deplored that Christians have not always respected the autonomy of science and that, as a result, some people have been misled into thinking that faith and science are at odds. He further expressed the hope that theologians and historians would "study the Galileo case more deeply and, in loyal recognition of wrongs from whatever side they came,"[2] in order to dispel the mistrust that still exists between the Church and the world.

The Pope's regrets were voiced three hundred and forty-six years after the trial. As someone remarked, "It's a pretty long time to say, 'Sorry!'" The Vatican's belated, and suitably orotund, expression of regret is itself a manifestation of the fashionable demand that we apologize—to natives, to minorities, to people whose forefathers were persecuted, ill-treated and slighted by other people who, no doubt, had grievances of their own. These days, it feels good to feel sorry, although we still have to see whether the recognition of past faults (not perpetrated by us, heaven forbid! but by distant ancestors) will translate into genuine tolerance and a practical respect for the ideas and lifestyles of people with a different ethnic or religious history.

Paradoxically, the Pope's address came at a time when some historians of science were giving Galileo a hard ride. In his best-selling *Farewell to Reason*, Paul Feyerabend paints an unflattering picture of Galileo as a pushy and dogmatic scientist. "It is a pity," he writes, "that the Church of today, frightened by the universal noise made by the scientific wolves, prefers to howl with them instead of trying to teach them some manners."[3] The Church has been the big loser in the Galileo Affair: Galileo's fame increased steadily while the Church lost prestige and ground.

A Pontifical Commission

In the wake of the Pope's address, a special Commission was established to reexamine the Galileo Affair. Presided over by Cardinal Gabriel Marie Garrone, it consisted of four sections: (1) an exegetical section headed by Carlo Maria Martini, the former Rector of the Pontifical Biblical Institute; (2) a cultural section under Paul Poupard, who later became a cardinal and head of the Pontifical Council for Culture; (3) a scientific and epistemological section chaired by Carlos Chagas, the President of the Pontifical Academy of Sciences, and Father George Coyne, the Director of the Vatican Observatory; (4) a historical and juridical section entrusted to Michele Maccarrone, the President of the Pontifical Academy of Historical Sciences, and the Jesuit historian, Edmond Lamalle. "The goal of the Commission," wrote the Secretary of State, Cardinal Agostino Casaroli, was "not a *revision* of the trial or a *rehabilitation*, but a serene and objective *reconsideration*."[4]

Impressive as was the goal, the four sections did not have the means to enlist historians who could devote themselves full time to the Galileo Affair. It is surprising, however, that not a single Galileo scholar was appointed to the Commission. Seven plenary meetings were held between 1982 and 1983, and none thereafter. Towards the end of the 1980s, the Commission grinded to a halt due to the retirement, the illness, or new assignments of several of its members. Cardinal Poupard was asked to take over as Chairman in 1990, and he soon came to the conclusion that the Commission had gone as far as it could, and should be disbanded. No official report was submitted, but a closing ceremony was held on 31 October 1992 at a meeting of the Pontifical Academy of Sciences.[5] Father George Coyne spoke on behalf of the academicians and their President.

After which Cardinal Paul Poupard made a speech in which he recalled that the goal of the Commission had not been to revise the trial, but to examine the Galileo Affair in honest recognition of errors, and in the hope of dispelling the prejudices that the Affair continues to foster. The Cardinal mentioned, on the one hand, that Galileo did not have definitive proofs for the motion of the Earth and, on the other hand, that the sentence of the Holy Office in 1633 was not cast in iron. It was gradually and slowly revised, but it was not until 1741 that the Vatican authorized the publication of the complete works of Galileo. Cardinal Poupard's speech ended with a paragraph that is printed in italics, as though it were intended to sum up what the Commission had achieved:

> In an historical and cultural framework that is far removed from our own times, Galileo's judges believed, quite wrongly, that the adoption of the Copernican revolution (not yet definitively proven) was such as to undermine Catholic tradition, and that it was their duty to forbid its being taught. They were unable to dissociate their faith from an age-old cosmology. This error of judgment, so clear to us today, led them to disciplinary measures from which Galileo "had much to suffer." These mistakes must be frankly recognized, as you, Holy Father, have requested.[6]

In reply, Pope John Paul II said that the errors committed in the Galileo Affair had long been recognized. But it cannot be ruled out, he added, that we may one day find ourselves in a similar situation. Problems can only be avoided if science and religion are aware of their own limitations. Galileo, added the Pontiff, made no distinction between the scientific and the philosophical approach to nature, and this is why he rejected the suggestion made to him to present the Copernican system as a hypothesis that awaited confirmation. John Paul II added that Galileo had showed himself more perceptive in theology than the experts who opposed his interpretation of Scripture. Modern-day theologians, said the Pope, must keep abreast of scientific advances, and ask themselves whether they should introduce changes in their teaching.

John Paul II reminded his audience that the Galileo Affair became a "myth," and the symbol of the Church's alleged rejection of scientific progress. The myth has played a considerable role in our culture, and has led scientists to assume in good faith that a scientific outlook is incompatible with the Christian faith. "*A tragic mutual misunderstanding,*" said the Pope, "has been seen as a fundamental opposition between science and faith. Recent historical studies enable us to say that this unfortunate misunderstanding now belongs to the past."[7]

Whereas the media generally saw as laudable the effort made by the Catholic Church to recognize past errors and attempt to face present problems, some scholars voiced criticism that we shall now consider.

The Commission Indicted

In 1992, James Reston, who was working in Rome on a biography of Galileo, requested an interview with Cardinal Poupard. Asked to submit his questions in advance, he sent in several, of which the most important is the following: Was the Pope's address of 31 October 1992 a formal apology? Reston claims that when he faxed his questions to the Cardinal, the hotel concierge looked at him in astonishment, as if he expected him to be burned on the Campo dei Fiori at dusk.[8]

When Reston met Cardinal Poupard a few days later, he was told that the Pope's address was not an official apology but the recognition of an error. Reston could not see the difference, and asked: "Could the Cardinal imagine the Church ever having to say anything further about the case?" "Why?" replied Poupard. "It is done. *Finito*."[9] Reston saw this answer as a dodge, a mere rehearsal of

> the standard Church line about Galileo that I had heard often in three years of writing: Galileo had been condemned because he insisted on treating his Copernican theory as truth rather than hypothesis, and he could not prove it. This position deflected attention from a simple fact: The Copernican theory *was* true, and the Church had used extreme and rigorous methods to crush that truth and protect its falsehood.[10]

Reston is either seriously misinformed or too eager to teach the Catholic Church a lesson to attend to the evidence. For instance, he declares that "until as recently as 1984, important documents of the Galileo case remained secret. It is still not known if other important documents in the case lay hidden in the forbidding secret archives of the Holy Office."[11] Any historian knows that this is not the case. Although the archives of the Holy Office were not opened for research until 1998, the documents of the Galileo Affair were published in the nineteenth century, and have long been available in the National Edition of the *Works of Galileo* edited by Antonio Favaro between 1890 and 1909.

Reston's comments on the Decree of the Index of 5 March 1616 that placed Copernicus's book on the Index deserves to be quoted in full as an example of the way that personal convictions can distort simple facts:

> The March 5 decree is the crucial moment in the whole saga known as the Galileo Affair. More than the inconclusive and unclear meeting with Bellarmine the week before, and more than the Galileo trial seventeen years later, this was the act that established the reputation of the Roman Catholic Church as antiscience and anti-intellectual. It is this fatal misstep from which the church has been trying to recover for 378 years. For Galileo, this became the operative document. It superseded his February 26 meeting with Bellarmine, both in its force and in his own memory. He would remember this edict sixteen years later, as the formal, written, and promulgated action of the church, and he would forget about his meeting with Bellarmine. . . . A few days after the formal edict Pope Paul V received Galileo for nearly an hour. . . . In the light of history, it amounted to entrapment. How was Galileo to bear in mind Bellarmine's February 26 verbal admonition in the face of these comforting flatteries?[12]

It is simply not true that Galileo, in 1633, had forgotten about his meeting with Bellarmine in 1616. He remembered it very well, and he had come to Rome with the testimonial that the Cardinal had given him. In his mind, it was to be the strongest weapon in his defense. What Galileo did not recall was whether the Commissary of the Holy Office, Michelangelo Segizzi, had added something else. Galileo's first deposition before the Inquisition on 12 April 1633 is clear about this point. "Cardinal Bellarmine," he declared,

> informed me that the opinion of Copernicus could be held hypothetically, as Copernicus himself held it. His Eminence knew that I held it hypothetically, namely in the same way as Copernicus, as you can see from his answer to a letter of Father Paolo Antonio Foscarini, Provincial of the Carmelites. I have a copy of the Cardinal's letter where we find these words, "It seems to me that Your Reverence and Galileo wisely limit yourselves to speaking hypothetically and not categorically."[13]

As we have seen in chapter four, a document in the Holy Office mentioned that after Galileo had been giving an injunction by Bellarmine, Commissioner Segizzi ordered him to refrain from teaching Copernicanism *in any way*. This is what Galileo did not remember:

> I do not recall that this precept was intimated to me by any other than by Cardinal Bellarmine. I remember that I was enjoined, "not to hold or defend," but there may also have been "nor teach." I do not remember that "in any way" was added, but this may have been the case. I did not give much thought to it or keep it in mind because I was given some months later the certificate of Cardinal Bellarmine dated 26 May that I have submitted, in which it is mentioned that I was ordered not to hold or defend the said opinion. As for the other two particulars of the precept now notified to me, that is "nor teach" and "in any way," I do not remember them, I think because they are not set forth in the certificate on which I relied and that I kept as a reminder.[14]

The writing on which Galileo relied all those years was not the Decree of the Index, but Bellarmine's testimonial or certificate.

Further Queries

What is at the root of Reston's deep discontent is his belief that by the summer of 1991 the Vatican wished that the subject would simply go away. "The issue," he writes, "was on the verge of being buried alive for another four hundred years. The church had come up against a question that, in all its wisdom, it could not answer: How does a divine institution confess error?"[15] But this is a red herring. In recent times the Church has repeatedly recognized and deplored errors made in the past. For instance, in December 1999, the International Theological Commission, chaired by Cardinal Joseph Ratzinger (now Pope Benedict XVI) issued a statement entitled *Memory and Reconciliation: the Church and the Faults of the Past*, where we find an ample repertoire of faults that the Church acknowledges and pledges itself to avoid in the future.

Reston also wanted to know from Cardinal Poupard why neither he nor John Paul II mentioned Urban VIII. Poupard answered that he felt that the assessment of the specific role of individuals should be left to professional historians. "All those involved in the trial, without exception," the

ILLUSTRATION 17   Galileo's tomb in Santa Croce.

Cardinal stressed, "have a right to be considered as being in good faith unless there is evidence to the contrary."[16]

It is important to recall that the Commission did not submit a report, although the way the session of closure was conducted may have given the impression that Cardinal Poupard was presenting the Pope with conclusions reached by the Commission. This misunderstanding could have been avoided if the work of the Commission had been terminated in another way, say by a letter from the Pope thanking the members for what they had done. The only "result" that Cardinal Poupard presented to the Pope was a list of publications, where we do find numerous references to Popes Paul V and Urban VIII, to Cardinal Bellarmine and other Church officials. But the Commission, as such, never intended to judge their individual behavior. Poupard did not speak of *conclusions*, only of results. This went largely unheeded, and an official publication of the Vatican went so far as to add the following subtitle to the Cardinal's address: "Cardinal Paul Poupard, President of the Pontifical Council for Culture addressed the Holy Father on behalf of the Pontifical Commission on the Galileo Case, and provided a summary of the conclusions reached."[17]

Galileo Rehabilitated?

A harsh criticism of the alleged "rehabilitation" of Galileo by the Catholic Church has been voiced by Antonio Beltrán Marí in his Spanish translation of Galileo's *Dialogue*.[18] According to Beltrán, the "rehabilitation" was engineered by the Vatican, and is no more than a shocking piece of propaganda, for now "most people believe that Galileo did something wrong and that the Church, showing her kindness, decided to forgive him."[19] Beltrán takes issue with John Paul II's claim that recent historical studies enable us to say that the unfortunate misunderstanding between science and religion belongs to the past. Beltrán sees things otherwise: "The intellectual audacity concealed in this comedy is so enormous that it almost conceals its moral baseness." Not mincing his words, Beltrán declares that John Paul II shared the frame of mind of "the inquisitors who condemned Galileo."[20]

Rehabilitation was not the word that the Commission used, but it has caught on, probably because it is the most understandable term that can be used to indicate a process of undoing a wrong inflicted on somebody. In *Retrying Galileo*, Maurice Finocchiaro devotes the last chapter to the Pontifical Commission, and calls it *"More Rehabilitation*: Pope John Paul II (1979–1992)."[21] The name may well be here to stay, but it is fraught with ambiguity.

In order to buttress his criticism of the Pontifical Commission, Beltrán refers to Annibale Fantoli, the author of an excellent biography of Galileo, who has his own reservations about what was achieved. Fantoli is disappointed by what Cardinal Poupard and the Pope had to say. According to him, they are guilty of having kept quiet about Paul V and Urban VIII, the two Popes who were responsible for the Galileo Affair.[22]

Poupard described the steps taken by the Church to come to terms with the Galileo Affair in the 18th and 19th centuries, but left in the shadow responsibilities "at the top." For Fantoli, Paul V and Urban VIII, the Holy Office and the Congregation of the Index, are virtually whitewashed. He points out that when the Holy Office finally allowed the publication of Galileo's *Works* in 1741–1742, it did so half-heartedly. The *Dialogue* appeared for the first time with ecclesiastical authorization, but only on condition that Galileo's sentence and abjuration be included. Furthermore, this edition did not contain Galileo's *Letter to the Granduchess Christina*, his most important writing on science and religion. Therefore, it cannot be said that this authorization was an "implicit reform" of the sentence of 1633, as we read in Cardinal Poupard's address. Neither can it be said, for the same reasons, that "this implicit reform became explicit" when the Congregation of the Index decreed in 1757 to remove the general prohibition on Copernican books. This decree says nothing about the 1633 sentence, and works of Copernicus, Galileo, and Kepler continued to appear on the list of condemned books. The first edition of the Index that did not include books by these three authors did not see the light of day before 1835.

Galileo's condemnation is called a disciplinary measure by Poupard. Fantoli believes that the 1616 decree of the Index had a doctrinal character, and that Pope Paul V and the members of the Holy Office considered it as definitive. Fantoli relies here on the interpretation of Francesco Beretta, for whom the decree of the Index of 1616 and the sentence of the Holy Office of 1633 were both acts of the Pontifical Magisterium. On this view, the responsibility of the Pope is indeed a problem.

Responsibility "At the Top"

The Pope presided personally over the Holy Office and set its agenda. Paul V in 1616, and Urban VIII in 1633 actively intervened in the Galileo Affair. This is what led Beretta to claim that decisions of the Holy Office were magisterial acts of the Pope. We find this argument unconvincing because the decrees of 1616 and 1633 were only published under the names of the cardinals of the Holy Office or the cardinals of the Congregation of the Index. The absence of the Pope's signature or of any reference to him, was not accidental, and limited the theological import of the document. "Infallibility" was never an issue. Cardinal Poupard did not refer to ultimate responsibilities "at the top," but to interpret this as an attempt to exonerate the Church is wrong. Poupard is the former president of a Catholic university in France, and a distinguished historian in his own right. He seems to have exercised the kind of restraint that is becoming in a scholar whose field of expertise lies outside the seventeenth century.

Fantoli and Beretta are convinced that authoritarianism is the main source of the evils that have afflicted the Church since the time of Galileo and they would like to see this denounced. Hence their objection that the official conclusion of the Galileo Commission left unfulfilled John Paul II's wish that there be a "loyal recognition of wrongs from whatever side they come." Fantoli grants that most of the studies published under the auspices of the Commission frankly admit errors committed, not only by anonymous "theologians" or unspecified "judges of Galileo" but by senior officials and the Popes themselves. Fantoli thinks that the Cardinal and the Pope minimized the gravity of Galileo's condemnation by presenting it as a simple "disciplinary measure."[23] But what if the Pope and the Cardinal were right?

Fantoli's critiques have been echoed by Father George Coyne, the director of the Vatican Observatory, who translated into English Fantoli's *Galileo for Copernicanism and for the Church* and his essay *Galileo and the Catholic Church: A Critique of the "Closure" of the Galileo Commission's Work*. Coyne was a member of the Pontifical Commission and he speaks in the light of personal experience:[24]

> Neither the final report nor the papal discourse appears to reflect the majority of the conclusions enunciated in the official publications of the commission, the conclusions stated in the final report and repeated in the papal discourse were never submitted, as best I know, for comment to the members of the commission . . . these two documents cannot justifiably be considered to be conclusions of the commission's work.[25]

We have already pointed out that the Commission did not submit a report, and that Cardinal Poupard's discourse cannot be considered a summary of conclusions that never existed. Poupard was well aware of this, as we can see from the letter he wrote to the Secretary of State in 1992. "We should," he writes,

> distinguish clearly and persuasively the historical problem from another problem that could be called eternal, philosophico-theological, often ideological. This process requires maturing and time, beyond the real possibilities of a Commission, whatever this may be. Cultural facts with roots in history cannot be changed by decree or by a Commission. We can only help their historical evolution with opportune initiatives, as doubtless has been done by the work developed by the Commission created by the Holy Father during this fruitful decade.[26]

The Commission might have achieved more, but it would be unfair not to recognize that important research was encouraged, and that the outcome was a number of important publications. One of the most significant contains the documents of the Vatican File on Galileo's trial,[27] while another provides the documents related to the vicissitudes of Copernican books from the 1600s until the present day.[28] The documents of the Holy Office on the Settele Affair,[29] and the Louvain lectures of Cardinal Bellarmine have also been published.[30] We find books on the interpretation of Scripture in Galileo's time,[31] on Galileo and the Council of Trent,[32] on Galileo's epistemology,[33] and on Galileo's trial.[34] The Galileo Affair was reassessed by Mario d'Addio,[35] Walter Brandmüller,[36] and Annibale Fantoli.[37] Several useful essays on different aspects of the Galileo Affair were also edited.[38] Last but not least, the Commission had the Archives of the Holy Office opened for research in 1998. This was a decisive step in furthering fresh and unhindered study of the Holy Office and the Congregation of the Index.

Can we say therefore that the Galileo "myth" has been laid to rest as the Pope wished? Michael Segre doubts this because the problem is not merely one of knowing who was right or wrong but the right to hold and defend one's own opinions. "What the Church should do, if it wishes to reconcile its teaching with science," writes Segre, is "to grant that Galileo had the right to state his scientific views, even if they were mistaken and despite any damage they may have caused to the church."[39] For the real issue is, "Freedom of thought, inquiry, and expression, rather than Galileo's failure to prove the motion of the earth."[40]

We are back to the contemporary demand that apologies be given, as if this could be the role of someone who lives almost four hundred years after the event. Freedom of expression is a right that was won over a long period of time, and we should perhaps be more anxious to see that it is maintained and extended than to proffer apologies for people long dead. Science and religion should learn from each other, not indulge in endless recrimination about the past.

NOTES

1. John Paul II, Address to the Pontifical Academy of Sciences, 10 November 1979, in *Papal Addresses to the Pontifical Academy of Sciences 1917–2002* (Vatican: Pontifical Academy of Sciences, 2003), p. 241. Earlier editions of this chapter appeared in Mariano Artigas, Rafael Martínez, and William R. Shea, "New Light in the Galileo Affair," in John Brooke and Ekmeleddin Ihsanoglu, eds., *Religious Values and the Rise of Science in Europe* (Istanbul: Research Centre for Islamic History, Art and Culture, 2005), pp. 145–166, and in Ernan McMullin ed., *The Church and Galileo* (Notre Dame, Indiana: University of Notre Dame Press, 2005), pp. 213–233.
2. *Ibid.*, pp. 241–242.
3. Paul Feyerabend, *Farewell to Reason* (London and New York: Verso, 1987), p. 260.
4. Quoted by: Melchor Sánchez de Toca, "Un doble aniversario: XX aniversario de la creación de la Comisión de Estudio del Caso Galileo y de su clausura," *Ecclesia*, 16 (2002), p. 146.
5. *L'Osservatore Romano*, 1 November 1992, pp. 1 and 6–9.
6. Cardinal Paul Poupard, Paul. Address to Pope John Paul II reporting on the work of the Galileo Commission, 31 October 1992, in *Papal Addresses to the Pontifical Academy of Sciences 1917–2002* (Vatican: Pontifical Academy of Sciences, 2003), p. 348.
7. John Paul II, Address to the Pontifical Academy of Sciences, 31 October 1992, in: *Papal Addresses to the Pontifical Academy of Sciences 1917–2002* (Vatican: Pontifical Academy of Sciences, 2003), p. 341.
8. James Reston, *Galileo. A Life* (London: Cassell, 1994). Bruno was executed on the Campo dei Fiori in 1600.
9. *Ibid.*, p. 285.
10. *Ibid.*
11. *Ibid.*, p. 140.
12. *Ibid.*, pp. 168–169.
13. Galileo Galilei, *Le Opere di Galileo*, edizione nazionale, Antonio Favaro, ed., 1890–1909, reprint (Florence: Barbèra, 1968), vol. XIX, p. 339.
14. *Ibid.*, p. 340.
15. Reston, *Galileo*, p. 142.
16. Cardinal Paul Poupard, Paul. Address to Pope John Paul II reporting on the work of the Galileo Commission, 31 October 1992, in *Papal Addresses to the*

Pontifical Academy of Sciences 1917–2002 (Vatican: Pontifical Academy of Sciences, 2003), p. 347.

17. *Ibid.*, p. 344.
18. Antonio Beltrán Marí, "Introducción" to Galileo Galilei, *Diálogo sobre los dos máximos sistemas del mundo ptolemaico y copernicano* (Madrid: Alianza, 1994), pp. LXX–LXXIV. See also by the same author, *Una reflexión serena y objetiva.* "Galileo y el intento de autorrehabilitación de la Iglesia católica," in Antonio Beltrán Marí, *Galileo, ciencia y religión* (Barcelona: Paidós, 2001), pp. 203–248.
19. Beltrán, "Introducción," p. LXX, footnote 223.
20. *Ibid.*, pp. LXXII–LXXIV.
21. Maurice Finocchiaro, *Retrying Galileo, 1633–1992* (Berkeley: University of California Press, 2005).
22. Annibale Fantoli, *Galileo and the Catholic Church: A Critique of the "Closure" of the Galileo Commission's Work* (Vatican: Vatican Observatory, 2002).
23. *Ibid.*, pp. 20–21.
24. George Coyne, "The Church's Most Recent Attempt to Dispel the Galileo Myth," in: *The Church and Galileo*, Ernan McMullin, ed. (Notre Dame, Indiana: University of Notre Dame Press, 2005), pp. 340–359.
25. *Ibid.*, p. 354.
26. Cardinal Paul Poupard, *Letter to the Cardinal Secretary of State, 13 July 1990.* Quoted by Sánchez de Toca, "Un doble aniversario," p. 158.
27. *I documenti del processo di Galileo Galilei*, Sergio Pagano and Antonio Luciani, eds. (Vatican: Pontifical Academy of Sciences, 1984).
28. Pierre-Noël Mayaud, *La condamnation des livres coperniciens* (Rome: Università, Gregoriana, 1997).
29. *Copernico, Galilei e la Chiesa*, Walter Brandmuller and Egon Johannes Greipl, eds., (Florence: Olschki, 1992).
30. Ugo Baldini and George Coyne, *The Louvain Lectures (Lectiones Lovanienses) of Bellarmine and the autograph copy of his 1616 declaration to Galileo* (Vatican: Vatican Observatory, 1984).
31. Rinaldo Fabris, *Galileo Galilei e gli orientamenti esegetici del suo tempo* (Vatican: Pontifical Academy of Sciences, 1986).
32. Olaf Pedersen, *Galileo and the Council of Trent* (Vatican: Vatican Observatory, 1983).
33. Józef Zycinski, *The Idea of Unification in Galileo's Epistemology* (Vatican: Vatican Observatory, 1988).
34. Richard S. Westfall, *Essays on the Trial of Galileo* (Vatican: Vatican Observatory, 1989).
35. Mario d'Addio, *Il caso Galilei. Processo, Scienza, Verità* (Roma: Studium, 1997). Previously published as *Considerazioni sui processi a Galileo.*
36. Walter Brandmüller, *Galilei und die Kirche oder Das Recht auf Irrtum* (Regensburg: Verlag Friedrich Pustet, 1982). New enlarged Italian edition: *Galilei e la Chiesa ossia il diritto ad errare* (Vatican: Librería Editrice Vaticana, 1992).

37. Annibale Fantoli, *Galileo, for Copernicanism and for the Church*.
38. *Galileo Galilei: 350 ans d'histoire, 1633–1983*, Paul Poupard, ed. (Tournai: Desclée, 1983); *The Galileo Affair. A Meeting of Faith and Science*, Proceedings of the Cracow Conference 1984, George V. Coyne, Michael Heller and Józef Zycinski, eds. (Vatican: Vatican Observatory, 1985); *Après Galilée. Science et foi: nouveau dialogue*, Paul Poupard, ed. (Paris: Desclée de Brouwer, 1994).
39. Michael Segre, "Light on the Galileo Case?", *Isis*, 88 (1997), 497.
40. *Ibid*.

Galileo and the Dialogue between Science and Religion

We have found the accounts of Galileo's life to be so numerous and so different that the reader may well ask whether we have managed to see him as he was. We hope to have taken a step in the right direction but we recognize that our vision, *any* vision, of the world is the outcome of ideas that we lug about, often unconsciously, and that provide us with our bearings in a pluralistic and sometimes terrifying world. A movie with no clearly recognizable "good guys" and "bad guys" might be more true to life but it would stand no chance of establishing a record at the box office. Commercial films sacrifice historical authenticity for broad audience appeal, simplifying the complex patterns of the past, and telling the public what it wants to hear.

We inhabit a present-tense culture, but we need to know the past to escape the fetters of past prejudice. It is only when we wrestle with an historical event that has been understood in a variety of ways that we come to realize that our current viewpoint is neither obvious nor always anchored in hard facts. In the seventeenth century, the Protestant Reformation used the Galileo Affair to deal a blow to the claims of the papacy. A hundred years later, the secular Enlightenment turned it into a stick to trounce Christianity in general and, by the nineteenth century, it had become a battleaxe to shatter any kind of religion. Those who shared this view believed that progress was only possible if the human mind was liberated from the trammels of religious creeds and made to rely exclusively on science, the embodiment of rationality.

No characterization of the relationship between science and religion has proved more seductive and tenacious than that of conflict. The two "classic" works discussed in Chapter One carry the title, *History of the Conflict between Religion and Science* (1874), and *A History of the Warfare of Science with Theology in Christendom* (1896). The former, which passed through twenty editions and was translated into nine languages, was written by the chemist-historian John William Draper, who saw Christianity and especially Roman Catholicism as the arch-enemy of science. The history of Science, for him, was the record of the conflict between two contending powers, the expansive force of the human intellect on one side, and the compression arising from religious faith. The author of the second work, Andrew Dickson White, was equally convinced that war was inevitable. As the first President of Cornell University, White was dedicated to the creation of a center of higher knowledge free from the constraints of religious creeds. In an age when the American establishment was still largely Protestant, this raised comprehensible opposition, and White came to see himself as another Galileo battling the arrayed forces of obscurantism. On his view, Yankee divines who objected to his plans behaved like the Italian clerics who had persecuted Galileo. White was confident that he would overcome and, more importantly, he nurtured the hope that this would happen during his lifetime, not after his death like Galileo.

Both Draper and White acknowledged that the historian must enter into the minds that he studies and that this requires an appreciation of the ideas, ambitions and prejudices of the past. What they failed to grasp is that this can only be achieved if the historian is critically aware of his own ideas, ambitions and prejudices. Self-knowledge is difficult at all times, but Draper and White had swallowed whole a view that made it impossible for them to exercise self-criticism. They believed that the "scientific method," ushered in by the Scientific Revolution, provided them with a way of understanding not only nature but history. This view thrived well into the first half of the twentieth century, and received its canonical formulation (and geometrical garb) in George Sarton's *The Study of the History of Science* that was published in 1936:

> Definition: Science is systematized positive knowledge or what has been taken as such at different ages and in different places.

Theorem: The acquisition and systematization of positive knowledge are the only human activities which are truly cumulative and progressive.

Corollary: The history of Science is the only history which can illustrate the progress of mankind. In fact, progress has no definite and unquestionable meaning in fields other than the field of science.[1]

The notion that science is always and necessarily the motor of progress suffered a blow after the first atomic bomb fell on Hiroshima. The unease that "enlightened" people had felt about revealed religion since the eighteenth century shifted to science whose enormous power was being increasingly recognized as a mixed blessing at best. Science can work wonders for the good of mankind; it can also cause untold damage. From the naive assumption that freedom to carry out any scientific experiment would inevitably result in a better world, people came to question the right of science to tamper with nature. The issue is no longer more science, but more *good* science, namely sound knowledge that will benefit all mankind and not only a few (bad?) guys.

The notion of goodness has been discussed since the Greeks invented philosophy over two thousand years ago, but our vision of the world never was and never will be completely shaped by a debating society, however sharp, witty or wise. We need the experience and the support of systems that can cope with our emotional as well as our intellectual needs. The great religions that have emerged over the course of centuries have grappled with the use and abuse of power, and there is a diffuse, if sometimes inarticulate, feeling that we need their insights. But we can only learn from what religion has to tell us if we listen with an open mind. This implies, for instance, the willingness to entertain that religion may have something important to say about the perils of rash experimentation.

In this new climate, where an increasing number of people seriously query the advisability of making science the ultimate source of appeal when moral issues are at stake, we are at liberty to re-examine the Galileo Affair from a different standpoint. We are no longer under any compulsion to hail it as a glorious episode in the battle of scientific light against religious darkness. Or let us put it this way. In Galileo's day the challenge was to find room for a new form of knowledge (what we call modern science) in a worldview shaped by another way of knowing, namely religion. The challenge nowadays is to reintroduce this older kind of knowledge into an intellectual context structured by science. How do we fit spirituality into

197

a conceptual scheme of things that many assume to rest on purely mate- rialist assumptions? Are we to speak of two independent but complemen- tary ways of coming to terms with reality? Or should we pursue the more radical hypothesis that science and religion are convergent paths that lead to the same ultimate answer? There is no easy solution.

Religion, in the twenty-first century, is asked to show its credentials and there is little agreement on what counts as genuine, as distinguished from putative, insight. The reverse was the case in Galileo's day when vir- tually everyone took it for granted that the Bible was literally true unless there were compelling reasons for considering some passages as mere figures of speech. Scripture mentions that the Sun rises and sets, and since this agrees with everyday observation, it was reasonable to ask why we should not believe our senses. Galileo was convinced that he could prove that the Sun merely appears to move from east to west. His main ar- gument for Copernicanism was that tides could not occur in the ocean un- less the Earth rotated on its axis and revolved around the Sun. It was an ingenious argument. Unfortunately, it was also completely wrong. Galileo clung passionately to his spurious demonstration, and Pope Urban VIII maintained with as much vigor that any statement in the Bible was to be considered literally true unless shown otherwise.

We have had for some time definite proof that the Earth really goes around the Sun, and Christians have long come to realize that the Bible is not meant to be read as a scientific textbook. It is a pity that scientists and theologians did not learn the lesson earlier, but it would be equally sad if they did not take the lesson to heart and combine their insights about the baffling richness and diversity of the world. Someone who tried to be faithful to Scripture while leaving room for eventual reinterpretations in the light of fresh scientific evidence was Cardinal Robert Bellarmine (1542–1621). When a friar named Paolo Antonio Foscarini sent him a pamphlet in which he argued that the Motion of the Earth was not at vari- ance with the teaching of the Bible, the Cardinal wrote back to express a view that was eminently sensible in the light of current beliefs. Whatever his disagreement with Lutherans and Calvinists, Bellarmine was at one with them in stressing that Christianity is a revealed and, hence, a his- torical religion. The acts of God occurred at a given time and were recorded in a series of books that have a peculiar kind of veracity, which is conveyed by the word *inspired*. This meant, for Bellarmine and the generation prior to Galileo's telescopic discoveries, that apparently straightforward statements in the Bible were to be taken as such unless shown to have a different or a looser meaning. Here is how Bellarmine put it: "Someone who denied that Abraham had two sons and Jacob twelve would be just as much a heretic as someone who denied the virgin birth of Christ, for both are declared by the Holy Ghost through the mouths of the prophets and the apostles."[2] When Galileo saw this letter, he commented on the difficulty as follows: "It is much more a matter of faith to believe that Abraham had sons than that the Earth moves. . . . For since there have always been men who have had two sons, or four, or six, or none . . . there would be no reason for the Holy Spirit to affirm in such matters anything contrary to truth. . . . But this is not so with the mobility of the Earth, this being a proposition far beyond the comprehension of the common people."[3]

We can appreciate Galileo's point today, but was it convincing in the seventeenth century? Bellarmine, however mistakenly, believed that the Old Testament book of *Ecclesiastes* had been written by Solomon, "who not only spoke by divine inspiration," he stressed, "but was also a man wise above all others, and learned in the human sciences and in the knowledge of all created things. This wisdom he had from God."[4] This is why, when he read the verse, "The Sun rises and the Sun sets, and hurries back to where it rises,"[5] he wanted to think twice before denying that it was literally true. In the twenty-first century we take our cue from astrophysicists; in the seventeenth century Bellarmine took it from Solomon. He was willing, however, to acknowledge that if a genuine proof that the Earth moves were found, then we would have to reinterpret passages that appear to state that it is at rest. The rub is that neither Foscarini nor Galileo had such a proof. The argument from the tides did not hold water, as Bellarmine was told by the contemporary scientists whom he consulted.

Copernicus's book on the motion of the Earth had appeared way back in 1543 and the theory had been found mathematically interesting but physically out of step. There was a remote chance that it might turn out to be right in the long run, but until this was demonstrated it was unwise to jettison the traditional reading of biblical passages that referred to the Sun as rising and setting. This way of speaking is still deeply imbedded in our language, and we go on talking about sunrise and sunset although we know that the Sun is at rest. The Scriptures, written to be understood by everyone, naturally use popular rather than scientific or technical descriptions.

The lesson (if history can teach us anything) is that theologians should not make pronouncements about the laws of nature, and scientists should not demand that religion be tailored to fit current speculative ideas about physics. By recognizing that the Bible contains what is necessary for salvation, but that all that it contains is not necessary, and by acknowledging that science provides us with know-how but not with moral guidance, we may be on the road to rediscover the records of moral experience that we find in religion. We are sanguine enough to think that this is what Galileo would have wanted.

NOTES

1. George Sarton, *The Study of the History of Science* (Cambridge, Mass.: Harvard University Press, 1936), p. 5.
2. Cardinal Bellarmine to Antonio Foscarini, 12 April 1615, *Opere di Galileo*, vol. XII, p. 172.
3. Galileo, *Considerazioni circa l'Opinione Copernicana, ibid.*, vol. V, p. 368.
4. Cardinal Bellarmine to Antonio Foscarini, 12 April 1615, *ibid.*, vol. XII, p. 172.
5. *Ecclesiastes*, ch. 1, v. 5.

Bibliography

Addio, Mario d'. *Il caso Galilei. Processo, Scienza, Verità*. Roma: Studium, 1997.

Artigas, Mariano. "Un nuovo documento sul caso Galileo: EE 291," *Acta Philosophica*, 10 (2001), pp. 199–214.

Artigas, Mariano; Martínez, Rafael; and Shea, William R. "New light on the Galileo affair." In *The Church and Galileo*, edited by Ernan McMullin, Notre Dame, Indiana: University of Notre Dame Press, 2005, pp. 213–233.

Baldini, Ugo and Coyne, George. *The Louvain Lectures (Lectiones Lovanienses) of Bellarmine and the autograph copy of his 1616 declaration to Galileo*. Vatican: Vatican Observatory, 1984.

Baldini, Ugo and Spruit, Leen. "Nuovi documenti galileiani degli Archivi del Sant'Ufficio e dell'Indice," *Rivista di storia della filosofia*, 56 (2001), pp. 661–699.

Beltrán Marí, Antonio. *Galileo, ciencia y religión*. Barcelona: Paidós, 2001.

Beretta, Francesco. "*Omnibus Christianae, Catholicaeque Philosophiae amantibus.*" Le *Tractatus syllepticus* de Melchior Inchofer, censeur de Galilée, *Freiburger Zeitschrift für Philosophie und Theologie*, 48 (2001), pp. 301–325.

Beretta, Francesco. "L'archivio della Congregazione del Sant'Ufficio: Bilancio provvisorio della storia e natura dei fondi d'antico regime." In *L'Inquisizione romana: Metodologia delle fonti e storia istituzionale*, edited by Andrea Del Col and Giovanna Paolin. Trieste: Università di Trieste, 2000, pp. 199–244.

Beretta, Francesco. *Galilée devant le Tribunal de l'Inquisition. Une relecture des sources*. Fribourg: Université de Fribourg, 1998.

Biagioli, Mario. *Galileo Courtier. The Practice of Science in the Culture of Absolutism*. Chicago: The University of Chicago Press, 1993.

Brandmüller, Walter and Greipl, Egon Johannes, eds. *Copernico, Galilei e la Chiesa. Fine della controversia (1820). Gli atti del Sant'Uffizio*. Firenze: Olschki, 1992.

Brandmüller, Walter. *Galilei und die Kirche oder Das Recht auf Irrtum*. Regensburg: Verlag Friedrich Pustet, 1982. Enlarged Italian edition: *Galilei e la Chiesa ossia il diritto ad errare*. Vatican: Libreria Editrice Vaticana, 1992.

Brecht, Bertolt. *Life of Galileo*. Translated by John Willett and edited by John Willett and Ralph Manheim. New York: Arcade Publishing, 1994.

Brecht, Bertolt. *Galileo*. English version by Charles Laughton, edited with an introduction by Eric Bentley. New York: Grove Press, 1966.

Bruno, Giordano. *The Ash Wednesday Supper*. Edited and translated by Edward A. Gosselin and Lawrence S. Lerner. Toronto: University of Toronto Press, 2001, first published in 1977.

Cesarani, David. *Arthur Koestler: The Homeless Mind*. New York: The Free Press, 1999.

Coyne, George V.; Heller, Michael; and Zycinski, Józef, eds. *The Galileo Affair. A Meeting of Faith and Science*. Proceedings of the Cracow Conference 1984. Vatican: Vatican Observatory, 1985.

Drake, Stillman. *Discoveries and Opinions of Galileo*. New York: Doubleday, 1957.

Draper, John William. *History of the Conflict between Religion and Science*. New York: D. Appleton and Co., 1890.

Duhem, Pierre. *To Save the Phenomena: an Essay on the Idea of Physical Theory from Plato to Galileo*. Translated by Philip P. Wiener. New York: Atheneum, 1962.

Fabris, Rinaldo. *Galileo Galilei e gli orientamenti esegetici del suo tempo*. Vatican: Pontifical Academy of Sciences, 1986.

Fahie, J. J. *Galileo His Life and Work*. London: John Murray, 1903.

Fantoli, Annibale. *Galileo and the Catholic Church: A Critique of the "Closure" of the Galileo Commission's Work*. Vatican: Vatican Observatory, 2002.

Fantoli, Annibale. *Galileo, for Copernicanism and for the Church*, 2nd ed. Vatican: Vatican Observatory, 1996.

Finocchiaro, Maurice A. *Retrying Galileo, 1633–1992*. Berkeley: University of California Press, 2005.

Finocchiaro, Maurice A. *The Galileo Affair. A Documentary History*. Berkeley: University of California Press, 1989.

Firpo, Luigi. *Il processo di Giordano Bruno*. Roma: Salerno Editore, 1998.

Galilei, Galileo. *Le Opere di Galileo*. Edited by Antonio Favaro, 1890–1909. Reprint, Florence: Barbèra, 1968.

Galilei, Galileo. *Dialogue Concerning the Two Chief World Systems*. Translated, with notes, by Stillman Drake, 2d revised ed. Berkeley: University of California Press, 1967.

Galilei Galileo. *Diálogo sobre los dos máximos sistemas del mundo ptolemaico y copernicano*, translated with introduction and notes by Antonio Beltrán Marí. Madrid: Alianza, 1994.

Gallagher, Michael Paul. "Note in margine al caso Galileo," *La Civiltà Cattolica*, 144 (1993), vol. I, pp. 424–436.

George, Marie I. "The Catholic Faith, Scripture, and the Question of the Existence of Intelligent Extra-terrestrial Life." In *Faith, Scholarship, and Culture in the 21st Century*, edited by Alice Ramos and Marie I. George. Washington: The Catholic University of America Press, 2002, pp. 135–145.

George, Marie I. *Christianity and Extraterrestrials? A Catholic Perspective*. New York: Universe, 2005.

Gingerich, Owen. *The Book Nobody Read. Chasing the Revolutions of Nicolaus Copernicus.* New York: Walker & Company, 2004.

Gosselin, Edward A. and Lerner, Lawrence S. "Galileo and the Long Shadow of Bruno," *Archives Internationales d'Histoire des Sciences,* 25 (1975), pp. 221–246.

Gould, Stephen Jay. *The Hedgehog, the Fox, and the Magister's Pox. Mending the Gap between Science and the Humanities.* New York: Harmony Books, 2003.

Grant, Edward. *The Foundations of Modern Science in the Middle Ages. Their Religious, Institutional, and Intellectual Contexts.* Cambridge: Cambridge University Press, 1996.

Howell, Kenneth J. *God's Two Books: Copernican Cosmology and Biblical Interpretation in Early Modern Science.* Notre Dame: University of Notre Dame Press, 2002.

Johnson, Paul. *Intellectuals.* London: Weidenfeld and Nicolson, 1988.

Koestler, Arthur. *The Sleepwalkers.* London: Penguin Books, 1988, originally published in 1959.

Koyré, Alexandre. *Galileo Studies.* Atlantic Highlands, N.J.: Humanities Press, 1978.

Kuhn, Thomas S. *The Copernican Revolution. Planetary Astronomy in the Development of Western Thought.* Cambridge, Mass.: Harvard University Press, 1997.

Lerner, Lawrence S. and Gosselin, Edward A. "Giordano Bruno," *Scientific American,* volume 228, April 1973, Number 4, pp. 86–94.

Machamer, Peter, ed. *The Cambridge Companion to Galileo.* Cambridge: Cambridge University Press, 1998.

Martínez, Rafael. "Il Manoscrito ACDF, *Index, Protocolli,* vol. EE, f. 291 *r-v,*" *Acta Philosophica,* 10 (2001), pp. 215–242;

Mateo-Seco, Lucas F. "Galileo e l'Eucaristia. La questione teologica dell'ACDF, *Index, Protocolli,* EE, f. 291 *r-v,*" *Acta Philosophica,* 10 (2001), pp. 243–256;

Mayaud, Pierre Noël. *La condamnation des livres coperniciens et sa révocation, à la lumière de documents inédits des Congrégations de l'Index et de l'Inquisition.* Rome: Pontificia Università Gregoriana, 1997.

McMullin, Ernan. "Bruno and Copernicus," *Isis,* 78 (1987), pp. 55–74.

McMullin, Ernan, ed. *Galileo: Man of Science.* New York: Basic Books, 1967.

McMullin, Ernan, ed., *The Church and Galileo.* Notre Dame: University of Notre Dame Press, 2005.

Mercati, Angelo. *Il sommario del processo di Giordano Bruno con appendice di documenti sull'eresia e l'inquisizione a Modena nel secolo XVI.* Vatican: Biblioteca Apostolica Vaticana, 1942.

Mereu, Italo. *Storia dell'intolleranza in Europa,* 6th edition. Milan: Bompiani, 2000.

Montesinos, José and Solís, Carlos, eds. *Largo campo di filosofare: Eurosymposium Galileo 2001*. La Orotava, Tenerife: Fundación Canaria Orotava de Historia de la Ciencia, 2001.

Pagano, Sergio and Luciani, Antonio, eds. *I documenti del processo di Galileo Galilei*. Vatican: Pontifical Academy of Sciences, 1984.

Pedersen, Olaf. *Galileo and the Council of Trent*. Vatican: Vatican Observatory, 1983.

Poupard, Paul, ed. *Après Galilée. Science et foi: nouveau dialogue*. Paris: Desclée de Brouwer, 1994.

Poupard, Paul, ed. *Galileo Galilei: 350 ans d'histoire, 1633–1983*. Tournai: Desclée, 1983.

Redondi, Pietro. *Galileo Heretic*. Princeton: Princeton University Press, 1987. Original Italian 1983.

Reston, James. *Galileo: A Life*. London: Cassell, 1994.

Routledge Encyclopedia of Philosophy. London: Routledge, 1988.

Russell, Colin A. "The Conflict of Science and Religion." In *Science and Religion. A Historical Introduction*, edited by Gary B. Ferngren. Baltimore: The Johns Hopkins University Press, 2002, pp. 3–12.

Sánchez de Toca, Melchor. "Un doble aniversario: XX aniversario de la creación de la Comisión de Estudio del Caso Galileo y X de su clausura," *Ecclesia*, 16 (2002), pp. 143–164.

Santillana, Giorgio de. *The Crime of Galileo*. London: Heinemann, 1961.

Segre, Michael. "Light on the Galileo Case?", *Isis*, 88 (1997), pp. 484–504.

Shea, William R. "Melchior Inchofer's *Tractatus Syllepticus*: A consultor of the Holy Office answers Galileo." In *Novità celesti e crisi del sapere*, edited by Paolo Galluzzi. Florence: Barbèra, 1983, pp. 283–292.

Shea, William R. "Galileo e l'atomismo," *Acta Philosophica*, 10 (2001), pp. 257–272.

Shea, William R. and Artigas, Mariano. *Galileo in Rome. The Rise and Fall of an Uneasy Genius*. New York: Oxford University Press, 2003.

Sobel, Dava. *Galileo's Daughter. A Historical Memoir of Science, Faith, and Love*. New York: Walker, 1999.

Westfall, Richard S. *Essays on the Trial of Galileo*. Vatican: Vatican Observatory, 1989.

White, Andrew Dickson. *A History of the Warfare of Science with Theology in Christendom* [1896]. Buffalo, N.Y.: Prometheus Books, 1993.

Wohlwill, Emil. *Der Inquisitionsprozess des Galileo Galilei*. Berlin: Oppenheim, 1870.

Yates, Frances A. *Giordano Bruno and the Hermetic Tradition*. London: Routledge, 1964.

Zycinski, Józef. *The Idea of Unification in Galileo's Epistemology*. Vatican: Vatican Observatory, 1988.

Index